A Journey to the Roots of Rastafari:
The Essene Nazarite Link

The Apocrypha
Authorized (King James) Version
Translated out of the original tongues and with the former translations
diligently compared and revised by His Majesty's special command
Appointed to be read in churches
Cambridge, England: University Press
Pitt Brevier edition
Being the version set forth 1611
International Standard Book Number (ISBN) 0-521-50674-3 hardback

The Oxford Annotated Apocrypha of the Old Testament
Revised Standard Version
Translated from the Greek and Latin tongues
Edited by Bruce M. Metzger
New York: Oxford University Press, Inc., 1965
Being the version set forth 1611, revised 1894, compared with the most
ancient authorities and revised 1957
Library of Congress Catalog Number (LCCN) 65-12463

The Holy Bible
(Gideons Bible)
Authorized (King James) Version
Containing the Old and New Testaments
Translated out of the original tongues and with the former translations
diligently compared and revised [by His Majesty's special command]
[Appointed to be read in churches]
Nashville: National Publishing Co., 1978
For the Gideons International
Being the version set forth 1611

Essene Holy Bible
The Holy Megillah: The Nasarean Bible of the Essene Way, English
translation available through www.essene.org/essnmstr.html
Dec.21, 2013. Includes: *Essene New Testament: The Gospel of the Holy Twelve*
Translated from the original Aramaic by Gideon Jasper Ouseley
in the late 1800s
Pamphlet produced c/o Rev. Brother David Owen, Creswell, Oregon, 1980

A Journey to the Roots of Rastafari:
The Essene Nazarite Link

Copyright © 2014

* * *

Written, Compiled and Illustrated by
Abba Yahudah Berhan Sellassie
Edited by Vik Slen

Order this book online at www.trafford.com
or email orders@trafford.com

Most Trafford titles are also available at major online book retailers.

© Copyright 2014 Abba Yahudah Sellassie.
All rights reserved. No part of this publication may be reproduced,
stored in a retrieval system, or transmitted, in any form or by
any means, electronic, mechanical, photocopying, recording, or
otherwise, without the written prior permission of the author.

Portions of this book have been previously published in the *Bedford-Stuyvesant Current* (Volume 2, No. 5), "Feminine Mysticism in Art: Artists Envisioning the Divine" by Victoria Christian, and other publications.

Printed in the United States of America.

ISBN: 978-1-4907-3316-6 (sc)
ISBN: 978-1-4907-3315-9 (hc)
ISBN: 978-1-4907-3317-3 (e)

Library of Congress Control Number: 2014906558

Because of the dynamic nature of the Internet, any web addresses or
links contained in this book may have changed since publication and
may no longer be valid. The views expressed in this work are solely those
of the author and do not necessarily reflect the views of the publisher,
and the publisher hereby disclaims any responsibility for them.

Any people depicted in stock imagery provided by Thinkstock are models,
and such images are being used for illustrative purposes only.
Certain stock imagery © Thinkstock.

See more of Abba Yahudah Sellassie's art online at:
www.thirdeyecolortherapy.com
www.abbayahudah.com

Book design by: www.gotbrandsolutions.com

Trafford rev. 07/01/2014

Trafford PUBLISHING® www.trafford.com
North America & international
toll-free: 1 888 232 4444 (USA & Canada)
fax: 812 355 4082

A Journey to the Roots of Rastafari

For all the hungry children

In memory of Loran Hector

One should never make the mistake of assuming or pretending that a human being emanates from a deity.

Haile Sellassie I in an interview with Bill McNeil in 1967 broadcast by the Canadian Broadcasting Corporation

Believe nothing, no matter where you read it or who has said it, not even if I have said it, unless it agrees with your own reason and your own common sense.

Attributed to the Buddha

CONTENTS

Found Art, Maps and Photos xvi
Original Art, Maps and Photos xvi
Foreword by Mutabaruka xix
Foreword by the Editor xxi
About the Author xxv
Preface xxvii
Acknowledgements xxxi

Chapter 1: Introduction to the Essenes 1
    The Essenes of All Ages 2
    Enoch 3
    The Essenes 8
    The Rastafarians: Essenes of Today 10

FIRST EPOCH: B.C. 15

Chapter 2: Mother Ethiopia 17
    Ethiopia: As Eden 17
    Ethiopia: The Land 21
    Ethiopia: The People 23
    Ancient Axum 28

Chapter 3: The Old Testament 31
    Salem: The Kingdom of Melkizadek 32
    Egypt and the Prophecy of the Mashiakh 35
    Nazarites 42
    David Establishes Jerusalem 47
    King Solomon and the Queen of Sheba 49

Chapter 4: The Ark of the Covenant 55
    The Ark as an Object 57
    The Ark as a Living Testament 60

SECOND EPOCH: IN THE YEAR OF OUR LORD 63

Chapter 5: The Man Yahowshua and His Times 65
    Pharisees 65
    Sadduccees 66
    Essenes 68
    John the Baptist 73
    Yahowshua ha Mashiakh 74
    Why Yahowshua was Rejected 75
    Yahowshua the Ethiopian 76
    Miriam of Magdala 80

Chapter 6: Christianity 89
    The Disciples of Yahowshua 89
    Nazarenes 90
    The Gnostics and the Canon of Scripture 92
    Fate of Israel's Levitical Priesthood 95
    Christianity and Egypt 98
    Egyptian Monasticism 103
    Creeds and Definitions 104
    Egypt Passes the Torch 106

Chapter 7: The Hebrew Christian Empire 109
    Ethiopia's Conversion 110
    Ethiopian Christians in Jerusalem 111
    Anciency of Ethiopian Christianity 111
    Egypt's Legacy of Monasticism in Ethiopia 113
    Bahtawis 114
    Saint Tekle Haminot 118
    Saint Gebre Menfes Kidus 119
    Timkat 120
    Stone Churches and Knights Templar 123

Chapter 8: The Immaculate Conception 127
    Understanding the Immaculate Conception 129
    Woman/Ethiopia: The Cosmic Ark 133
    Sacred Geometry 137
    Super-Natural? 142
    The Feminine 143

Chapter 9: The Two Messiahs 149
    Yahowshua ha Mashiakh: Archetypal Son 149
    Yahowshua: The Faithful Witness to Haile Sellassie I 154

THIRD EPOCH: A.D. **161**

Chapter 10: The Man Haile Sellassie I **163**
    The Rising 163
    The Coronation 166
    The Giving of the Law 179
    The Calamity 181
    Return of the Conquering Lion 185
    The Battle of Adowa 189
    No Country but Ethiopia 193
    Two Questions 195
    Weakness in the International System 196
    Why Ethiopia? 203

Chapter 11: Rastafarian Founders **209**
    The Birth of African Zionism in Jamaica 209
    Alexander Bedward 214
    The Right Honorable Marcus Mosiah Garvey:
    Father of Black Nationalism 219
    Brother Leonard Percival Howell: First Patriarch of Rastafari 225
    Brother Joseph Natiel Hibbert: Patriarch of Rastafari 234
    Brother Henry Archibald Dunkley: Patriarch of Rastafari 235
    King Emmanuel: The High Priest 237

Chapter 12: The Rastafarians: The Essenes Reincarnated **241**
    Rastafarians as the Essenes Reincarnated 241
    Messianic Consciousness: The Uprising 245
    Nazarites Today 246
    The Re-emergence of the Mystics 251
    The Ordinances of the True Church 252
    Vegetarianism 257
    The Tree of Life 260
    Holy Baptism 263
    Levitical Priesthood 268
    The Sabbath and the Number Seven 271

Chapter 13: Reasonings In Black and White **275**
    Europe vs. Africa 275
    The Fascist Spirit 279
    Colonial Christianity 285
    Armageddon 288
    Esau and Jacob 290
    White Privilege 295
    Black Supremacy vs. White Supremacy 299
    Jesus: The Myth vs. Yahowshua: The Life 304

Appendix A: The Authenticity of the Bible 326

Appendix B: Little-Known Facts about the Apostles of Yahowshua 337

Appendix C: Notes On Original Art 339
    The First Supper 339
    Behold an Ethiopian 341
    The Gathering 343
    Revelation 12 345

Appendix D: The William Lynch Letters 348

Bibliography 359
    Ancient Scripture 359
    Writings and Speeches of H.I.M. Haile Sellassie I 362
    The National Geographic Magazine 363
    Modern Apocrypha 363
    Other Sources 364

FOUND ART, MAPS AND PHOTOS

The Fidel	27
Coronation Portrait of their Imperial Majesties	167
1632 Map of Africa	278
1886 Map of the World	280-281
Ancient Map of Africa	282-283
The Classic Image of Jesus (found art)	304
Ethiopian Sticker I (found art)	318
Ethiopian Sticker II (found art)	319

ORIGINAL ART, MAPS AND PHOTOS

Abba Yahudah Sellassie	xxiv
The Four Winds	xxxii
Medieval Castle in Gondar	5
Before the Beginning	16
Map of Ethiopia 1928	21
Ethiopian Tribes	24-25
Kushitic/Sabean Alphabet	26
The Blessing	30
The Nursing Goddess Isis	34
Wooden Bust of the Child King Tutankhamen	37
Nyiah-Man	45
Eyes Upon You	54
Behold an Ethiopian	64
Map of Qumran	71
Yahowshua Son of David	77
Miriam of Magdala	81
Church of St. George	88
Map of Egypt and Surrounding Area	99
Egyptian Goddess	100
The Seal and Emblem of the Royal Apostles of Haile Sellassie I	108
Bahtawi Priest	115
The Hebrew Christian Seal	121
A Window of St. George's Monolithic Church	124
The First Supper	126
She Gives Birth Unto Magic	131

Revelation 12	135
The Matrix of Planes and Dimensions	139
The Separation of the Trinity and the Creation of Dimensions	140
The Matrix of 7 in Conjunction with 3 and the Trinity	141
The Resurrection	148
The Trilateral Time Wheel	151
Haile Sellassie I	155
Lij Tafari	162
Empress Menen	176
Unto Us A Child Is Born	183
The King of Kings Slays the Beast	186
Menelik II	190
Map of Africa 1914	198
Past For Now	208
Map of Jamaica	210
Marcus Mosiah Garvey	221
Patriarch Leonard Percival Howell	227
King Emmanuel	236
This People	240
The Rastaman	249
The Gathering	253
The Fruitful Essene Tree of Life	261
Black Market Triangle	274
YHVH (הוהי), The Tetragrammaton	305

"Original Art, Maps and Photos" are by the author. All rights reserved.

FOREWORD BY MUTABARUKA

The Rastafari movement has become a worldwide phenomenon. Over the years, many books have been written with the intention to give readers an understanding and an historical perspective of who these strange people are — as one Rasta elder, Mortimo Planno, said and wrote, *The Earth's Most Strangest People: The Rastafarians*.[1]

Who are the Rastafarians? — claiming that a king thousands of miles from Jamaica, their place of origin, is Divine, and that Ethiopia is the birthplace of humanity. Most of the books that attempt to answer these questions are written by non-Rastas, either from an anthropological perspective, often as study papers, or by soldiers of a new army of black nationalists seeking liberation from white dominion. While I would consider the black nationalists' perspective to be the true one, there is much more to the Rasta movement than meets the eye, as you will see in this book, written by a Rastafarian. Abba Yahudah has gone where no book has gone before in documenting different aspects of the Rastafarian phenomenon.

In this book, you will be presented with information about what preceded the Rastafarians and see how this prehistory helped shape the philosophy and livity[2] (life) of the Rastafarians, both in their original beginnings and in their present evolution. Abba Yahudah will take you to Ethiopia — to Egypt — to Palestine. He examines the role of Christianity in shaping the movement, and the movement's connection to ancient Egypt. See how the redactors of the King James Bible usurped the original intent of the scribes writing some three to four thousand years ago.

---

1 Author's note: *The Earth Most Strangest Man: The Rastafarian* is a 1969 hand-written report by the elder Rastafarian Mortimo Planner or Planno, Bob Marley's spiritual advisor. Planno was convinced that it was essential to make a written record of the oral tradition and culture of the Rastafarians. Mortimo's work has been published as a book and is available on-line.
2 *Livity*: The word used by Rastafarians for their way of life, which is the manifestation of pure thoughts, words and deeds: their *ital* or wholistic life activities.

For this book does not start at 1930, when the Emperor of Ethiopia was crowned. It does not start even with the ancient union of King Solomon and the Queen of Sheba. Abba Yahudah will take you on a journey through truly epic time. He writes about connections and influences that most books on the Rastafarians have never linked with this movement, such as the concept of the feminine, the Kemetic[3] origins of the Trinity, and the Essenes. He shows how this group of people, simply by living and experiencing their spirituality, was able to shape an esoteric philosophy in a society not conducive to such.

The Rastafarians, in spite of the oppression of the colonial past and the scorn of neocolonial minds, have created an important movement fast. It is said that the influence Rastafarians have had on world culture, in the seventy-odd years of their movement's existence, is much greater than the influence the three major religions of the West had in their first seventy years. Take the *Journey*. You might just find something that will help shape your consciousness.

Mutabaruka
Poet, Author and Activist

---

3 Author's note: Kemetic means ancient Egyptian from *Kemet*, the Egyptian word for Egypt

FOREWORD BY THE EDITOR

Dear Reader:

The Journey to the Roots of Rastafari is a journey like no other. I know. I have taken it!

I joined Abba Yahudah's *Journey* shortly after receiving a phone call from his wife Tsadae Neway in 2012. I was excited. I have long been intrigued and delighted by the Rastafarians. Abba Yahudah's manuscript was breathtaking in its scope, only my second complete book-length manuscript to edit, and the greatest, first to be published, and first to give me public credit.

But I had reservations. I am mostly interested in writing and commenting from what I consider an orthodox, though mystical and progressive, Christian point of view. Wouldn't working with Abba Yahudah bring my credentials as an orthodox Christian into question? And how would it be seen in the mainstream academic community?

Ultimately I concluded I can't let worrying about others, how they mis/understand my motivations and me, stop me from doing what I'm called to do. My heart said to be open to Abba Yahudah and to see what I could learn from him and give to him.

My job as editor is to help Abba Yahudah make his voice be heard and his vision be seen as clearly and strongly as possible. Others will judge how successful I have been.

But I have a personal interest in the things Abba Yahudah says. It is hard to see how I could have persisted to the point of bringing this book to light, with Abba Yahudah and Buggsy and the others who have contributed, if I didn't care about the stories and ideas and images in this book.

Abba Yahudah and I share a love of great books, of big ideas, of bringing together theology and philosophy, psychology and anthropology, history and scripture, mythology and ritual, art and language, mathematics and science, and the problems of ecstasy and action in the world: a deep long-standing footing in the Judeo-Christian tradition and in the mystical traditions of the West, Africa, Near East, Far East and beyond: a love of diversity, family and tribe, a preferential option for the oppressed, and a commitment to the liberation and flourishing of all mankind.

Abba Yahudah has indeed read and mastered many of the most important and fascinating books: be sure to check out the footnotes and bibliography. I love how he knows and marshals the most fascinating facts and arguments to build a vision far above most people's view.

What I admire perhaps most in Abba Yahudah's vision is his insistence on the image and light of God which is within every person, the potential all people have for divinization, and the need to coordinate all fields of study and action, faith and practice to support that singular goal.

Abba Yahudah is not one to shy away from the impossible, much less the difficult. He courageously brings his passions and inspiration to bear on problems like white supremacy, the conjoined issue of colonialism, and the sexism entrenched in much of traditional, classical, medieval and modern society. Many, not least many "white" folks, may get their hackles up during his nuanced discussion of black supremacy. Feminists will cheer any number of passages, while celibates and other sexual minorities, along with advocates of "family planning" and "safe sex," question the drift of a few. His ideas and beliefs are his own[4], but I am convinced he balances within himself a love for genuine traditional values, a zeal for justice and progress, and a liberated, liberating spirit and lifestyle.

---

[4] The author is likewise responsible for copyright and attribution, as well as the final form of the book.

As for the journey toward the *Journey* — which has been of course a journey within the *Journey* — I can assure you that it has been intense. As you may infer from reading these pages, Abba Yahudah is an intense man. He is a man of big ideas, an intense teacher, artist, family man and more, but significantly, he escapes the tendency great men can have to abuse or talk down to those around him. He keeps his compassion, sense of humor and mellow poise through the vicissitudes of human frailty on every side.

This has been a big project for both of us, and we have had growing pains. Each of us was prone to bouts of gloom, frustration and uncertainty, punctuated by periods of warm elation. But, in a sign of the work of the Spirit among us? each was always ready to help the other in his hour of darkness.

My *Journey* has been a long one, and Abba Yahudah has walked it much longer still. I thank Abba Yahudah for allowing me to work with him. I am happy and proud to see the *Journey* come to press.

You will hear wondrous tales, see great marvels, and encounter hard sayings in this book. I hope you will find it also a source of wisdom, joy and hope, and a pleasure and inspiration.

Vik Slen

Bachelor of Arts, St. John's College, Santa Fé, New Mexico; author of essay *Cybernetic Incarnation: Toward a Systems Approach to the Economy of Salvation* (1983)

Master of Urban Planning, San José State University, San José, California; author of interdisciplinary report *Systematic Zoning Administration* (1992)

Master of Arts, Ethics and Social Theory / Religion and Society, Graduate Theological Union / Church Divinity School of the Pacific, Berkeley, California; author of thesis *The Local Church, the Middle Judicatory and the City of God: Lessons of Cooperative Ministry in San Francisco* (2011)

Abba Yahudah Sellassie

ABOUT THE AUTHOR

An African Jamaican male with a feminist perspective, Abba Yahudah is a conscious visionary heart brother, deeply committed to the rebirth of the Goddess. He has deep empathy for the suffering of black women, in particular, as well as for the pain of the larger collective body of African people. The African Diaspora, Ethiopianism, mysticism, and the Rastafarian experience inspire his art and writings.

He believes in the ultimate unity of all spiritual traditions, but as a Jamaican, he was unable to escape the Catholic and Baptist missionaries and therefore has been particularly influenced by Christianity. He could be considered a Rastafarian Gnostic, in the sense that he has retained the jewels of truth in Christianity, but radically dissected the false patriarchal ideologies in Christianity (and elsewhere) that subjugate the feminine principle. He prefers to take history all the way back to the emergence of humanity from the primordial womb of the Mother — the land of Ethiopia.

He has felt the pain of his heritage and has spent most of his life developing an artistic identity that transcends borders, labels and stereotypes, not an easy task for an African Jamaican male.

Born in St. Catherine, Jamaica, to a family of artists and builders, Abba Yahudah vowed early on to devote himself entirely to art, making everything he did a creative exercise. By the age of ten, he developed a very detailed eye, showing remarkable skill with the pencil, and able to draw the exact likeness of anything he saw.

He migrated to the United States in 1981 and at the age of fifteen took his first job as a sign painter, intimately exposing him to typography and layout. Several of his works were published in local and national media such as *Sights and Sounds*, *The Apprentice*

Writer and *Student Voice*. In 1985, while living in New York, he enrolled in Parsons School of Design, majoring in graphic design. A year later, he enrolled in the School of Visual Arts, where he majored in design and illustration. In 1987 Abba Yahudah began working as an illustrator and art director for one of the larger design firms in Manhattan. He designed and illustrated for companies such as Sony, Sharp, Revlon, Maxwell House and Pepsi, to name a few. In 1996, he opened the first Rastafarian art gallery in Park Slope in Brooklyn, calling it Lalibela after the monolithic churches of Ethiopia's New Jerusalem.

Today Abba Yahudah divides his time between Jamaica, Oregon and California, where he principally resides in the San Francisco Bay Area. His art has traveled internationally, to Italy and Spain, to Ethiopia, where it has been exhibited at the Habesha and Lela Art Galleries, and to Jamaica, with an exhibit at the University of the West Indies. He has also exhibited at the Smithsonian Museum of Natural History in Washington, D.C., and numerous galleries in the San Francisco Bay Area. He had an amazing and very successful show at the California Institute of Integral Studies. He is also a talented musician and loving father.

Victoria Christian

Artist and author of the 2013 coffee table book, *Feminine Mysticism in Art: Artists Envisioning the Divine,* and of the 2008 video with the same title

PREFACE

It was in the summer of 1997 that I was asked to write an article about the Rastafarians by Jean Patrick Icart-Pierre, a fellow artist and an editor who heard me speak on the subject at a conference in New York. I outrightly refused, stating I wasn't a writer, but I later succumbed to his entreaties since I had the information and felt it was my duty to share it. He convinced me that I could do it, promising that, if I did, he would publish it in the winter issue of his paper, the *Bedford-Stuyvesant Current*, a local Brooklyn publication that featured articles on issues that affected communities of color.

The first part of *A Journey to the Roots of Rastafari* was printed in the winter of 1997. That issue, Volume 2, Number 5 of the *Bed-Stuy Current*, caused a stir among the readership. Subsequently, calls began to come in from as far as Chicago, IL. One particular incident that registered in my mind was the day a professor of African history at NYU walked through the doors of my place of business, Lalibela, to address me with questions about my article. Questions like, How do I know the things I wrote about? which he, a teacher of African history at a distinguished institution of higher education, was totally ignorant of. After talking for a bit, he asked if I could come lecture to his class. At first I declined. I found it a bit surreal and somewhat bewildering that he wasn't schooled in basic African history, especially the history of Ethiopia, considering that he was a professor of African history at a quite prominent university.

After deep contemplation on how to approach the subject of Rastafari in the small space given me, keeping it to a few words without compromising the essence of the culture, I decided to break the *Journey* into parts, each part broken down into chapters dealing with specific points. The newspaper articles developed into half page to full center spreads. It was the feedback from that series of articles, and from the lectures based on them I gave in that professor's class and elsewhere, that compelled me to publish this book.

Throughout the *Journey* you will find that I use the common name *Jesus* when referring to the son of God from a conventional Christian perspective. However, *Yahowshua*[5] is used, from the perspective of the original name of the Jewish mystic, to denote the difference between the mythical European version portrayed in the King James Version of the Holy Bible (KJV) and the historical Essene master portrayed by the Essene scriptures, according to which He had a natural sexual birth and was more human than is normally believed of *Jesus*.

Thus, my reference to *Jesus* throughout the *Journey* is within the context of colonial Christianity and the KJVs perspective, which is the general public's understanding of Him. In contrast, I use *Yahowshua* as the Essene representation. Throughout the *Journey* I also use *Mashiakh*[6], the Hebrew word, interchangeably with *Christ*, so as to not create confusion or unnecessary complication for my readers. I use *God* and *Yahweh* much in the same way I use *Jesus* and *Christ*.

The first chapter of the text unfolds in a rudimentary and simple style, approaching the subject matter from a very matter-of-fact perspective. I did this deliberately, not taking for granted that you will have any background on which to contextualize the information I am imparting.

The chapters increase in depth and intensity as the subject matter is explored in scriptural and historical texts, looking at them from angles ranging from the pragmatic to the highly esoteric. I

---

5 Author's note: *Yahowshua* is the original, unadulterated Hebrew name from which we get *Jesus*.

6 Author's note: *Mashiakh* is the Hebrew word meaning Messiah. *Christ* is the Greek equivalent (as it has found its way into conventional English).

choose to write in a language that is at times inconsistent with the general Rastafarian jargon, since that jargon can, if you are not familiar with it, complicate an already complex phenomenon.

My research for this project started long before I knew this book would be written. The basic materials were compiled from my lifelong love affair with metaphysics, theology, psychology, iconography, sacred geometry, world history and the esoteric, my insatiable appetite for knowledge and burning desire to know. The resources for this manuscript have been gathered from numerous sources from around the world, from Ethiopia, Jamaica, Austria, the UK, Egypt and the Americas, for the last two decades. My eyes have seen some very rare manuscripts; some I have acquired, while others were simply unobtainable. I use my Jamaican childhood exposure to Rastafarians in the sixties to measure the growth and development of the movement from its early days to its global impact today. Parallels are drawn between the ancient Essenes and the Rastafarians to clearly illustrate the undeniable fulfillment of the former by the latter as the promise manifest. These claims are based on an assessment of the available facts and of the subtle truths embedded between the lines on the pages of history.

From 1930 to 2020 makes ninety years since the coronation of their Imperial Majesties Haile Sellassie I and Empress Menen. These nine decades are symbolic of the conception and incubatory stages of the Rastafarian faith, as in the cycle of nine months or three trimesters of a woman's pregnancy. At the end of the third trimester a rebirth of Rastafari is inevitable, with an organized and centralized consciousness, fulfilling the Emperor's direct commandment to the movement, *organize and centralize*.[7] I believe that is in fact the primary need of the movement, which when achieved will propel the group into its next level of infrastructural growth and development. In this

---

[7] Author's note: *Organize and centralize*: The advice reportedly given to the select few Rastafarians that had the privilege of an audience with Haile Sellassie I during His visit to Jamaica in 1966.

Journey however I am focused on exposing the significant parallels that lead us to the conviction that the Rastafarians of today fulfill the ancient Essenian prophecies, and are the only group that can claim to do so.

A Journey to the Roots of Rastafari is a concise compilation of thoughts inspired by a wealth of knowledge gleaned from many different sources to support one point: Ancient prophecies are being fulfilled in our times, right before our eyes, yet they go unnoticed; and the Rastafarians, through Haile Sellassie I, are the fulfillment of such prophecies. The parallels I draw throughout this *Journey* from the available facts will illustrate just that.

These writings were compiled to help dispel the myths, academic dishonesty, and general misinformation about the Rastafarians, as well as to shed light on the movement's legitimacy based on the African origins of the Messianic lineage.

Abba Yahudah
The Author

ACKNOWLEDGEMENTS

A world of love and gratitude pours out from the wellspring of my being for all the women of the world, especially the mothers.

Those to whom I owe my life and the multiplicity of my love: my mothers, the mothers of my children, my daughters, sisters, aunties and nieces. I would like to specifically thank Wendy Ashley and Tsadae Abeba Neway, the two women in my world, without whom none of my work would be possible.

I would also like to acknowledge my earthly father Horace Hall for instilling in me, from early childhood, a deep and lasting love interest in everything African, and for consciously guiding me into the blackest depths of my being — where I found the value, beauty and meaning of my African history and heritage.

Thanks to my brother Garfield Hall, whose critical and objective mind was a valuable asset which contributed importantly to this work. A world of thanks to Michael *Buggsy* Malone, whose faithfulness and devotion has been more than a strength to this project. I also like to extend appreciation and gratitude to Vik Slen, my editor, who through intense and at times extreme conditions found ways to overcome many challenges in the process of the preparation of the manuscript — thank you.

In recognition of the numerous sacrifices made for the liberation of the Africans, I thank Harriet Tubman, Sojourner Truth, Queen Nzinga, Princess Nyabinghi, Vita Kimba, Empress Taitu, the Rt. Hon. Marcus Mosiah Garvey, H.I.M. Haile Sellassie I, Leonard P. Howell, Nanny of the Maroons, King Emmanuel and John Brown.

Abba Yahudah

The Four Winds

CHAPTER 1

INTRODUCTION TO THE ESSENES

Were the thoughts of Plato and Socrates, the beliefs of Christianity and Judaism not harmonized with Hindu Philosophy: were Yoga and its previous stages not exposed to Western thought; had Western religion and philosophy not been exposed to the philosophy and religion of the East ... how much the poorer would human thought have been!

Since nobody can interfere in the realm of God, we should tolerate and live side by side with those of other faiths. In the mystic traditions of the different religions, we have a remarkable unity of spirit. Whatever religion we may profess, we are spiritual kinsmen. While the different religions in their historic form bind us to limited groups and militate against the development of loyalty to the world community, the mystics have already stood for the fellowship of humanity...in harmony with the spirit of the mystics of ages gone by. No one should question the faith of others, for no human being can judge the ways of God. However wise or however mighty a person may be, he is like a ship without a rudder if he is without God.

— H.I.M. Haile Sellassie I[8]

---

[8] H.I.M. is an acronym for His and/or Her Imperial Majesties, used for the Emperor and Empress of Ethipia. Haile Sellassie I was the last Emperor of Ethiopia and ruled Ethiopia in that office from 1930-1974.

The Essenes of All Ages

Existence as we know it is a cycle, a constant evolutionary process with no break. There are peak moments in this sequence, such as the expression of the Mashiakh in the material realm, which represent paradigm shifts. In some cultures individuals who embody such shifts are called Avatars or Buddhas. These mystic manifestations enrich our lives still today, and shape the history of the world, as in the case of the order of the Essenes.

There is evidence that all religions preceding Rastafari contributed to the unfolding of the Essene cycle, and share responsibility for where it has led today. Life has been happening according to a plan of cause and effect that has been continuously unfolding from before the beginning of time, and is the reservoir of universal wisdom that gave Yahowshua, an Essene prophet, the authority to declare that *before Abraham was, I AM.*[9]

This dynamic universal teaching from beyond the distant past, which is timeless in its application and ageless in its wisdom, has benefited humanity as a standard by which to live in Divine consciousness. It is the theological blueprint upon which the Hamitic, Shemitic and Kushitic kingdoms were built, and traces of it can be found in Egyptian hieroglyphs within the heart of the pyramids dating back some eight to ten thousand years. Many of the elemental symbols, such as those for the sun, moon, air, water and other natural forces, are from an even earlier age, the Atlantean civilization, which preceded the cataclysm that ended the predominately Kemetic period.

It is unknown for how many thousands of years this teaching existed previous to that. But we do know that its traditions are present with us today, via the sages and mystics who have

---

9 *I AM* is the Old Testament name of God revealed to Moses on Mt. Sinai, Exodus 3:13-14. It signifies that God is presence.

lived throughout the ages. Many are credited with contributing to this mystic practice of the Essenes, but the name of Enoch surfaces as the cornerstone of the Essenes' ancient Hebraic monotheistic order.

Enoch

Enoch, whose Hebrew name means *initiator*, *founder* or *teacher*, is declared in the Bible to have been the first prophet, seven generations from Adam.[10] He is the one to whom all the mysteries were revealed. His revelations gave birth to the concepts of the Tree of Life, astronomy, angelology, the promise of the Mashiakh, and the imminent clash of good and evil forces classically known as the apocalypse.[11]

Enoch handed these teachings down to his children:

> And now, my children, I know all things, for this is from the Lord's lips, and this my eyes have seen from beginning to end. I know all things, and have written all things into books, the heavens and their end, and their plenitude, and all the armies and their marchings.
>
> *The Secrets of Enoch* ch. 40, vv. 1, 2

The *Book of Enoch* was virtually unknown to Europe for nearly a thousand years. James Bruce discovered it in Ethiopia and brought three copies, written in Ge'ez, home to Scotland in 1773.

---

10 Genesis 5:1-24

11 "Apocalypse" has come to refer to the end time or "eschaton," in many religions a cosmic war between good and evil preceding a day of judgment, like the one depicted in the Apocalypse or Revelation of St. John the Divine in the New Testament.

He wrote:

> Amongst the articles I consigned at the library at Paris, was a very beautiful and magnificent copy of the prophecies of Enoch, in large quarto; another is amongst the books of Scripture, which I brought home, standing immediately before the Book of Job, which is its proper place in the Abyssinian Canon; and a third copy I have presented to the Bodleian Library at Oxford by the hands of Dr. Douglas, the Bishop of Carlisle.
>
> by James Bruce, *Travels*, vol. ii, quoted by Richard Laurence in his edition of Enoch p. xiv

James Bruce was a Scottish explorer, scholar and writer, and a Freemason. He was said to be from the lesser aristocracy, of the Kinnaird family, from which he inherited enough of a fortune to facilitate his passion for overseas journeys. He traveled to Ethiopia in 1768 in search, he said, of the source of the Blue Nile. However, this was a mere façade covering up his hidden agenda of finding out what became of the Ark of the Covenant. Over a period of seven years he managed to carry out a meticulous study, documented in his journals, of the faith of the Falashas,[12] a group of mysterious Ethiopian Jews. During this period he also discovered some very rare and ancient Ethiopian manuscripts, namely the *Kebra Negast* and the *Book of Enoch*. These books James Bruce literally stole from amongst the royal treasures at Gondar and brought back to Europe.

Yet the priceless manuscript of the *Book of Enoch*, destined to reveal the forgotten source of many Christian dogmas and mysteries, rested in obscurity for over half a century more, until revealed to the world in 1821 through an English translation by Dr.

---

[12] *Falasha*, meaning Wanderer, is the term commonly used for the Ethiopian Jews. It is a misnomer. These people prefer to be called *Beta Israel*, Amharic for House of Israel.

Medieval Castle in Gondar

Richard Laurence, one-time Archbishop of Cashel and professor of Hebrew at Oxford University. Dr. Laurence was apparently unaware that he was giving mankind theological fossils through which we, in the clearer light of our generation, may study the evolution of Christianity.

> There I beheld the ancient of days, whose head was like white wool, and with him another, whose countenance... was full of grace, like that of one of the holy angels. Then I inquired of one of the angels, who went with me, and who shewed me every secret thing, concerning this Son of man; who he was; whence he was; and why he accompanied the Ancient of days. He answered and said to me, This is the Son of man, to whom righteousness belongs; with whom righteousness has dwelt; and who will reveal all the treasures of that which is concealed: for the Lord of spirits has chosen him; and his portion has surpassed all before the Lord of spirits in everlasting uprightness.
>
> *Book of Enoch* ch. XLVI, vv. 1, 2

> And trouble shall seize them, when they shall behold this Son of woman sitting upon the throne of his glory. Then shall the kings, the princes, and all who possess the earth, glorify him who has dominion over all things, him who was concealed; for from the beginning the Son of man existed in secret, whom the Most High preserved in the presence of his power, and revealed to the elect. He shall sow the congregation of the saints, and of the elect; and all the elect shall stand before him in that day. All the kings, the princes, the exalted, and those who rule over the earth, shall fall down on their faces before him, and shall worship him. They shall fix their hopes on this Son of man, shall pray to him, and petition him for mercy. Then shall the Lord of spirits hasten to expel them from

his presence. Their faces shall be full of confusion, and their faces shall darkness cover. The angels shall take them to punishment, that vengeance may be inflicted on those who have oppressed his children and his elect.

Book of Enoch ch. LXI, vv. 9-14

These passages of the ancient teachings of Enoch undeniably parallel prophetical writings in the *Holy Bible*, including, among others, the prophetical book of *Daniel* and the *Revelation of St. John the Divine*. The Ethiopic *Book of Enoch* is the oldest record of Enoch in history. It was quoted by the prophets of Old and New Testament times; yet it was omitted from the selection of books from which was compiled the holy scriptures of Western Christianity. However, *Enoch* was and continues to be part of the Ethiopian canon of Holy Scripture, and all existing versions of this book come from the Ethiopic text[13].

Enoch was fundamental to the evolution of Judaism, Christianity and Islam. In Ethiopia, these writings are much more than liturgical texts, they are at the core of Ethiopian Orthodoxy, both Judaic and Christian.

Through many generations, these apocalyptic writings were chronicled and handed down to the time of Moses,[14] who used them to construct a nation of *children of light*.[15] The people did not keep

---

13 The *Secrets of Enoch*, or *Second Book of Enoch*, preserved in full only in the Slavonic, but Coptic fragments of which have been found, contributes significantly to the ancient Ethiopic tradition about Enoch.

14 *Moses* is not a Hebrew name; it is Egyptian for *son of*. For example, *Ramses* means *son of Ra* and *Tutmoses* means *son of Tut*, god of wisdom. Moses was actually named after one of the Egyptian gods, and after he converted to belief in the god of Israel, the god of his forefathers, he slashed off the prefix and became just Moses. In Hebrew, however, Moses means *to draw out*. Exodus ch. 2, v. 10 states that "the child grew, and she brought him unto Pharaoh's daughter, and he became her son. And she called his name Moses: and she said, because I drew him out of the water."

15 1 Thessalonians ch. 5, v. 5: *Ye are all the children of light, and the children of the day: we are not the night, nor the darkness.*

his ordinances, but a group evolved under the esoteric teachings of this first Law, emerging as the vanguard of all prophetical fulfillments of the Law. This mystical body of people was known in Egypt as *Therapeutae*[16] or worshippers; in Greece as *Esseion* and *Assaya* or physicians; and in Palestine and Syria as *Essenes*.

The Essenes

The Essenes lived knowing of the Mashiakh as a principle manifest in their communal body, paving the way for the coming of the Mashiakh as a Personality.

The task of this small group was to embody a consciousness that would allow the Anointed to manifest through the womb, so the Essenes surrounded and protected their children. They preserved their collective consciousness by thus raising the children as nazarites, from which resulted the ultimate manifestation, the Christ Child, Yahowshua.

Within the context of a messianic movement, it is the duty of the devotees of the principle to usher in the incarnation of the cosmic Divine ego. The Essenes were the group of consecrated initiates bestowed with the duty of fulfilling the most glorious task, cradling the Christ Child, thus ushering in the Christian faith. In this respect, they were the Christians before the coming of the Christ. The historically recorded entry of the Power of the Mashiakh into the organic structure of the human race — a power the Essenes cradled — gives Christianity its unique distinction from other major world religions.

The Essenes saw that liberation was the destiny of humanity. Therefore the possibility for every individual to work out their salvation and attain their goal by virtue of sublime deeds became the focus of their discipline. At the heart of this mission is the

---

16 Some modern scholars refer to the Therapeutae as *healers*; however, their name actually means "worshippers."

assistance of the Messianic Consciousness in achieving this state, and thus the devotee continues the ministry and teachings of the Messiah (Mashiakh). The Essenes were thus both the forerunners and preservers of the true teachings of the Mashiakh.

They revered the Sun (Son) as a symbol of light and fire. They chanted hymns of praises facing the rising sun, marking a time of communion with the higher realms in keeping with reverence for the Sun as habitation for the Light of the World. They are still famous for their celebrations of the solstices.

The actual name *Essene* is not found in many of the sacred chronicles because the secretive Essenes were often the ones producing these writings. And so for thousands of years the Essenes have remained in the background, even though they are at the heart of events that continue to reshape the world. Today they are re-emerging, revealing the true importance of the contribution they made to the spiritual evolution of humanity, which was clearly seen through the ascension of the Mashiakh to His Throne. This historic apparition stimulated a reincarnation of ancient souls, creating an elect body of those who have *eyes to see* and *ears to hear*, making them witnesses to the Mashiakh in his second Advent.

The Essenes having always existed in one form or another, even though their teachings may not be acknowledged by many of the historical records. Newly discovered texts such as the *Dead Sea Scrolls* and the *Nag Hammadi Library* reveal that the Essene Mashiakh, Yahowshua, vastly differs from the Jesus Christ of the King James Version. Although the word Essene does not appear in contemporary translations of the *Holy Bible*, the presence and teachings of the Essenes are evident in the history of the prophets and judges of Israel, for example, Elijah, Ezekiel and countless others including the prophets of the New Testament. Many of these differences are perfectly preserved in the lifestyle of the present mystics of the Ethiopic glory.

... God is in the generation of the righteous.

Psalm 14, v. 5

The ancient Essenes are mystically present even today and are shaping the direction of the coming age. When a civilization or culture is transitioning from one stage or phase into another, as is the case in our time, matters pertaining to such developments are not only a concern of scholars and scientists, they are for everyone's consideration.

Such cognitions are important when we recapitulate the work of the historical Essenes over 2,000 years ago. They helped to lay the foundations for the dawning of the Piscean Age, which has now drawn to a close. Today we must help lay the foundation for the Aquarian Age.

The Rastafarians: Essenes of Today

Continuing the teachings of Yahowshua, the Priestly Mashiakh, the Rastafarians have emerged as the reincarnated souls of the ancient Essene masters, to become the illuminated heralds of the gospel of the new age. Their pre-Adamic consciousness has come down through the ages, linking time and space, and bringing us to today's natural manifestation, the Essene Nazarite Monastic Order of Melkizadek.[17]

It is not necessary to undergo the experience of Rastafari, nor of any organized religion, to become enlightened. Religions in fact can become

---

[17] The Essene Nazarite Monastic Order of Melkizadek (E.N.M.O.M.) is the Rastafarian Essene sect. Their understanding of Haile Sellassie I as King of Kings has brought them full circle to the Divine Feminine, which manifested and was embodied in the emperor's wife, Empress Menen as Mother Divine. This particular fulfillment is to Rastafarians evidence of the equality of the sexes as well as the revelation of Queen Omega. In Rasteology (Ras Theology), the emperor, being the expressed figure of King Alpha, was instrumental in raising the standard of the Ethiopian woman while exposing Her as the right hand of God. The Royal Apostles have accepted this image and reality and are devoted to the balance of the Trinity, being the image set before them in Haile Sellassie I's coronation portrait of 1930. The Essene Nazarite Monastic Order of Melkizadek is the priestly order devoted and surrendering to the male and female Divinity.

huge stumbling blocks to salvation by closing one to the many other ways and means to know God. However, Rastafari, as a manifested way, is one of the quickest paths to immediate enlightenment, in that it forces one to come to grips with the God within humanity, and the Divine connection of all life as part of a whole. But one must first see the God within in order to see the Divinity in another.

Salvation comes through the power of transcendence, which is the vehicle to bliss. Without the power to transcend obstacles, one cannot truly become enlightened. The power of transcendence comes by taking chances, by testing the limits and strength of the boundaries set by the programmed mind: which means one will have to lose one's own mind in order to know oneself.

These writings seek to educate all who seek the truth about the ancient Essenes and the Rastafarians, that *peculiar people*[18] that chooses to walk the earth in the light of Haile Sellassie I.

Rastafarians encounter all manner of diverse opinions, hearsay and half-truths about themselves, usually from those who see them from the perspective of spectators rather than faithful disciples. Regardless of how sympathetic or empathetic a person is, their ignorance will always handicap their pursuit of understanding. This is true for anything. Therefore *the Journey to the Roots of Rastafari* is a *Journey* you must take for yourself.

This is why I accepted the challenge of writing on the subject Rastafari — the object being understanding. After accepting the challenge, I realized I could simply write a few paragraphs outlining the religious cultural expression of the Rastafarians, but this would not even begin to scratch the surface. As a matter of fact, anything I wrote would leave most readers with more questions than answers — which is a step in the right direction.

---

18 Deuteronomy 26, v. 18: "And the Lord hath avouched thee this day to be his *peculiar people*, as he hath promised thee, and that thou shouldest keep all his commandments."

Throughout this *Journey*, at various points and at different levels, the origins and focus of the Rastafarians will be discussed. In an attempt to shed more light on the roots of Rastafari, we will discuss in some depth:

1. Ethiopia: The Place
2. The Ark of the Covenant: The Thing
3. Yahowshua ha Mashiakh/Haile Sellassie I: The Man
4. The Rastafarians, Reincarnation of the Ancient Essenes: The People

> Until ignorance has been eradicated, understanding and sympathy cannot truly exist among men, without tolerance and comprehension, oppression will continue to exist, and peace will not be assured. To love and to seek learning is thus to love and to seek peace.
>
> — H.I.M. Haile Sellassie I, 1963[19]

The struggle to conquer ignorance proceeds through a series of reasonings,[20] in order that we may know peace by the way of the truth. Ignorance has given birth to many myths about the *Place*, the *Thing*, the *Man* and the *People*. Through ignorance, fear has taken root in the minds of many, creating vain imaginings and misconceptions about who the Rastafarians really are.

The Rastafarians reason: the lion, although not the largest, strongest or fastest animal in the jungle, is without dispute, the king of the jungle. Without trickery or stealing, often without even having to fight or kill, the lion ascended to the throne of kingship by the Divine will and power. Over the ages, mankind has come

---

19 H.I.M. Haile Sellassie I's 1963 speech on education.

20 Reasoning — A process by which one draws a conclusion based upon one's ability to think logically. Reasoning can proceed between two or more people, through calm and rational verbal exchange, or internally, through a series of questions and answers within oneself.

to understand this through careful observation and reasoning, and has not hesitated to give the lion his crown and glory. It is simply because he has accepted the truth as it is that the lion rules by Divine order. That is why even mankind, the ruler of the earth through Divine right, fears the lion. If man, through reason, can discern between the lion and the rest of the jungle, then surely he can, and must, be able to identify which man is the Lion King amongst men, the Ruler and Lord of the hearts of men by Divine right and natural order.

I suggest that you process this information within yourself and jot down your comments and questions,[21] which will be addressed after the completion of A.D., the Third Epoch, the final leg of this *Journey*. In chapter 12, entitled *The Rastafarians: The Essenes Rencarnated*, I will elaborate in depth on the ideals, traditions, aspirations and history of Rastafari, the manifestation of the ancient Essene prophecies living in Jamaica and abroad. I will outline some essential beliefs and rituals both groups have in common, establishing that modern Rastafarians are indeed the reincarnated souls of the ancient Essenes.

For everyone that takes this journey, a few essentials are recommended: an open mind, the *Holy Bible,* and the Ethiopian *Kebra Negast* (The Glory of Kings), from which I shall quote. I will also quote the *Book of Enoch* and the *Essene (Nazarene) Holy Bible*, just recently translated and published in its entirety. I make these suggestions so that you may analyze the writings for yourself and draw your own conclusions. I am aware that many people are not familiar with many of these writings. Therefore, I find it appropriate to periodically quote passages from these most informative, indeed sacred, books. The information in these ancient manuscripts augments my points while broadening our views and perspective of the subject.

---

21 Your *comments* and *questions* can be jottted down on the blank pages for notes at the back of the book. Please send your notes to: info@wordswordpublishing.com, where they will be addressed and considered in the revision process — as the *Journey* continues.

It is not the intention of this book to add to the already complicated web of religious theology by overwhelming you with occult semantics and difficult dogmas — though unavoidably some will be overwhelmed. I beseech you to take the *Journey* to its final destination and judge what sense it makes only when you arrive.

FIRST EPOCH

B.C.

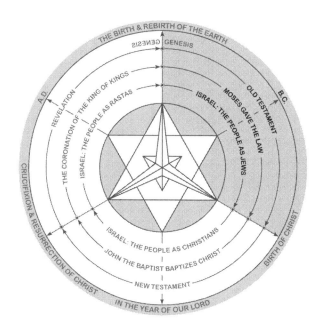

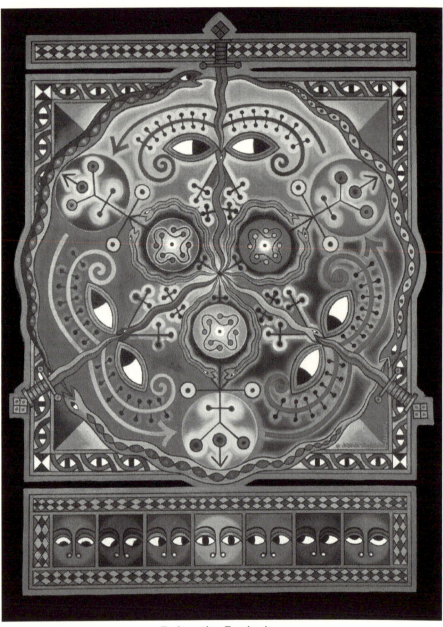

Before the Beginning

CHAPTER 2

MOTHER ETHIOPIA

Ethiopia: As Eden

From the remote times to the present, one of the most celebrated and yet most mysterious nations was Ethiopia. In the early traditions of nearly all civilized nations the name of this distant people is found.

They are the remotest nation, the most just of men, the favorite of the Gods, and when the faint gleam of tradition and fables gives way to the clear light of history, the luster of the Ethiopian is not diminished, they still continue as the object of curiosity and admiration; the pen of cautious, clear sighted historians often paint them in the highest rank of knowledge and civilization.

The Physical History of Mankind
By the historian of antiquity Hereen[22]

A study of the ancient kingdom of Ethiopia is of paramount importance for understanding Rastafarians' faith in Her as Holy Mount Zion the Tabernacle of the Living God.

It is evident that more and more people are leaving the countryside and flooding the cities. In the modern world, people live far from nature, far from the world that shaped the traditions of primordial Ethiopia. Nevertheless, dreams of an earthly paradise persist. All societies and religions across the ages aspire to return to a Garden

---

22 Arnold Hermann Ludwig Hereen was a German historian born October 25, 1760 and died March 6, 1842. He was known to be a calm and impartial man who possessed vast and varied learning. It is said that his chief merit as an historian was his ability to look at the ancient world with fresh eyes and a new perspective.

of Eden, a place that lives in and beyond our imaginations, and one that can still be found along the headwaters of the Nile. *In our beginning is our end, and the end of all our exploring will be to arrive where we started and know the place for the first time.*[23]

The earliest known human fossils are all from East Africa. Anthropologists have found fragments of human bones and teeth from around four million years ago in various regions of Ethiopia and as far as South Africa.

The birthplace of humankind, said Darwin, *was most likely Africa. He found that in each great region of the world, the living mammals are closely related to the extinct species of the same region. He concluded that, as [the gorilla and chimpanzee] are now man's nearest allies, it is somewhat more probable that our early progenitors lived on the African Continent than elsewhere.*[24]

Darwin arrived at this theory though no human fossils had yet been found anywhere in Africa. The only human fossils known in Darwin's time were from the Netherlands, representing a relatively late stage of human evolution.

Because of the anti-African prejudices of the colonial mind, anthropologists intensely disliked Darwin's suggestion of an African origin for humankind. The so-called *Dark Continent* was not viewed as a suitable place for the origin of such a noble creature as *Homo sapiens*. This attitude prevailed for decades, until Louis Leakey, a European born and raised in Kenya, in the early nineteen-thirties ignored the advice of scholars and set out

---

23 Adapted from T. S. Eliot, *Four Quartets* ("East Coker" and "Little Gidding"). Thomas Sterns Eliot (1888-1965) is one of America's best-known poets, and said to be one of the most daring innovators in twentieth-century poetry. He was born in St. Louis, Missouri, but later moved to England where he became a British citizen.

24 In *The Descent of Man* (1871) p. 199, Charles Robert Darwin, Fellow of the Royal Society, was an English naturalist. He established that all species of life have descended over time from common ancestors, and proposed the scientific theory that this branching pattern of evolution resulted from a process that he called natural selection.

to establish East Africa as the vital link in the history of human evolution.

The finds of human fossils on the continent in recent years have indeed proven Darwin's theory to be correct and established East Africa, and specifically Ethiopia, as the Mother of human existence. As Mother, Ethiopia represents the roots of mankind, shedding light and pouring life into the many branches of the human family tree.

Ethiopia is the land where the sun rises from the lowest depths of the earth to the highest heights of the heavens, a land of gods and goddesses, kings and queens, princes and princesses. She is the land of the Conquering Lion of Judah, the womb and Mother of the human race. Genesis ch. 2, vv. 7-13 gives a specific location for the original Garden (the home of Adam and Eve) as *eastward in Eden*, at a place where the head of the river is parted into four:

> And the Lord God formed man of the dust of the ground, and breathed into his nostrils the breath of life; and man became a living soul. The Lord God planted a garden eastward in Eden; and there He put the man whom He had formed. And out of the ground the Lord God made to grow every tree that is pleasant to the sight and good for food; the tree of life was also in the midst of the garden, and the tree of knowledge of good and evil. And a river went out of Eden to water the garden; and from thence it was parted, and became into four heads. The name of the first is Pishon: that is it which compasseth the whole land of Havilah, where there is gold: And the gold of that land is good. There is Bdellium and the onyx stone. And the name of the second river is Ghion (Nile): The same is it that compasseth the whole land of Ethiopia.

So Moses, the presumed author of the Book of Genesis, names Ethiopia as the place where God placed Adam after He breathed the breath of life into his nostrils. Logically speaking, if Adam, symbolically the first begotten Son of God, is an Ethiopian, then God, the Father and Mother of all, must have resided there before him. Ethiopia, then, is the earthly Zion, the Mother, and the place God has chosen for Himself. Upon their transgression of the original Law, Adam and Eve were cast out into the rest of the earth, but God's presence, or *Shekinah*, remained in that land. Genesis ch. 3, vv. 23, 24 states:

> Therefore the Lord God sent him forth from the Garden of Eden to till the ground from whence he was taken. And so he drove out the man; and he placed at the East of the Garden of Eden cherubim and a flaming sword, which turned every way, to keep the way of the tree of life.

The Garden of Eden in Ethiopia is a sacred and protected place, one reserved for the Almighty. After a period of time, however, mankind — being purified in the Life of the Word, the second Adam, Yahowshua ha Mashiakh, the Keeper of the Way to the Tree of Life — will be able to return to that land.

For Rastafarians, the biblical Promised Land is therefore not Old Jerusalem in Palestine, but Ethiopia. She is that place that has never been conquered by the evil forces of the colonial powers of the world, the place that Jacob yearned to dwell. She is the place where Jah rules as High Priest and King, on the Throne of Melkizadek.[25]

Ethiopia holds within Her bosom very deep mysteries yet to be fully revealed. We must take these into account when evaluating Her true importance to human spiritual evolution if we are to understand the Judaeo-Christian psychology we find in ourselves.

---

[25] *Melkizadek* is from two Hebrew words — *melki*, meaning *king*, and *zadek*, meaning *righteousness*. Thus *Melkizadek* translates to *king of righteousness*.

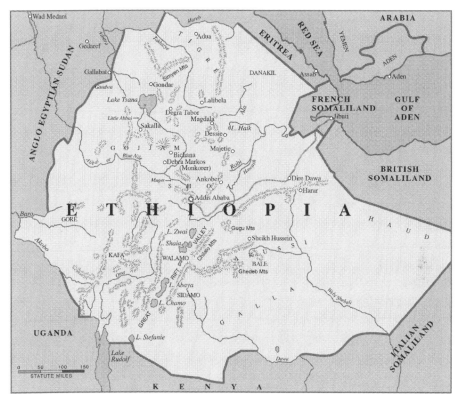

Map of Ethiopia 1928

Ethiopia: The Land

The most common misconception of Ethiopia is that it is nothing but a desert, plagued by famine and misery. This myth was created during the war years following the Italian invasion of 1936. Certain European journalists entered Ethiopia after the war, in the years of Haile Sellassie I, with the intention of casting Ethiopia and Her Emperor in a negative light.

Reputable, well-established publishers such as the National Geographic Society documented Ethiopia's rich cultural heritage in numerous issues describing Her as a country of almost unlimited resources. In 1925, American agriculturists were sent there to collect highly valued seeds and grains with the intention of cultivating them in the United States. Both Britain and the U.S. sent scientists there to study rare species of plants and animals found there.

Agents of the mass media nevertheless have spent much time and effort perpetuating the myth that Ethiopia is a desert plagued by disease, poverty and famine. Even before the 1936 invasion, the fascist Italian government's propaganda machine was diligent in developing the lie that Ethiopia is a worthless, barren, and deserted land of savages. This they did to justify their malicious intentions against this ancient civilization.

Contrary to Western propaganda, Ethiopia's elevated central plateau, which stretches over more than half of Her land area and supports a large majority of Her population, is extremely fertile, possibly the most fertile part of Africa.

Ethiopia's highlands and lowlands are lush, fertile and densely cultivated. Her southern and western highlands boast the most extensive indigenous forests to be found anywhere in the eastern half of the African continent. Her central highlands are more open, but still heavily vegetated, especially during the rainy season.

The Great Rift Valley, located between the southern Ethiopian Plateau to the north and the northern Somalian Plateau to the south, south of Addis Ababa,[26] is dominated by grassy vegetation and decorated with flat-topped acacia trees. The Ethiopian Rift Valley Lakes (which have no outlets) are at the northernmost point of the African Rift Valley Lakes, and occupy the floor of the

---

26 *Addis Ababa*, the name of Ethiopia's capital city, is Amharic for "new flower."

plain in the valley between the highlands, creating a very fertile environment well vegetated for wildlife and native people alike. The western lowlands are very tropical in appearance, covered with a variety of indigenous plants. There are indeed deserts in Ethiopia: they stretch from the base of the plateau, near the borders of Kenya, to the Red Sea. As one would expect, these areas are sparsely populated, so they have little impact on the lives of most Ethiopians.

The Ethiopian highlands provide an insulated habitat for rare mammals such as the Simeon fox and the Gelada baboon, as well as for thirty of the eight hundred or more species of birds that are found in Ethiopia, twenty-three of which are found nowhere else.

Ethiopia's capital, Addis Ababa, situated in the central highlands in the heart of the country, sits at an altitude of 2300 meters, making it the third highest capital city in the world. The population of the country is estimated at over fifty million people, the third highest of any country in Africa, exceeded only by Nigeria and Egypt.

Ethiopia: The People

The historian Graham Hancock notes that in the twelfth century a French explorer ventured into the heart of Abyssinia (Ethiopia). When he returned to Europe he said that he saw the Ark of the Covenant being carried about there by men with blue eyes and red beards.

The expedition that brought the French explorer into the mountainous country of Kush in the twelfth century had brought him into the cradle of African civilization. Africans in fact are quite diverse in terms of culture, ethnicity and skin color, but for the most part, Africans are richly pigmented, leading to their description as *black*.

Ethiopian Tribes

Oromo

Karrayyu

Amhara

Hamar

Ethiopian Tribes

Abore   Afar

Like many African societies, Ethiopia is Mother to a mosaic of tribes and nationalities, each with its own language, over seventy-five to be specific. Linguists have divided the languages into four groups, three of them tracing their roots to a language called Proto-Afro-Asiatic or Lismaric. These three language groups are known as Kushitic, Omotic and Semitic.

Kushitic and Omotic are the two oldest language groups spoken in the Ethiopian region. The Kushitic-speaking people were dominant in ancient times. The Agaw, a Kushitic speaking people, have now assimilated into the dominant Semitic culture with a few groups scattered in the Gojam region. Other Kushitic-speaking tribes are the Afar, the Saho, the Hadiya and the Kambata in the region of Shewa.

Kushitic/Sabean Alphabet

The Oromo constitute the largest single nationality in Ethiopia. Although they have never taken Ethiopia's royal throne they have influenced the political system, intermixing with the ruling class Amharas and exercising great influence on the Ethiopian government. In terms of linguistics, the Oromo are closest to the Somali.

Omotic-speaking people, the Oromo, derive their name from the Omo River, situated in the southwestern area of Ethiopia, in the Omo Valley, where human fossils dating some two and a half million years ago have been found.

The Semitic languages belong to an independent family called Nilo-Saharan. For the most part, the Semites have played the dominant role in the country's history. The empires and kingdoms that have emerged in Ethiopia have been invariably under the control of Semites, especially the Tigrinya and Amharic-speaking people. And while Ge'ez, the language of ancient Axum, is the oldest of the Semitic languages, today Ge'ez is in use only as the liturgical language of the Orthodox Church. Amharigna or Amharic, along

The Fidel

with Tigrinya, are the Semitic languages derived from Ge'ez (which has its roots in ancient Sabean text) that are most important in Ethiopia today. Amharic is the official language of Christian Ethiopia and is spoken by many members of other tribes.

The Semitic languages of Ethiopia are written using a script quite unique to the country. It consists of over two hundred characters, each representing a syllable as opposed to a letter. This group of languages allows speakers to express themselves and articulate emotions and feelings much more precisely than do languages based on Latin or German.

Ancient Axum

Ethiopia's cultural, historical and linguistic identity is quite distinct from that of the other countries on the continent, mostly because She has spent prolonged periods of Her timeless history in virtual isolation.

Ethiopia's oral tradition states that Ethiopia (Kush) was settled by Ethiopic (Kushitic), the son of Ham, the son of Noah, in the year 6,280 B.C. — which would make Her 8,200 years old, three times as many years as have elapsed since the birth of Yahowshua ha Mashiakh. Ethiopic's son Aksumai then founded the capital of Axum and also a dynasty of rulers that ruled from its fifty-second to its ninety-seventh generation.

As early as 1000 B.C., northern Ethiopia supported a thriving agricultural civilization of extraordinary magnitude. Archeological sources have left little doubt that this pre-Axumite culture, as much as any external influences, laid the foundation for the Axumite Empire that followed. Although archeologists are not certain when Axum was founded, Ethiopians believe they know this and many more details of their early history, and will quickly provide them to any *firenghi* (foreigner) who would dare to question their traditions.

The last and greatest of the monarchs of this dynasty, and the mother of a new dynasty, was Queen Makeda in the tenth and eleventh centuries B.C., who had a caravan of five hundred and twenty camels and a fleet of seventy-three ships that traded with places as far away as India and Palestine. This great Queen ruled Ethiopia, and what is called Yemen, for thirty-one years from her capital on the outskirts of modern-day Axum, a place Ethiopians also know as Saba (Sheba). We will hear a great deal more about Makeda *Queen of Sheba* and her offspring in the story and reasonings ahead.

The ancient Axumite kingdom, situated in the rocky hills of northern Ethiopia, had strong links with ancient Egypt, Greece, and Semitic civilizations in the Middle East, blending those with traditional African influences as early as 600 B.C. or even before. In particular, the Ethiopia of today is heavily influenced by ancient Judaism, an influence that is evident in her Orthodox Christian Church, which was established in Axum in the early fourth century A.D.

The pre-Christian Jewish community in Ethiopia, *Beta Israel*[27], commonly known as *Falashas*, preserve basic traditions dating back to Moses that were lost by Jews outside Ethiopia.

---

27 See note 12 on p. 4.

The Blessing

CHAPTER 3

THE OLD TESTAMENT

His foundation is in the holy mountains. The Lord loveth the gates of Zion more than all the dwellings of Jacob. Glorious things are spoken of thee, O city of God. Selah. I will make mention of Rahab and Babylon to them that know me: behold Philistia, and Tyre, with Ethiopia; this man was born there. And of Zion it shall be said, This and that man was born in her: and the highest himself shall establish her. The Lord shall count, when he writeth up the people, that this man was born there. Selah. As well the singers as the players on instruments shall be there: all my springs are in thee.

Psalm 87

We have seen that the biblical Garden of Eden, man's true and original home, is to be found in Ethiopia; and that She has preserved many ancient traditions that enable us to understand what Old Testament life was like centuries ago.

The teachings of Enoch were also preserved in Ethiopia, while being suppressed elsewhere by the Church of Rome and only rediscovered recently.

This chapter will discuss the traditions of the Old Testament that apply to our *Journey*, specifically the Kingdom of Melkizadek, the Prophecy of the Mashiakh, the Ark of the Covenant, the founding of the Nazarites, the establishment of Throne of David, and the mysterious union of King Solomon and the Queen of Sheba.

Salem: The Kingdom of Melkizadek

Of all biblical figures, one man stands out as a particularly vague and mysterious character. Not much is written about him; but he is, without a doubt, one of the missing links to the mystery of the biblical fulfillment of the living God of all ages. As we go into Genesis ch. 14, vv. 18-20, we read:

> Melkizadek, King of Salem, brought forth bread and wine: and he was the priest of the most high God. And he blessed him, and said, Blessed be Abram of the most high God, possessor of heaven and earth: and blessed be the most high God, which has delivered thine enemies into thy hand. And he gave him tithes of all.

Again, we read in the Letter to Hebrews ch. 7, vv. 1-3:

> For this Melkizadek, King of Salem, priest of the Most High God, who met Abraham returning from the slaughter of the kings, and blessed him; to whom also Abraham gave a tenth part of all; first being by interpretation king of righteousness, and after that also king of Salem, which is, king of peace; without father, without mother, without descent, having neither beginning of days nor end of life; but made like unto the Son of God; abideth a priest continually.

Salem is Jerusalem or Zion; they are all the same place, where Melkizadek ruled as King and High Priest. This man represents the actual receptacle of God Almighty, in His Holy Habitation of Zion.[28] As we shall see, in its deepest sense Zion is in the land of Ethiopia.

According to the *Dead Sea Scrolls*, Melkizadek was the leader of God's army of angels of righteousness who fought in the heavenly

---

[28] Zion being the habitation of Yahweh's Shekinah, His presence made it a holy place.

war against the angels of darkness. Melkizadek is also referred to in these antique scrolls as the *Elohim* (Hebrew for god) of the sons of light. In the *Melkizadek Document*, a fragmented manuscript found amongst these scrolls in the caves at Qumran, dating to 100 BC, we get a glimpse of the Priest King in the context of the heavenly hierarchy. It is the only other source, apart from those mentioned above, which gives us any mention of Melkizadek:

> [And it will be proclaimed at] the end of days concerning the captives as [He said, To proclaim liberty to the captives (Isa. 61.l). Its interpretation is that He] will assign them to the Sons of Heaven and to the inheritance of Melchizedek; f[or He will cast] their [lot] amid the po[rtions of Melchize]dek, who will return them there and will proclaim to them liberty, forgiving them [the wrong-doings] of all their iniquities. And the Day of Atonement is the e[nd of the] tenth [Ju]bilee, when all the Sons of [Light] and the men of the lot of Mel[chi] zedek will be atoned for. [And] a statute concerns them [to prov]ide them with their rewards. For this is the moment of the Year of Grace for Melchizedek. [And he will, by his strength, judge the holy ones of God, executing judgement as it is written concerning him in the Songs of David, who said, ELOHIM has taken his place in the divine council; in the midst of the gods he holds judgement [Ps 82:1]. ... And Melchizedek will avenge the vengeance of the judgements of God... and he will drag [them from the hand of] Belial.

It was said that Yahowshua was to be a priest forever *after the order of Melkizadek* fulfilling Psalm 110, v. 4 which states:

> The Lord hath sworn, and will not repent, thou art a Priest forever after the Order of Melkizadek.

The Old Testament

The Nursing Goddess Isis

Metaphysically, Melkizadek is an office of ascendance to the Divine, ascendance which can be attained by living out the Divine Will. This Will is established in righteousness, justice and peace, ruling in supreme consciousness and maintaining right action through self-remembering. It is also called the Mind of the Mashiakh or Super-Consciousness. Melkizadek is the King and Priest of Salem, and in the realm of the esoteric, Salem is Consciousness of spiritual peace, wholeness and perfection, the mountaintop Habitation of the Divine I AM.

When one takes hold of the in-dwelling Mashiakh, one is raised out of the fallen nature of the Adamic consciousness, on the first stage of the journey into the numerous levels of the Mashiakh. The seventh stage is unfoldment, in which one finds rest and peace.

Melkizadek is not an office that can be given by another but is a space that one must claim and affirm for onseself, in a lifestyle that will be recognized and confirmed by those who *have eyes to see and ears to hear*.[29] It is the office of the Elect of God, but not one established according to the will of men, as was the Levitical Priesthood on which I will elaborate later.

Egypt and the Prophecy of the Mashiakh

The Old Testament can only be understood in the light of the civilization of ancient Egypt, which was the major influencing power for the books of Genesis and Exodus.

Amun, Amon or Amen was the ancient Egyptian god of breath and air who was also known as the *hidden one*. His consort was Amaunet or Ament, whose name reveals her as the feminine aspect of Amun.[30] In the 21st century B.C. Amun rose to prominence as

---

29 Ezekiel ch. 12, v. 2

30 In the Ogdoad of Hermopolis, Amun and Amaunet form a Divine couple.

the primary deity, replacing Monthu, the former deity of Thebes. Amun continued to rise in national importance and would soon attach himself to Ra, the Sun god, as Amun-Ra.

By the 20th century B.C. Amun-Ra had become the patron god of Thebes, which would later become the capital of ancient Egypt. As the prominence of Thebes grew, so did the power and popularity of Amun-Ra, who now became the god of a new dynasty that attributed all its victories and successes to him. Amun-Ra, the god of breath or spirit, would eventually become the ultimate symbol of the self-created god, and finally crowned as God of Gods.

Over time the word *Amun* became the Ethiopian and Egyptian word for God, which has good and evil, physical and spiritual as well as male and female counterparts.

The doctrine of Divine duality was also based upon the tradition of the Egyptian Pharaoh as the Father, and the Prince the Heir apparent born to be King. The Father was the King of Egypt and the Son was the Prince of Ethiopia.

> The first born, Osiris and his twin, Isis, formed a couple and ruled peacefully over the earth, which is to say over Egypt. Seth and Nephthys formed a sterile couple, although Seth embodied the turbulent and uncontrollable forces of nature and showed evidence of an overweening but utterly disorganized sexuality.
>
> Nephthys appeared to be more attracted to Isis as well as to Osiris; with him she conceived a child who is the fruit of a relationship that is both incestuous and adulterous. This child is the dark dog Anubis the Divine mummifier.

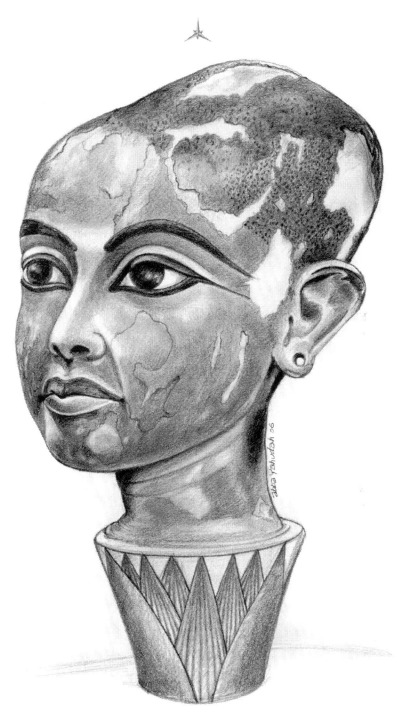
Wooden bust of the Child King Tutankhamen

Seth, who was jealous of Osiris for more than one reason, decided to overthrow him and rule in his place. He used a ruse to draw him out and seal him within a chest that he sunk into the flooded Nile. Isis and Nephthys, in distress, went off in search of the missing one, whom the waves have carried off to the banks of Byblos, where the chest had been caught in the root of a tamarisk tree.

They returned to Egypt with the chest, but Seth discovered it. He hurled himself upon his brother a second time and cut his body in sixteen pieces which he again throw into the Nile, convinced he had eliminated his rival once and for all. But Seth failed to take into account the determination of the faithful Isis, who was, moreover, a magician in her own right.

Isis gathered together all the pieces of her husband, with the exception of the phallus, which was swallowed by a fish, the oxyrhynchus. It is at this point of the legend where the sources diverge — either Isis finally rediscovers Osiris's virile member, or she manufactured a substitute; in any event the Divine body was reconstituted through her efforts with Anubis.

Isis then took the form of a bird and magically revived the generative ardor of Osiris, to whom the beating of her wings restored the vital breath. Isis and Osiris finally obtain a heir, the god Horus, the young son.

Meanwhile Osiris returned to the bowels of the earth in order to recharge his energies with an eye to a new cycle, symbolized by the image of a germinating Osiris. In this way Osiris who shares the same energies as Ra, incarnated his terrestrial, latent potential in Anubis and reveals his dynamic, celestial face in Horus.

Isis raised her son alone and in hiding in the Chemmis Swamp in order to evade the attacks of Seth. On reaching adulthood, Horus reclaimed his father's throne and immediately entered into conflict with his uncle Seth.

Schumann Antelme and Rossini,
Sacred Sexuality in Ancient Egypt, pp. 14-17

Recorded in the annals of the 18th dynasty of Egypt is the marriage of King Ahames to Queen Neferti of Ethiopia. Now Queen Neferti was seen as the spiritual wife of the God Amon (Amen), so the offspring of their union was named Tut-ankh-amon.[31]

According to the tradition of the Egyptian royal house, Moses also married an Ethiopian Princess, one whose father, Jethro, was a Midianite[32] Priest-King, a direct descendant of the Kushite race. So the Jews, as a nation, took their idea of religion from the Egyptians who, in turn, got theirs from Ethiopia, Egypt's Mother Country. It is Ethiopia's lifeblood, the Nile, which is also the source of life for Egyptian civilization. Hence, Egypt became the glory of Ethiopia.

It was Jethro, Moses' father-in-law, who instructed him in setting up the first governmental system for ruling the Israelites in the wilderness. This system consisted of breaking down the people into groups of thousands, hundreds, fifties and tens, creating a hierarchy of appointed rulers over each group, with ultimate authority lying in the hands of the Negus (King) or Emperor. This type of hierarchy, as described in Exodus ch. 18, vv. 17-24, is the age-old tradition of ancient Ethiopia as well.

---

31 Actually many young princesses of the royal house of Ethiopia dedicated themselves as spiritual wives of the God Amon, but not in the way a nun does. Being the spiritual wife of Amon did not destroy a woman's right or privilege to marry, but the sons born to her union with a prince took the name of the spiritual husband, the god, instead of the real father.

32 Some scholars believe that Midian is located in the Egyptian Sinai peninsula. The location is not certain, but the Midianite people are believed to be descendants of Abraham from his wife Keturah and their son Midian.

The Old Testament

It has also been a long-standing tradition for the Pharaohs of Egypt to take their wives from Ethiopia. Now Pharaohs in Egypt were very religious.[33] Tirakha, the Ethiopian pharaoh, for example, would baptize his soldiers before going into battle. The reason the Pharaohs of Egypt took their wives from Ethiopia is that Ethiopia was to them, as the land where their fore-parents once dwelt, the Holy Land. An Egyptian Pharaoh who married an Ethiopian wife looked forward to the time that a Crown Prince would be born as the second Adam who would restore the lost paradise and universal brotherhood among the nations of the earth.

All Nations of the Ancient East looked for a second Adam. They expected Him to come from Ethiopia or to be of an Ethiopian lineage.

David, in Psalm 87, v. 4, says:

> I will make mention of Rahab and Babylon to them that know me; behold Philistia and Tyre with Ethiopia; this man was born there.

The doctrine of the coming Mashiakh, the Son of God, thus did not originate with the Jews in Palestine but with the ancient Egyptians and Ethiopians.

Messianic comes from the Egyptian root word *Messu*, as does the Hebrew word *Mashiakh*, which means *anointed, consecrated by vow, endowed with a special mission*. *Mashiakh* has become *Messiah*, or in its Greek form *Christ*. So *Messu* signifies the son or the Heir Apparent, the Prince of Ethiopia.

The Line of *Messu*, the ancestors of Yahowshua ha Mashiakh, were of the Ethiopian race, according to Josephus, who says

---

[33] Many were actually selected from among the Priests.

that Canaan, the fourth son of Ham, inhabited the country now called Judea and called it Canaan from his name. Ragmus, the Son of Canaan, had two sons, one of which was *Judadas* and his descendants were called *Judadean,* a nation of Western Ethiopians. The name Judean or Jew is short for Judadean, for the Hamites and Semites were one and the same people, and the early Jews were a direct branch of the Ethiopian race.

And Cush begat Nimrod: he began to be a mighty one in the earth: He was a mighty hunter before the Lord: wherefore it is said, Even as Nimrod, the mighty hunter before the Lord. And the beginning of his kingdom was Babel, and Erech, and Accad, and Calneh, in the land of Shinar. According to this passage the early Chaldaeans should be Hamites, not Semites — Ethiopians not Aramaeans: they should present analogies and points of connection with the inhabitants of Egypt and Abyssinia, of Southern Arabia and Mekran, not with those of upper Mesopotamia, Syria, Phoenicia, and Palestine....

Now a large amount of tradition — classical and other — brings Ethiopians into these parts, and connects, more or less distinctly, the early dwellers around the Persian Gulf with the inhabitants of the Nile Valley, especially with those upon its upper course. Homer, speaking of the Ethiopians, says that they were "divided," and dwelt "at the ends of the earth, towards the setting and the rising sun."

This passage has been variously apprehended. It has been supposed to mean the mere division of the Ethiopians south of Egypt by the River Nile, whereby some inhabited its eastern and some its western bank. Again, it has been explained as referring to the east and west coasts of Africa, both found by voyagers to be in the possession of Ethiopians, who were "divided" by the vast extent of continent that lay between them. But the most satisfactory explanation is that which Strabo gives from Ephorus, that the Ethiopians were considered as occupying all the south coast both of Asia and Africa, and was "divided" by the Arabian Gulf (which separated the two continents) into eastern and western — Asiatic and African.

> *The Five Great Monarchies of the Ancient Eastern World*
> ch. 3, pp. 44-48, by George Rawlinson

Nazarites

After the Israelites were led to Palestine, the people were ruled for a while by judges. An important figure emerging during the time of the judges was the Nazarite.

There are two basic types of Nazarites. The first is what we term the *Birthright Nazarites*, who took their vows through their mothers, via Divine intervention. Samson was an early Birthright Nazarite, consecrated in this way. Samuel, John the Baptist and Yahowshua are later examples.

The Old Testament Book of Judges tells the story of the Birthright Nazarites:

> And the angel of the Lord appeared unto the woman, and said unto her, Behold now, thou art barren, and barest not: but thou shall conceive and bear a son. Now therefore beware, I pray thee, and drink not wine nor strong drink, and eat not any unclean thing: for, lo, thou shall conceive, and bear a son; and no razor shall come on his head: for the child shall be a Nazarite unto God from the womb: and he shall begin to deliver Israel from

out of the hands of the Philistine...And the woman bare a son and call his name Samson: and the child grew, and the Lord blessed him. And the spirit of the Lord began to move him at times in the camp of Dan between Zorah and Eshtaol.

Judges ch. 13

And it came to pass, when she pressed him daily with her words, and urged him, so that his soul was vexed unto death; that he told her all his heart, and said unto her, There hath not come a razor upon mine head; for I have been a Nazarite unto God from my mother's womb: if I be shaven, then my strength will go from me, and I shall become weak and become like any other man... And she made him sleep upon her knees; and she called for a man, and she caused him to shave off the seven locks of his head; and she began to afflict him, and his strength went from him...But the Philistines took him, and put out his eyes, and brought him down to Gaza, and bound him with fetters of brass; and he did grind in the prison house. However the hair of his head began to grow again after he was shaven...And Samson called unto the Lord, and said, O Lord God, remember me, I pray thee, and strengthen me, I pray thee, only this once, O God, that I may be once avenged for the Philistines for my two eyes...And Samson said Let me die with the Philistines. And he bowed himself with all his might; and the house fell upon all the people that were therein. So the dead which he slew at his death were more than that which he slew in his life.

Judges ch. 16

There is a deep esoteric meaning to the story of Samson and Delilah. Samson's birth as a Nazarite, due to the vow that his (previously barren) mother took for him, made Samson a special gift of the Holy Spirit. But he defiled his covenant vow by not living in the consciousness of it. He is a poor example of a judge in Israel, falling short of the Nazarite precepts and stipulations.

His failure led directly to his deception by Delilah and cost him his covenant with God. Only in his moment of powerlessness, having fallen out of grace with God, was he able to realize the power of his locks and thereby consciously make the vow for himself. Upon then renewing his vow, he was able then to shed the blood of thousands of Philistines and make atonement for his faltering ways.

The second group of Nazarites are those who consecrate themselves by virtue of personal tribulation or by direct revelation from the Spirit. A period of at least forty days of fasting and abstinence in the wilderness was standard procedure for this type of Nazarite. These could be called *Temple Nazarites,* due to the fact that their initiation into Nazariteship came with all the basic ordinances stated in Numbers ch. 6:

> And the Lord spake unto Moses saying, Speak unto the children of Israel, and say unto them, when either man or women shall separate themselves to vow a vow of a Nazarite, to separate themselves unto the Lord … all the days of the vow of his separation there shall no razor come upon his head: until the days be fulfilled, in the which he separateth himself unto the Lord, he shall be holy, and shall let the locks of the hair of his head grow.

This type of covenant was traditionally made before a priest and in the presence of a witness. It was also necessary to sacrifice animals as a trespass offering, as stipulated by the laws governing

Rastafarians are naturally covenant keepers. All Rastas wear locks as a symbol of the covenant to live the life of the mystic. Those who claim "to be" Rastas that are not locked are mere sympathizers, because one must make a vow to separate oneself, through the Nazarite vow, which makes locks mandatory unto the Most High.

the vow. If for any reason he defiled himself by being exposed to anything dead, his head had to be shaved as per the Mosaic law governing the Nazarite.

To say that Nazarites can be broken down into two basic groups is not to disclaim that within these two groups variations exist. In the Bible, many different vows were made and there were numerous reasons why they were made the way they were. To have *a vow*, as it is sometimes expressed in the scriptures, as in Acts ch. 18, v. 18, oftentimes, though not always, means that the individual is a Nazarite. All Nazarites however do carry the vow of the covenant; and this covenant always takes on the form of coils of matted hair, which distinguished the Nazarite vow from the many other vows of the ancient Hebrews.

> And he put forth the form of a hand, and took me by a lock of my head; and the spirit lifted me up between the earth and the heaven, and brought me in the visions of God to Jerusalem.
>
> Ezekiel ch. 8, v. 3

In the days when judges ruled the people of Israel, a covenant of locks was the outstanding sign of every judge, setting them apart from every other man.[34] For the judges, wearing the covenant of locks was an insignia of high moral and spiritual conduct. The prophet and mystic Samuel, who was the last to judge Israel under the Mosaic law, handed Israel over to a new era of judgment, wherein the judge rules as king under the covenant of a crown, as king. Henceforth, the new judges of Israel, the kings who sat on the royal Throne, wore a new covenant, the covenant

---

[34] This tradition may have been mimicked by the Europeans and is evident in British governmental bodies, where magistrates wear the wigs of judgment as symbols of their official rank as judges over the affairs of the state. The term *bigwig* has its roots in the wig-wearing practice of European imperial authorities.

of the crown.³⁵ Even after Israel became a kingdom, however, the Nazarites continued to exist, their locks a judgment and a reminder of the Law, especially to corrupt kings who were to rule over Israel. Elijah was a prophet of this type, the forerunner of many others that were to come.

David Establishes Jerusalem

Jerusalem, or *Yah-Rule-Salem*, in Hebrew means Habitation of Peace. In the days of Melkizadek and Abram, it was known as Salem, but it was captured by the Jebusites,³⁶ for whom it was called Jebus, meaning *trodden down, trampled, profane* etc.

Esoterically, their conquest of Salem symbolizes the disturbance of Peace (Salem) in the higher realms of the spirit of human consciousness, which manifests itself as the fallen, animalistic Adamic nature of mankind. This disturbance takes on many carnal forms, and it is not until one is able to bring one's beastly nature under control that any restoration of balance will be experienced leading back to the Eden paradise of peace.

How did David and his descendants come to rule Israel?

> All the elders of Israel gathered together and came to Samuel at Ramah, and said to him, "Look, you are old, and your sons do not walk in your ways. Now make us a king to judge us like all the nations."
>
> 1 Samuel ch. 8, vv. 4-5

---

35 It is because Haile Sellassie I wears a crown that he does not wear the covenant of locks, yet those who bear witness to Him do, in a spiritual covenant called by Rastas *livity*.

36 Jebusites refers to the descendants of Jebus, the third son of Canaan, the fourth son of Ham.

The children of Israel besought the Priest-Judge, Samuel, to anoint them a King so that they might be as other nations, having a King not only to judge them but to lead them into battle. In that very day, they gave their power over unto a man to be their absolute ruler. The King was Elect of God and had ultimate power, subject only to the Priest, who represented the Voice of God. The fact that a king was appointed to rule over the people of Israel created a whole new dynamic, eventually leading to the coming of the messianic King.

The first king was Saul, a son of Kish the Benjaminite, who was chosen more or less by the will of the people. The scriptures describe him as a *choice young man, and a goodly man: and there was not among the children of Israel a goodlier person than he* (1 Samuel ch. 9, v. 2). It also describes him as handsome and tall, standing head and shoulders above the rest of the people. At the people's request, he was anointed king, and therefore became the first ruler of Israel to govern from the seat of a sovereign, and a perfect example of a monarch chosen by the people.

He was unable to establish the sovereign throne of Yahweh for a number of reasons however. (1) He was not of the tribe of Judah, and according to the prophecies, the king must come from Judah. (2) He was disobedient to the voice of God heard through the Prophet Samuel; thus the kingdom was wrenched from his grasp. (3) David had already been anointed in the spirit as a *man after God's own heart* and was destined to be the fulfillment of the *promise*.

Saul wanted to secure the kingdom in his own name, and stopped at nothing to eliminate David as a threat. He conspired to kill David and declared to Jonathan — whose affinity with David was complicated by this, considering that as Crown Prince he would have reaped his father Saul's success — that:

... As long as the son of Jesse liveth upon the ground, thou shalt not be established, nor thy kingdom. Wherefore now send and fetch him unto me, for he shall surely die. Jonathan answered Saul his father and said unto him, Wherefore shall he be slain? What hath he done?

I Samuel ch. 20, v. 31

But David did establish his throne, and once he established his throne he conquered the Jebusites and restored the peace of Salem. He made his chief city Jebus, also known as Salem, where Melkizadek had been Priest and King before. Thus Salem became the City of David. As the City of David, Salem also became the Holy Tabernacle of Zion, for under David's rule Jerusalem became the home of the Ark of the Covenant. David brought the Ark there in a tent, but his conquest brought forth the balance of peace that enabled his son, Solomon, to build Yahweh a temple of stone. By building the temple, King Solomon, the Wisdom of David, shed forth the Glory of Yahweh from Zion, in peace and prosperity — the very meaning and essence of *Jerusalem*.

After Solomon, many more kings governed the people of Israel through the tradition of hereditary Sovereign via King David's lineage. Some of these kings ruled in tyranny and corruption, and their impure leadership tainted the Davidic lineage, until, as we shall see, Haile Sellassie I ascended to the Imperial Dignity.

King Solomon and the Queen of Sheba

Ethiopia's history stretches so far back into the past that much of what is said about Her can neither be proved nor disproved. There are many beautiful and wonderfully mysterious legends that are permanently interwoven into the history of Ethiopia. The stories of King Solomon and Queen Makeda of Sheba and of their only son Bayna Lehkem (Son of the Wise) are to be found woven into nearly all aspects of Hebraic-Judaic and Hebraic-Christian life in Ethiopia.

The *Kebra Negast* gives us this account of Queen Makeda's visit to King Solomon in Jerusalem:

> And she arrived in Jerusalem, and brought to the king many precious gifts which he desired to possess greatly. And he paid her great honor and rejoiced, and he gave her an habitation in the royal palace near him. And he sent her food both for the morning and evening meal, each time fifteen measures of finely ground white meal, cooked with oil and gravy and sauce in abundance, and thirty measures of crushed white meal wherefrom bread for three hundred and fifty people was made...

> Queen Makeda spake unto King Solomon, saying: Blessed art thou, my Lord, in that such wisdom and understanding have been given unto thee. For myself I only wish I could be one of the least of thy handmaidens, so that I could wash thy feet, harken to thy wisdom, apprehend thy understanding, serve thy majesty and enjoy thy wisdom. King Solomon answered and said unto her: Wisdom and understanding spring from thee thyself. As for me I only possess them in the measure in which the God of Israel hath given them to me because I asked and entreated them from him...

> And the Queen said: From this moment I will not worship the sun but will worship the Creator of the sun, the God of Israel. And that tabernacle of the God of Israel shall be unto me My Lady, and unto my seed after me, and unto all my kingdoms that are under my dominion...

And the Queen departed and came into the country of Bala Zadisareya nine months and five days after she had separated from King Solomon. And the pains of childbirth laid hold upon her, and she brought forth a man-child, and she gave it to the nurse with great pride and delight.

In I Kings ch. 10, vv. 1-13, we read of the same royal encounter. Verse 13 tells us:

King Solomon gave the Queen of Sheba all her desire, whatsoever she asked, beside that which Solomon gave her of his royal bounty. So she returned and went to her own country, she and her servants.

Two questions come to mind after reading this verse:

1. What is the geographical location of Sheba, Queen Makeda's *own country*?
2. What exactly is meant by King Solomon's *royal bounty*?

It is quite certain that Ethiopia is the geographical location of the Queen's *own country*. It is equally certain that King Solomon's *royal bounty* was the royal seed he planted in the womb of the legendary Virgin Queen of Sheba.

One legend speaks of how King Solomon's son by Queen Makeda sojourned to Old Jerusalem from Ethiopia to visit him. It is said that, upon reaching Jerusalem, Bayna Lehkem was embraced by his father, who exclaimed that he looked more like King David, his father, than like him, King Solomon. Therefore he was called David II. By the will of God, the Ark of the Covenant was taken from Jerusalem back to Ethiopia with Solomon's son, and there it remains until this day.

The Old Testament

The ancient story of King Solomon and the Queen of Sheba gives strong evidence that the Ethiopian monarchs sit on the world's oldest continuously sovereign Throne, and that it is the Throne of King David. This throne was established in Ethiopia in the tenth year of King Solomon's reign, well before the birth of Christ. This represents the fulfillment of the promise God made to King David in Solomon, as we read in I Kings ch. 9, vv. 4-5:

> And if thou wilt walk before me, as David thy father walked, in integrity of heart, and in uprightness, to do according to all that I have commanded thee, and wilt keep my statutes and my judgments: then I will establish the throne of thy kingdom upon Israel forever, as I promised to David thy father, saying, There shall not fail thee a man upon the throne of Israel.

In order for this promise to be fulfilled, King Solomon had to give his seed to the beautiful Ethiopian Queen, who is the prototype of the First Queen Mother, Miriam (Mary), and her Davidic Christ Child, as we will explore further in a later chapter.

That Sheba, the Queen's country, should be Ethiopia makes perfect sense. With Biblical customs so perfectly preserved in the social, political and religious history of this ancient land (as is well known among historians and religion scholars alike), in fact, Ethiopia offers our most direct link to the cultural heritage of the Biblical Hebrews and the Jews of the Old Testament.

> A Queen shall be born to an Ethiopian woman; yea, not a queen with a worldly kingdom, but the Queen of the Universe. Our Lady, our Goddess, the Ruach-ha-Kodesh, the Shekinah, shall enter the world through the purified womb of an Ethiopian woman and the purified seed of an Ethiopian man. Behold: Our Goddess comes as a woman, to show the way of perfected woman. And

all women who emulate Her will find perfection; yea, and all men who humble themselves to learn from Her will find wisdom indeed.

Behold: Our Spiritual Queen shall be birthed from an Ethiopian womb; but the holy mother of our Goddess will need flee to Israel, for the animal sacrifice cult shall slay her holy husband in Ethiopia and will hunt her like an animal.

And from this day forward unto the end of time, any Ethiopian who gives aid to the Essene Nazarene remnant gives aid to the Holy Mother of our Goddess, and gives life to the martyred Father of our Goddess, and worships our Goddess in word and deed.

Taken from *The Holy Megillah*

What Palestine represents retrospectively is seen in the present experience of Hebraic-Christian Ethiopia, where biblical culture is perfectly preserved, even though this has impeded Her development according to the standard of Western civilization. Ethiopia's devotion to the maintenance of the ancient Hebraic Judaeo-Christian tradition both confirms and validates the history of the Israelites and makes Ethiopia a force to be reckoned with among the Hebrews and their various offshoots, the Jews, the Christians, and the Muslims.

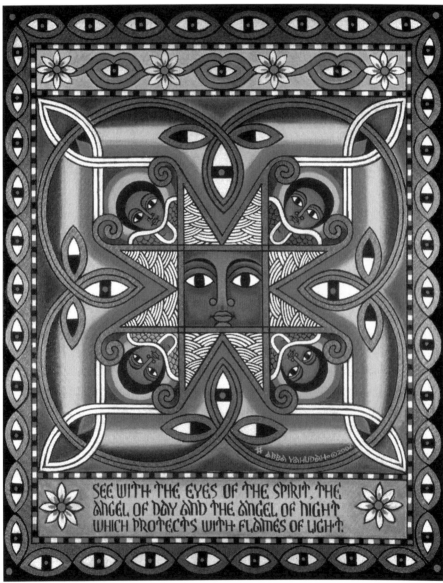

Eyes Upon You

CHAPTER 4

THE ARK OF THE COVENANT

> The Law, whether it rewards or punishes, must be applied to all without any exceptions... Loyalty inspires understanding, and understanding cooperation; these are the clearest evidence of strength. But the solid basis for all lies in education. It is education which allows people to live together, makes them avoid the pitfalls of immorality, and induces respect for the Law.
>
> — Haile Sellassie I, 1968

Chapter 1 gave a general overview of Ethiopia and Her early historical background, while Chapter 2 covered the Kingdom of Israel and the Throne of David. We will focus ever more closely on the way in which the ancient Hebraic traditions inherited from King Solomon provided the Ethiopian Empire with its basic religious and political structure. By *Journey's* end, I intend to establish and inform you by means of reason, giving solid grounds to the claim of the Rastafarians, their conviction that Ethiopia and specifically Haile Sellassie I are indeed the Body of the ancient Essenes proclaimed by Yahowshua the Priestly Mashiakh. Behind every claim there is a reason, and behind every reason a passion. It is therefore important that everyone's passion be governed by reason in pursuit of Truth.

First we must explore the Ark of the Covenant and its significance to the people of Israel. This will then take us into the deeper mysteries of the Ark as a crucial relic and a symbol of the earthly Zion, properly understood.

History now proves that the Ark of the Covenant, which Moses fashioned by his own hands according to patterns he saw in heaven, has been in its resting place in Ethiopia for centuries. (See *The Sign and the Seal*, written by the English writer and historian Graham Hancock.)

The following passage was written in the *Kebra Negast* concerning the Ark, the glory of Zion:

> ... The work thereof is marvelous, resembling jasper and the sparkling stone, ... the crystal and the light. It catches the eye by force and astonishes the mind and stupefies it with wonder. It was made by the mind of God and not by the hand of man. He himself created it for the habitation of His glory; it is a spiritual thing and is full of compassion; it is a heavenly thing and is full of light. It is a thing of freedom, and a habitation of the Godhead, whose habitation is in heaven and whose place of movement is on earth. It dwelleth with men and with the angels; a city of salvation for men, and for the Holy Spirit, a habitation.[37]

The *Holy Bible* gives us this description in Exodus ch. 25, vv. 8-19:

> And let them make me a sanctuary, that I may dwell among them. According to all that I shew thee, after the pattern of the tabernacle, and the pattern of all the instruments thereof, even so shall ye make it. And they shall make an Ark of shittim wood: two cubits and a half shalt be the length thereof, and a cubit and a half the breadth thereof, and a cubit and a half the height thereof. And thou shall overlay it with pure gold, within and without shall thou overlay it, and shall make upon it a crown of gold round about. And thou shalt cast four rings of gold for it, and put them in the four corners thereof; and two rings shall be in the one side of it, and two rings in the other side of it. And thou shalt make staves of shittim wood, and overlay them with gold. And thou shalt

---

37 *Kebra Negast*, published by Miguel F. Brooks, ch. 17.

put the staves into the rings by the sides of the Ark, that the Ark may be borne with them. The staves shall be in the rings of the Ark: they shall not be taken from it.

And thou shall put into the Ark the testimony which I shall give thee. And thou shall make a mercy seat of pure gold: two cubits and a half shall be the length thereof, and a cubit and a half the breadth thereof. And thou shalt make two cherubim of gold; of beaten work shalt thou make them, in the two ends of the mercy seat. And make one cherub on the one end, and the other cherub on the other end: even of the mercy seat shall ye make the cherubim on the two ends thereof.

Citing these lengthy descriptions of the Ark of the Covenant may seem a pedantic exercise at first, but to really take you through the mysteries of the Ark it was necessary to familiarize you with the general description of this ancient relic.

The Ark as an Object

The Ark of the Covenant is today the most sacred religious relic of the Ethiopians, as it once was of the ancient Hebrews. It is the symbol of the embodiment of the Almighty God, their source of strength, and the Glory of their Faith. It is an object of light and holiness in the perfection and beauty of the Godhead within, the Law from on high. The covenant God made with Israel is kept in the Ark, and it has delivered them out of countless tribulations. In centuries gone by, the Hebrews of the Old Testament would take the Ark of the Covenant upon the battlefield for a surety of victory over their enemies. It was taken upon the shoulders of the Priests (Levites), who were given the office of ministering around the Ark. The possession of the Ark of the Covenant made the Israelites a nation glorious unto God, and the Ark made its place of rest, Holy Mount Zion, in the city of David, Jerusalem, surpassingly glorious.

Possession of the Ark of the Covenant made the ancient Israelites victorious and powerful. Respect, fear and dread of them were universal amongst the nations and tribes of the ancient Eastern world. But in the period during which judges and priests governed Israel, supposedly by the Mosaic Law, and especially under the priestly reign of Eli and his sons, Israel became corrupt.

According to the Book of Judges, ch. 13, Israel did evil in the sight of the Lord and was thus delivered into the hands of their enemies the Philistines for forty years, and during one of their battles the Philistines took the Ark of the Covenant and kept it for seven months. The Bible says *the glory was departed from Israel* because the Ark of the Covenant was taken.[38]

It was the Ark, which for the ancient Hebrews represented the presence of the Lord, the Shekinah, which made them victorious as a holy people. On the other hand, we shall see in taking the *Journey*, the permanent absence of the Ark in latter days determined a negative fate for these people and a new destination for God's glory.

Every Divine force has its materialization on earth, resonating at one level or another. It is not significant what is considered to be the highest manifestation of this Divine matter, but for the Israelites, it was the Ark of the Covenant. Out of the Power and the Glory of the Ark come all other forms of material manifestation, corresponding to the various levels of consciousness.

The Sun, above the earth, was the source of the Glory and Power of the Ark. The Sun's energy was harnessed by the Ark within the Holy of Holies, the innermost chamber of the Tabernacle, and then of the Temple, where it was overlain, from floor to ceiling, with pure gold. I Kings ch. 6, vv. 14-35, gives a detailed description of

---

[38] The Philistines took the Ark of the Covenant when they defeated the Israelites in the Battle of Aphek. See 1 Samuel ch. 4-6

the temple and its specifications, that Solomon was to build to house the Ark of the Covenant. Verse 21 states: *So Solomon overlaid the house within with pure gold: and he made a partition by the chains of gold before the oracle; and he overlaid it with gold.* Gold was the element Moses prescribed for the most important applications. Gold symbolizes purity for it becomes purer and purer the more exposure to the sun (fire) energy it has.

The interior of the Holy of Holies, lain with gold, reflected the Sun's rays, creating a ball of light within the walls of the chamber. To the Israelites, this unapproachable light represented the power of Yahweh, the Almighty, who has the glory of the Sun. The phenomenon made the Holy of Holies a dangerous place for those unable to process energy waves at such high frequencies; exposure to this intense energy provided an instant shock or stroke to the unadapted nervous system, as if one were struck by lightning. It is for this reason that frankincense was perpetually burned, to form a thick cloud of darkness for the protection of the Priests who ministered around the Ark. The cloud of smoke functioned as a protective layer precisely as do clouds around the earth, which provide a screen through which we are able to receive the light of the sun, which is otherwise blinding. This is clearly illustrated in I Kings ch. 8, vv. 1, 9-12:

> Then Solomon assemble the elders of Israel, and all the heads of the tribes, the chief of the fathers of the children of Israel, unto king Solomon in Jerusalem, that they might bring up the Ark of the Covenant of the Lord out of the city of David, which is Zion. There was nothing in the Ark save the two tablets of stone, which Moses put there at Horeb, when the Lord made a Covenant with the children of Israel, when they came out of the land of Egypt. And it came to pass, when the priests were come out of the holy place, that the cloud filled the house of the Lord, so that the priests could not stand to minister

because of the clouds: for the glory of the Lord had filled the house of the Lord. Then spake Solomon, The Lord said that he would dwell in the thick darkness.

According to the Kabbalah, the Ark of the Covenant conducts a powerful force due to it being charged with the energy of the Sun. The Ark was designed and constructed so as to keep the force in a pure and undiminished form, so that, over a prolonged period of time, it has acted as a source of Divine power, of life itself. However, because the Ark does not transform and radiate this raw power at a frequency by which the average human can receive it, there remains a need for the archetypal Man or God-Man to rise as the ultimate transformer and mediator of the Power and Glory of God.

We read in the Book of Revelation ch. 1, vv. 7-8:

> Behold, he cometh with clouds; and every eye shall see him, and they also which pierced him: and all kindreds of the earth shall wail because of him. Even so, Amen. I am Alpha and Omega, the beginning and the ending, saith the Lord, which is, and which was, and which is to come, the Almighty.

This highly evolved personality is known as the Teacher and King of Righteousness, Melkizadek, the Mashiakh, and the Tree of Life.

The Ark as a Living Testament

For Rastafarians, the Ark of the Covenant is not merely a wooden box overlain in pure gold. It is an object of spiritual and Divine identification. Over the centuries, the Ark lost its function as the constant object and focus of Jewish and eventually also of the Ethiopian worship. But for Rastafarians it remains a sacred heritage and a compass pointing to the Earthly Zion, the place of Habitation for the Godhead in the flesh.

This vessel, made of shittim wood to prevent it from being eaten by worms, overlain in gold to symbolize purity, at an appointed time would take on flesh and become the Ark of the Living Testament, the embodiment of the Almighty, the Corporeal Living God, the High Priest *Yahowshua ha Mashiakh*. The Mercy Seat of pure gold symbolizes the golden rainbow circle throne of the Messianic King, who by His own power will take His rightful place as the Living Ark, seated between the cherubim. This will unfold in time through a trifold messianic advent, as we shall explain. Moses spoke of the Mashiakh's coming upon Israel in Deuteronomy ch. 18, vv. 18-19:

> I will raise them up a prophet from among their brethren, like unto thee, and will put my words in his mouth; and he shall speak unto them all that I shall command him. And it shall come to pass, that whosoever will not hearken unto my name, I will require it of him.

It is historically chronicled that the Ark of the Covenant has been in possession of the Hebrew Kings of Ethiopia since some time in the tenth century B.C. Ethiopia, since then and today, is the chosen land of God and the blessed Mother of all generations to come, and proven to be the Earthly Zion, as stated in the Gospel according to St. Luke, ch. 1, vv. 28, 48:

> And the angel came in unto Her, and said, "Hail thou that are highly favored, the Lord is with thee: Blessed art thou among women..." Mary replied, "For he has regarded the low estate of his handmaiden: for, behold, from henceforth all generations shall call me blessed."

Miriam's giving birth to the Mashiakh revealed Her to be our Lady Zion, the wife of Yahweh, married unto God Himself, the First Lady of the universe, and the Mother of God.

In the Second Epoch we shall learn of the further development of the idea of the Ark under the notion of the Immaculate Conception. As we shall see, the Immaculate Conception was the means of manifesting, by the power of the Holy Spirit, the earthly Body of the Almighty, which became one with Miriam within Her pure virgin womb and came forth again as the Mashiakh and the Tree of Life.

SECOND EPOCH

IN THE YEAR OF OUR LORD

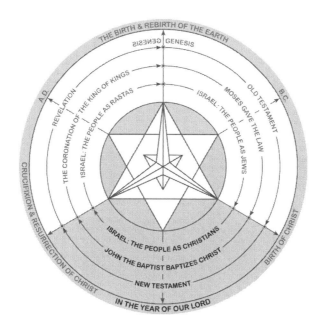

Behold an Ethiopian

CHAPTER 5

THE MAN YAHOWSHUA AND HIS TIMES

In the generation of Yahowshua ha Mashiakh, the Jews were divided into various sects. The classical Jewish historian Josephus, in his latter years, joined the Pharisees, and it is from him that we encounter the first historical mention and reference, in his historical chronicles, of the *four schools of thought* or *four sects* of Jews. The three main sects of Jews were the Pharisees, the Sadducees and the Essenes. The New Testament records Yahowshua's interactions with the Pharisees and the Sadducees.

Pharisees

Pharisee is derived from *pharisaeus*, which is Latin from the Hebrew *Perushim*, meaning: *separate* or *set apart*.

The Pharisees existed alongside the Sadducees, with whom they had various conflicts, dating from the days of the Babylonian captivity up until the life and times of Yahowshua. Of the three major sects, the Pharisees were the group most aligned with the office of government and social policy, and were at one point in part a political movement, though never primarily. In contrast to the Sadducees, the Pharisees were firmly aligned with the Mosaic Law and took their standard and interpretation from it, versus the Sadducees, who relied on the privilege of their priestly office and the etiquette established by the Zadokites in the days of King Solomon.

The Pharisees were supported and favoured by the Jewish masses based, more or less, on their old school attitude towards the Law and their down-to-earth approach of association with the common folks. Unlike the Sadducees, who were the elitist priestly caste, the Pharisees could be considered the preservers of the pre-Hellenistic Judaism, the Oral Teachings of Moses, handed down through generations. In addition, the Pharisees held onto various beliefs and interpretations of the Torah which were more flexible than those the Sadducees were able to accept, or recognize at all. The Pharisees accepted such ideas as the resurrection of the dead, individual spiritual revelations, the existence of angels and demons, final judgment, hell and an afterlife.

Progressive thinking on the other hand, allowed the Pharisees, to revamp the laws of Moses to suit their situation in their own dispensation. Through the re-interpretation of the Oral Law, the Pharisees found a way to create new developments in the arena of Jewish laws and precepts. They were scholars and metaphysicians of Jewish law and, for them, the synagogue was the preeminent institution of spiritual and religious worship. It was from the sect of the Pharisees that the rabbinical order developed, and it can also be said that they developed the synagogue to the eminence and importance it now enjoys in Jewish life.

The Pharisees were politically connected and sought to use Roman rule to gain control over the Jewish communities. For them, the laws of the Torah had to be studied in depth, and they trusted scholarship to inform their strategic political positions with the Romans as well as with the common Jew. The mere fact that they held onto the Oral Tradition and exercised a rigorous interest in studying the laws made them a force to reckon with in latter years. After the destruction of the second Jewish Temple in 70 A.D. the Pharisees rose to prominence and their teachings were eventually incorporated into Jewish Law.

Sadduccees

In the time of Christ, official Judaism was a colonial Judaism in the hands of a self-centered traditional priesthood, which the people of Israel found to be a yoke around their necks — much like colonial Christianity today is a yoke around the neck of the present generation.

The priestly caste of the *Sadducees* was a Jewish sect at the time of Christ which represented, on a metaphysical level, the concept of the intellect; they did not believe in the resurrection of the body or the immortality of the soul. They were the rationalists of their day, more preoccupied with materialistic aims and desires than with matters of the spirit. It is they who allowed traders to carry on their transactions in the holy places, a sacrilege that *Christ* confronted when he chased out the moneychangers from the temple. In a sense, you could say they held agnostic views pertaining to God, while professing to be Jews and the sons of Abraham and Zadok.

Sadducee is a Greek variant, or corruption, of the term Zadokite, from *Zadokim*, which is Hebrew meaning *righteous ones*. Zadok was the high priest under King David and the first of the priestly caste to serve in the temple of Solomon. Zadok's firstborn son Azariah was sent with King Solomon's first-born son, Bayna-Lehkem, along with the first-born sons of the nobles of Israel, to serve King Solomon's son Menelik the First at his court in Ethiopia.[39]

The Sadducees at the time of Christ, however, were not true to the trust of the noble priesthood of the Zadokites, aligning themselves with King Herod, the upstart monarch. Even more than the Pharisees, they enjoyed an easy and comfortable life of

---

39 The *Kebra Negast* (pages 53-54) gives us this account of the events concerning the departure of the sons of the nobles of Israel with Solomon's son Bayna-Lehkem, also called David, to the land of Ethiopia. "And the city rejoiced because the King had made his son King, and had appointed him king from his own territory to that of another. But the city sorrowed also because the King had commanded that they should give their children who were called "firstborn." And those who were on the right hand should sit in the same way as their fathers sat with King Solomon, even so should they sit at the right hand of his son David, the King of Ethiopia...And their rank should be like that of their fathers, and their names should be like those of their fathers...."

"...And then they made ready to set out, and (though) there was great joy with the nobles of the King of Ethiopia, there was sadness with the nobles of the King of Israel, because through the firstborn son of Solomon, King of Israel, that is to say, the King of Ethiopia, the firstborn sons of the nobles of Israel were given to rule over the kingdom of Ethiopia."

prestige and privilege, as they exercised a lucrative monopoly over the temple and everything that pertained to it. As the wealthy ruling class, they had no zeal for the Law. Under their influence, Israel found itself under the yoke of a corrupt and illegitimate monarchy served by a priesthood devoid of the Law, both of which were in turn puppets of pagan colonial Rome.

The Sadduccees preached no message of judgment upon Rome and dared not oppose the State because they were afraid to lose their prestigious priestly positions. Worse, despite their opposing theological views of the Torah, both the Sadducees and the Pharisees, or many of them, are implicated in the Roman crucifixion of Yahowshua.

This situation inevitably brought into prominence an opposing group of people, *Purists* who remained zealous and faithful to the Law. This group became known to history under a variety of names. It is the Qumran[40] writings that tell us they were *Zadokites*.

Essenes

For the true Zadokites, the Purists, were in fact the *Essenes*. They were the only one of the three major sects of Judaism that was not aligned with the State, that lived the esoteric aspect of the first Laws issued by Moses, and were actually the fulfillment of them. From the records of classical historians like Pliny and Josephus, we know the Essenes lived a communal life in a vow of poverty, sharing all things in common, unlike the Sadducees or the Pharisees. Though they were the least in numbers of the three sects, the Essenes had communes on the West side of the Dead Sea, throughout Judea, as well as in Egypt and Ethiopia.

---

40 The Qumran Caves in Palestine have produced archeological evidence such as the *Dead Sea Scrolls* giving us a new perspective on the origins and evolution of Christianity. There is much debate and speculation among scholars about the caves and their inhabitants. There is yet to be a consensus about its occupants, but archeologists and scholars alike agree that the Qumran Caves and the *Dead Sea Scrolls* in particular are some of the most significant finds pertaining to the culture and the lives of the early Christians and their forerunners the Jews.

John the Baptist and Yahowshua were in fact Essenes and spoke out against both the Sadducees and Pharisees, calling them *serpents* and a *brood of vipers* because they were void of the essence of the Law.

In the book of Matthew, ch. 23, Yahowshua poured out a lengthy sermon on the corruption of the Pharisees and Scribes saying: *Woe unto you, Scribes and Pharisees, hypocrites! For you pay tithe of mint and anise and cumin, and have neglected the weightier matters of the law: justice and mercy and faith. These you ought to have done, without leaving the others undone. Blind guides who strain out a gnat and swallow a camel.*

In the end shortly after 70 A.D., the Sadducees would become extinct, leaving no literature behind. The Pharisees became the Rabbis (and Rebbes) as we know them today.

The Essenes, who as we saw are of a much more ancient stock, and could be considered the *third part*, separate from both Pharisees and Sadducees, and the one that produced those mystics that pronounced fiery judgments upon the priestly ruling class in Jerusalem. The Essenes had nothing to do with state affairs and were more or less strangers to the temples and synagogues in Jerusalem where the Pharisees and Sadducees sat as rival heads. Their mission must be understood in the context of the mystical tradition of Kabbalah. Their mystical sources allowed them in fact to distill the essence of the Torah, as Yahowshua would illustrate in his ministry.

One must therefore ask: Why do the Pharisees and Sdducees alone and not the Essenes, appear by name in the New Testament? It may be because the Essenes were the authors of much of the scriptures and had no need to refer to themselves by name.

The Essenes eyed the chaos and moral and spiritual decline of Jerusalem under Rome and consciously and strategically paved the way for the new order to emerge while the Pharisees and Sadducees argued and debated issues of philosophy.

Until the discovery of the *Dead Sea Scrolls* in the twentieth century, everything we knew of the Essenes and their way of life came from classical writers who lived and wrote during the same period, primarily Philo of Alexandria, Flavius Josephus and Pliny.

There are varying opinions of the Essenes in the writings of Philo, Josephus and Pliny. It is said by some modern scholars that the inconsistencies in our understanding of the Essenes may be due to the philosophical biases of these authors. I would tend to agree with this assertion.

The oldest accounts of the Essenes came to us in Philo: *Quod Omnis Liber Probus Sit* (Every Good Man is Free) and *Hypothetica*, also known as *Apologia*. It is said that Philo wrote favorably of the Essenes because he had great respect for them and wished to accommodate their lives to his following of Greek readers.

The three major accounts of the Essenes written by Josephus are to be found in *Bellum Judaicum* "History of the Jewish Wars" c. 75 A.D. and *Antiquitates* ("Jewish Antiquities," c. 94 A.D.), as well *The Life of Flavius Josephus* (c. 97 A.D.). A Jewish historian who lived in Roman-occupied Jerusalem in the first century A.D., Josephus had spent some three years in an Essene commune and developed great admiration and respect for them but, in like manner, he later joined the sect of the Pharisees. He compared the Essenes to Pythagoras, the Pharisees to the Stoics, and the Sadducees to the Epicureans. Like Philo, he wrote from a perspective that would appeal to his Greek audience. In the writings of Josephus, the elements binding the ancient Essenes together were their zeal for

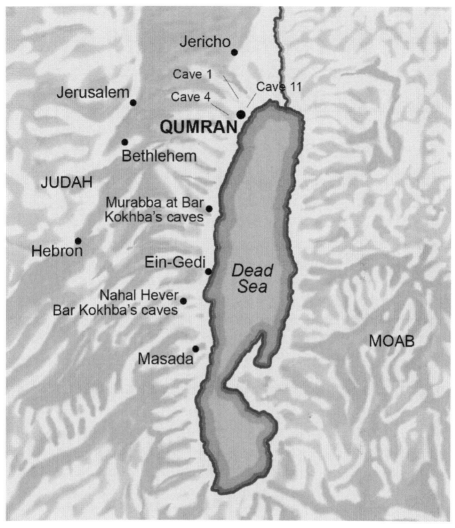

Map of Qumran

virtue and their love of mankind. The writings of Josephus are our most authoritative sources for the Essenes of the first century.

The Elder Pliny, a Latin writer, in his book *Natural History* mentioned the Essenes as an ascetic community living in the

Dead Sea area. Could Pliny have been referring to the Qumran community where the *Dead Sea Scrolls* were found?

There is no accepted Aramaic or Hebrew etymology of the name *Essene*. The root and derivation of the name perplexed even the writers of the classical era. Some modern scholars accept the theory that the term *Essene* comes from the Aramaic word *Assayya*, meaning *healers*, nevertheless this is only conjecture.

Extensive research shows that the word *Essene* does not appear anywhere in the Hebrew or Aramaic texts created by the Essenes, or specifically in the Essene scriptures found at the Qumran community; they employ a number of other Hebrew and Aramaic terms for their members. It seems that they did not have one definitive name for themselves, although they clearly did have a definite concept of who they were. Terms like Keepers of the Covenant, Keepers of the Way, and the Perfect of the Way occur frequently as references to themselves in their own writings. Another variation is *Osei-ha-Torah*, which in Hebrew means *Doers of the Law*. This phrase, in its plural form, is *Osim*, pronounced *Oseem*. It is probable that the name *Essene* came from this variation.

The Essenes led a separatist life beyond the reach of Jewish and Roman rule, and proclaimed that God was going to destroy the status quo and its supporters. Their radical apocalyptic message did not sit well with the Jewish authorities, who were supporters of the status quo.

In 100 B.C., the Essenes set out on a full messianic mission. Their leader was known as the Moreh Zadok,[41] Law Giver, Unique Founder, Anointed One, Master of Justice, Elect of God, and Teacher of Righteousness. He was the preserver of wisdom and the prophet and harbinger of the Mashiakh as the Lion of Judah[42]

---

41 *Moreh* is Hebrew for teacher; thus *Moreh Zadok* means *Teacher of Righteousness*.
42 Leo is the zodiacal constellation of Judah, and the sun is his symbol.

of the line of David. The Teacher of Righteousness was believed to be a Divine messenger who came to prepare the way for the Priestly Mashiakh. But the Essenes' teaching was so advanced compared to the conventional religious devotees of the time that they incurred major opposition from the priesthood at Jerusalem. The *Moreh Zadok* was condemned, stoned, and crucified on a cross, which was the customary punishment for blasphemers.

After the birth of Yahowshua, the Essenes disappear from the historical record, suppressed by the early Church under the authority of the state. According to the Bible, they became known as Nazarenes,[43] and are referred to by that name by fourth-century writers. Their name changed, but not their character; their inner vision remained.

John the Baptist

John the Baptist (Baptizer) was an Essene leader and a known eccentric, notorous for prophecy and baptism. He broke away from the traditional Judaic Essenian sect and retreated into the wilderness (see St. Luke ch. 1, v. 50), emerging only as a judgment on the conscience of the sacrificial priests, rulers, scribes and Pharisees. His soul was reincarnated from the ancient mystics who shone in Israel in the past and he was born a Nazarite.

In the Gospel of Matthew ch. 11, vv. 11-14, Yahowshua describes John the Baptist, who consecrated Him into the order of Essenes by baptism.

> Verily I say unto you, among them that are born of women there has not risen a greater than John the Baptist:

---

[43] Acts of the Apostles 24:5. See *The Oxford Dictionary of the Christian Church*, p. 1133. The word *Nasarean* is from the Hebrew root *Nasa* which means to *Ascend*. The word *Nazarene* is from the Hebrew root *Nezer* which means *Branch*. The word *Nazarite* is from the Hebrew root *Nazir* and means *Consecrated*. So, all three words, though they look and sound similar in English, are different words from different roots. All three words are used by the Essenes.

notwithstanding he that is least within the kingdom of heaven is greater than he... For all the prophets and the Law prophesied until John. And if ye will receive it, this is Elias, which was to come. He that has ears to hear, let him hear.

The passage above clearly depicts John as the reincarnation of Elijah (Elias) the prophet, who, don't forget, performed a resurrection centuries before Christ was born. Thus Elijah was an Essene in his day too.

Yahowshua ha Mashiakh

Yahowshua or Christ was the major force in the proclamation of a New Way, one that the priesthood in Jerusalem obviously did not accept. That priesthood was more aligned with the authority in Rome than with the teachings of this supreme Jewish Master. It was the Jews in Old Jerusalem that advocated the crucifixion of their king, vehemently declaring that if Pilate did not order his death, Pilate was no friend of Caesar. These Jews affirmed that, because they had no king but Caesar, Yahowshua had to be crucified. Supporting Caesar's kingdom, the Priesthood in Jerusalem denied their King in Yahowshua, making it impossible for Yahweh to establish His kingdom among them.

Yahowshua was crucified in the city that was once so glorious, the home of the Ark of the Covenant. Those glory days of Jerusalem were long before the birth of Christ, however. The Land of Israel in which he was put to death was already then, and survives today as, mere fragmented ruins of a once flourishing Jewish state. Invasions and occupations of Jerusalem created an ongoing atmosphere of tension and unrest before the time of Christ, in his lifetime, and continuing until the city was finally destroyed in 70 A.D.

The Romans crucified Yahowshua because the Jews declared it was not lawful for them to put a man to death, refusing to have

His blood on their hands — even though the Scribes and Pharisees made a number of attempts upon His life. On one such occasion Yahowshua fled from before an angry mob which was about to stone Him (to death) for claiming to be the Son of God. Stoning was/is a form of death sentence pronounced and executed on the spot, not unlike what is practiced today in some Arab countries. Stoning of the blasphemous, adulterers and infidels was customary punishment meted out by Jews among themselves, and was committed by them (lawfully or unlawfully) even under Roman rule. In fact, throughout their history the Jews, under the leadership of the ruling Priesthood, have killed many of their own prophets, mostly by stoning.[44]

Why Yahowshua was Rejected

Let us imagine for a moment the impact it would have had if the Jewish clergy had accepted Yahowshua as the Mashiakh. We can speculate that:

1. The acceptance of Yahowshua as the Elect One, the Anointed King of Israel, would have delegitimized the illegitimate Herod, the corrupt puppet king who ruled Judea under Rome; at the same time it would have undermined and even seriously threatened the imperial rule of Caesar himself.

2. The Romans, who held ultimate power over the priesthood, would have experienced an uprising, a full-blown revolution, but Rome with all her military force would have had the advantage. Thousands of Jews would have been slaughtered.

Neither outcome would have fulfilled the prophetic criteria or purpose for the Mashiakh in the First Advent however, so Yahowshua had to be rejected in Judea.

---

[44] The murder of the prophets is what Stephen would later charge them with, before he was martyred himself (Acts ch. 7, vv. 51-60).

When questioned by Pontius Pilate as to whether He was the King of the Jews, Yahowshua declared:

> ... If my kingdom were of this world, then would my servants fight, that I should not be delivered to the Jews: But now is my kingdom not from hence.
>
> John ch. 18, v. 36

His kingdom was already prepared, awaiting His appearance in glory, which was not in that place where He was crucified. His saying *then would my servants fight, that I should not be delivered to the Jews*, simply shows that His servants were not of the same sect of Jews, namely the clergy. In fact, the Jewish clergy became His persecutors and His enemies, from whom He had no protection. One should not make the mistake to think that all Jews denied Christ. However, it would appear that none of the Jewish rulers accepted Him as their savior.

Yahowshua the Ethiopian

Yahowshua may well have been crucified in Palestine, since most of His work and ministry on earth took place in that region. But there is absolutely no proof that He was born in Palestine. The scriptures state that He was born in Bethlehem of Judea, but history now shows that a new Bethlehem was established in Ethiopia, along with many other places whose names we know from the Bible. Places like Magdala, Nazareth and Jerusalem are also found in Ethiopia. Some of these places were established in the Kushite Empire upon the arrival of the Ark, long before Christ was born.

According to the Ethiopian histories, the tiny island of Tana Qirkos, situated in the eastern part of Lake Tana, safeguarded

Yahowshua Son of David

the Ark of the Covenant for centuries.⁴⁵ Places where Christ and the Holy Mother dwelt while hiding from King Herod have been made into shrines on this same island.

The Essenian scriptures, as well, declare both Yahowshua's mother and father to have been of pure Ethiopian blood, which makes perfect sense considering the virtual disappearance of Judaism from Palestine after the fall of Jerusalem in 587 B.C.

The Essene scriptures lead us to understand that Christ was not only a Nazarite from birth but black, and in fact, if one studies the ancient iconographic works of the Ethiopian Church, one will find that Christ was indeed depicted as both of black skin and a Nazarite. Those Ethiopian depictions of him as black-skinned and dreadlocked are likely the truest depictions ever made.⁴⁶ Yet no major Western Christian denomination has ever produced such an image of Christ.

> The queen of the south shall rise up in judgment with the men of this generation and shall condemn them, because she came from the uttermost parts of the earth to hear the Wisdom of Solomon, and behold a greater than Solomon is here.
>
> Luke ch. 11, vv. 31

In this passage, Yahowshua confirms that the Queen of Sheba (Makeda) did meet with King Solomon, and that from their union came a seed or offspring who would be a judgment unto the generation to which He came. This verse can only be understood

---

45 Until the fourth century A.D., when King Ezana ordered its transfer to the capital city Axum, where it remains today. Ancient sacrificial stone altars and various other artifacts, such as the tombs of Adam and of Enoch, are also to be found in the archeological treasure trove which is Ethiopia. Ethiopians have preserved the memory of historical events and places like this for centuries.

46 Chapter 4 explains the vow of the Nazarite. In this context, I use it particularly to denote the fact that He was a locksman – dreadlocked.

from the perspective that He, Himself, was that judgment from the said union of Solomon and the Ethiopian Queen.

It is also to be understood that Solomon, although famous for his wisdom and for the splendor God bestowed on his reign, attracted women from many peoples and nations, like the sun-worshiping Queen of Sheba and the Pharaoh of Egypt's daughter, whom he married, so that despite all, he was caught up in the web of idolatry and fleshly lust, and even he fell short of the true glory of God.

Therefore, Yahowshua declared that the judgment had come, because the Greater than Solomon was there — knowing that He was the fulfillment thereof. By examining his statement closely, one can see clearly that Yahowshua is confirming and verifying two facts of history:

1. That the Queen of Sheba was a real person, and that she met King Solomon.

2. That Yahowshua Himself arose from the royal union of the two.

These two points are important in tracing the true lineage and race of the one called Christ, as they show that Yahowshua was indeed an Ethiopian. How so?

Why would He say these things to the priesthood in Old Jerusalem? We conclude, because He was not of them, nor did He become one of them. In John ch. 9, vv. 28-30, the Jews declared that they *do not know where he (Christ) comes from.*

Spiritually, if He were one of them, they would know Him. Biographically, if He were from them, He would not have been the prophesied judgment He so boldly declared. Yahowshua was most definitely that Chosen One, Elect of the Most High, hailing out of the horn of the Lord's tabernacle.

The horn is metaphysically the highest region, the exalted and chosen land, the diadem of beauty to which the people shall cling for their redemption. Ethiopia, we see again, is the land revealed as the home and birthright of the true Davidic bloodline. And Ethiopia is precisely the *horn*, as biblically prophesied of the land of Judah. This new land of Judah represents *the third part* that was saved specifically for the purpose of re-establishing and purifying the nation of Israel through the pearl of David.

These facts taken together offer us virtual certainty that Yahowshua was from Ethiopia.

Miriam of Magdala

> Now when He rose early on the first day of the week, He appeared first to Mary Magdalene, out of whom He had cast seven demons.
>
> Mark ch. 16, v. 9

Miriam of Magdala played a hugely significant role in the life of Yahowshua. She embodied Sophia, the feminine aspect of who He was, as His most devoted, beloved disciple. The *Nag Hammadi Library's Gospel of Philip* states:

> As for the Wisdom who is called 'the barren,' she is the mother of the angels. And the companion of ... Mary Magdalene ... loved her more than all the disciples and used to kiss her often on her ... The rest of the disciples ... said to him, "Why do you love her more than all of us?"

Miriam of Magdala is the one he cured from seven demons. Demons here could represent a form of spirit possession, more or less what we in modern times call epilepsy or seizures. Kabalistically, the number seven is symbolic in this case of the seven-branched candle stand, the Menorah, which burns as the

Miriam of Magdala

seven seals are opened. After Yahowshua healed her, Miriam had no further blockages, and when the stone of the sepulcher was rolled away, she became the first to witness Him in His resurrected glory.

She is often confused with the adulterous woman whom Yahowshua saved from a public stoning. The misconception that Miriam was a harlot has caused the mystical nature and purpose of her life to be overlooked.

She is believed to have been the one who had the wisdom to wash His feet with her tears, dry them with her locks and anoint them with precious oil.[47] This was her way of expressing both her love and her acknowledgement of who He truly was, and fulfilling the witnessing role of the Divine priestess.

Miriam is the true Hebrew form of her name. *Magdalene* is English for *person from Magdala*; it is the name of the place she was from. It is not her name, even though it is often used as if it were her name.

Not much is written about her in the King James Version, but Essene scriptures, *The Holy Megillah,* show her to be one of holy birth from the Essene encampment of the Immaculate Conception in Ethiopia. And since she was always known as Miriam Magdalene, she must have been from the ancient Ethiopian city of Magdala.

> Lo: The Nasarean encampment in Ethiopia was called Eden in remembrance of the Garden of Eden, which had been in Kush. For, behold: the land that was called Kush, which came to be called Ethiopia, has had many names and many boundaries. Even so, to Nasareans this land

---

[47] The "woman with the alabaster jar," as she is often called, has become the subject of many legendary tales, and without a doubt has found a tender place in the hearts of many as a symbol of humility and love. She also displayed true recognition of the Master's spirit during his brief ministry. This passage can be found in the book of Matthew ch. 26, v. 7

will always be Kush, for that name came from the tongue of Cherubim.

Behold: in the Nasarean village of Eden were some families long devoted to The Order of the Immaculate Conception. For, lo: Eden was a tributary HomeCampus of that order. Now, besides the Nasareans, there were many Aaronite Jews in Ethiopia. Yea, the Aaronites greatly outnumbered the Nasareans, and hated the Nasareans. And the Aaronites were greatly outnumbered by the natives of Ethiopia, who were neither Nasarean nor Aaronite, but practiced their own Pagan rites of various varieties. Like the Nasareans, some of the natives worshipped both a God and Goddess and venerated the nature spirits, wherefore they respected the Nasareans and felt kinship with them. Yea, and these natives admired the discipline and holiness of the Nasareans. Wherefore these natives tried to protect the Nasareans from the violence and persecution of the Aaronites.

Behold: within the Nasarean encampment were prophets. And shortly before the birth of the Holy Babe Miriam, a prophet went forth from Eden and walked amongst the natives of Ethiopia. And he prophesied the coming of a Queen, saying: "Behold, a Queen shall be born to an Ethiopian woman of the Nasareans. Yea, not a Queen with a worldly kingdom, but the Queen of the All. Our Lady, our Goddess, shall enter the world through the purified womb of an Ethiopian woman and the purified seed of an Ethiopian man. Behold: our Goddess comes not as a Goddess, but as a perfected woman. And all women who embrace Her teachings will find perfection. And all men who humble themselves to learn from Her will find wisdom, indeed.

"Behold: our Queen shall be birthed from an Ethiopian womb. But the Holy Mother of our Goddess will flee to Galilee, for the Aaronites shall slay her holy husband in Ethiopia and will hunt her like an animal. "And from that day unto the end of time, any Ethiopian who gives aid to the Nasarean remnant gives aid to our Goddess and Her holy mission. This aid is in deed and truth and will not go unrewarded." And this prophet had no name, being called by the people simply "The Prophet."

Lo: the word of The Prophet was spread from village to village. In the Nasarean encampment of Eden there was great excitement; for, behold: this was the sixth generation since the founding of The Order of the Immaculate Conception. And according to the words of the angel Gabri'el, this generation would give birth to the seventh generation bodies suitable for the incarnations of the Lord and Lady. Though only Omen, our Jah-Jah, could know for certain, a number of bloodlines had apparently maintained the required level of purity for six consecutive generations. One of the young women from such a bloodline was named Zibiah. And Zibiah was of a pure Ethiopian bloodline, as was her husband Zemira, a harp player, though their names were Hebrew from Nasarean scriptures written in that tongue.

And lo: it was from the purified womb of Zibiah and the purified seed of Zemira that the Holy Babe Miriam came forth into the world. And the birth of our Goddess Immanent, Jahnah, as Miriam was as follows. Behold: The holy day ordained by Omen for the coming into the world of our Goddess had come.

The Nasarean Essene Scriptures describe the Ethiopian Essene community as one of the significant seven encampments because the Melki Zadok[48] of Alexandria already esteemed Ethiopia as Eden. It is important to understand the implications of this perspective, which suggests that Ethiopia/Eden continued the Judaic empire with many of the Mosaic laws intact, but serving also as the womb of the Divine Feminine. Ethiopia, as indicated above, had reached the sixth level of consecutive generation purity in order to give birth to Yahowshua, as well as His consort and Feminine aspect Sophia in the body of Miriam Magdalene, both of pure Ethiopian bloodlines. This is a significant revelation, which augments my claim and strengthens my point about Yahowshua being Ethiopian.

It is from these same Essene encampments, developed in the deserts of Egypt, sustained in Ethiopia, and preserved up until today that the Ethiopian hermits of today, the Bahtawis, come. They are remnants of a rare branch of Christians tied to the earliest roots of Christianity.

I believe that these scriptures prove that a platform and stage was already established in that Edenic paradise of Ethiopia that would not only give birth to the Mashiakh in the First Advent, the priestly Mashaikh, but also to the Kingly Mashiakh, as well as to their manifest Divine feminine counterparts as is the tradition of ancient Egyptian and Ethiopian theology. These Essene communes nurtured a sacred space for the promised Mashiakh of the Nazarene prophecies by preserving the true Way of the Tree of Life. The *Essene encampment of the Immaculate Conception* had to have been consistent with Essene commune tradition, where marriages and families were commonplace.

---

48 Melki Zadok — is a rank given to the Archbishop or Head of the Essene order. This was common practice in the priestly hierachy of the Essenes and is in direct relation to the Melkizadok or Melkizadek as we understand it.

It is said by some Rastafarians (Ras Michael and the Sons of Negus) as well as others that the marriage in Cana was the consecration of the union of Yahowshua and Miriam Magdalene. There is a Ras Michael song: *There was a marriage ina Cana, Yesus and His disciples was there...* This song in its lyrics asserted that the wedding where Yahowshua turned water into fine wine was in fact His own.

Miriam Magdalene, as the first witness of Yahowshua's resurrection, is the actual first apostle, and She laid the first cornerstone, if not the whole foundation, of the faith of the early Church. Yahowshua leaves nothing to the imagination in his reference to Miriam in the *Gospel of the Holy Twelve*:

Again I say unto you, I and my bride are one. Mary Magdalene, whom I have chosen, is one with me. She is my bride, ever one in Holy Union with me her spouse.

Church of St. George

CHAPTER 6

CHRISTIANITY

The Disciples of Yahowshua

The Jews hoped that the death of Yahowshua would eliminate the threat He posed by His radical lifestyle and teachings. This was a great miscalculation for them, however, in that He was glorified more in death than in life. The resurrection, which was practically manifested to the few He had chosen, remains the greatest force, internal or external, that the Jews would ever confront.

The priestly Jews were defeated in their attempts to stop the new wine of His gospel from being consumed by the many, causing Christianity to emerge as one of the biggest religious movements of all time.

As the devoted apostles persevered in spreading the new gospel of Yahowshua ha Mashiakh, many Jews, but even more gentiles, were baptized in the spirit of this vine. The events that led up to the establishment of the gospel can be found in the pages of the Acts of the Apostles.[49]

The disciples of Yahowshua were, in fact, Yahowshua's resurrected body. In all that they did, the life of Yahowshua was relived in them, and thus the martyrdom of faithful disciples began.

Stephen was the first to be tried in the courts of the unjust judges, who set up false witnesses against him. He was found guilty of blasphemy, in that he never ceased to preach this new gospel that Yahowshua, whom they crucified, was the Mashiakh. The

---

[49] Which, I may add, might equally be called the *Acts of the Essenes*, since the early Christians were Essenes.

high priest, the scribes and the Pharisees were pricked to the heart when Stephen pointed out their corruption and outrightly charged them and their forefathers with murdering the prophets. He declared:

> Which of the prophets did your fathers not persecute? And they killed those who foretold the coming of the Just One, of whom you now have become the betrayers and murderers, who have received the law by the direction of angels and have not kept it.
>
> Acts ch. 7, vv. 52-53

After this, he was cast out of the city where they stoned him to death. His last words were, *Lord, lay not this sin to their charge.*

The early church was not a structured or organized body of devotees, but a scattered group of people, sometimes living as outlaws, struggling in various pockets in the deserts of Egypt and along the Mediterranean coast. In its early days, various doctrines and dogmas, some based on their oral traditions, became a part of the scriptures used by the outposts of the developing cult. The early builders of the church inherited many ancient books considered sacred. The *Book of Enoch*, discussed earlier, is an example; the *Book of Jubilees* is another. Both were considered scripture.

For centuries Christians faced numerous onslaughts in the defense of their faith against many who questioned and doubted various aspects of their dogmas and beliefs.[50]

Nazarenes

> And when he had found him, he brought him unto Antioch. And it came to pass, that a whole year they

---

[50] On the flip side, however, in the dark ages in medieval Europe, the Catholic inquisition controlled the views and opinions of believers with an iron fist of cruelty.

assembled themselves with the church, and taught much people. And the disciples were called Christians first in Antioch.

Acts of the Apostles ch. 11, v. 26

We have found this man a pestilent fellow, and a mover of sedition among all the Jews throughout the world, and a ringleader of the sect of the Nazarenes.

Acts ch. 24, vv. 5-6

It is important to note that the New Testament is written in Greek, translating Hebrew or Aramaic ideas. While the Greek name *Christian* eventually became widespread for the followers of Yahowshua, *Nazarene* [51] is the older name.

Nazarene comes from Hebrew, meaning *one who is from Nazareth*. Yahowshua and His followers were called Nazarenes, not only because their home was in Nazareth, but because the gospel of the Messiah and its earliest communities of devotees were nurtured there in Nazareth. Thus, not only was the Messiah known as a Nazarene, His followers became His namesakes as well. *The Gospel of the Nazarenes,* which is still extant, became known as the fundamental Gospel of Christ, the true way. By the fourth century however *Nazarene* was understood as a Palestinian sect that was out of the Christian mainstream.

The root of *Nazareth* is *nazir,* meaning *branch* or *offshoot,* but also *shining, separate, guarded, defended* and *preserved. Nazir* is also the root of "Nazarite," but Nazarene should not be confused with Nazarite, since the Hebrew words have different connotations. One only becomes a *Nazarite* by taking a special vow to keep the true fast of abstinence according to the scriptures. Anyone

---

51 Josephus, in his memoirs, called them zealots. The Romans, of course, called them outlaws, terrorists, and brigands.

may take the vow, but not all do. Therefore not all Nazarenes are Nazarites, but every Nazarite is a Nazarene, a Nazarene who has attained the true consciousness of the Mashiakh through the vow he keeps.

Archeological discoveries have provided deeper insights into the lives of the ancient Nazarenes and Nazarites. The Nazarenes are metaphysicians of the spirit, while the Nazarites are the manifestation of that spirit that follows the Gospel of the Nazarenes through vows of abstinence and of growing their locks as a sign of material renunciation.[52]

The Gnostics and the Canon of Scripture

Gnosis is Greek for *knowledge*. Thus *Gnostic* is translated to mean *one who knows*. The mystical Jews and Christians known as *Gnostics* considered themselves masters of their own faith. Many were Essenes as well.

Their interpretation of the scriptures was often apocalyptic, undermining the priests and high priests (= bishops) through whom the Romans exercised rule. *Gnostics* also believed that by knowing themselves they could chart their own path to salvation, and thus, they had no need for priests and bishops. They clung to radical ideas of the imminent end of the Roman Empire by Divine intervention.

Like the Essenes, they claimed that the Teacher of Righteousness, the Messiah, was coming to gather the Children of Light to rise up against the Children of Darkness in an apocalypse.

The sacred books of the early believers in the Messiah varied. The church was divided into factions based on their doctrines of the nature of Christ and differing collections of scriptures.

---

52 See the section on "Nazarites" in ch. 3, beginning on p.

This young movement, having to struggle to establish itself under oppressive pagan Rome and a corrupt Jewish clergy, suffered a great many growing pains, and numerous threats to its early development.

The goal of Emperor Constantine the Great was to unify the church both religiously and politically, placing it firmly under his control as Roman emperor. It was he that called to order the Council of Nicaea and consolidated the four gospels of Matthew, Mark, Luke and John as the only gospels worthy to be considered scripture. He had fifty copies of this approved Bible hand-copied and published.

Actually, the so-called four Gospels are believed by experts not to have been written by their accredited authors. They may be even later than the *Gospel of Thomas*, although some scholars believe that the four Gospels of Matthew, Mark, Luke and John were penned as early as 40 A.D. to 60 A.D.

Yet in 382 A.D., under the Christian emperor Theodosius, devotees of the faith were banned from reading any of the so-called scriptures that were not included among the books hand-picked by the emperor. The omitted books were outlawed by the bishops, and severe sentences, even sentences of death, were pronounced upon the guilty.

For nearly two thousand years, most Christians have believed that there were only four Gospels; while the banned hieratic or priestly scriptures lay buried, unknown to the world. In 1896 the *Gospel of Peter*, one of the first lost gospels to be rediscovered, emerged from the sands of Egypt, awakening the Christian world to endless controversy and debate about the earliest beginnings of Christianity.

This Gospel and many of the other scriptures rediscovered in the last hundred years were products of Gnostics. The *Gospel of Peter* is said to have been written by Simon Peter, the one hand-picked by Christ to be leader of the apostles and the first pope. It claims to give an alternative eyewitness account of the resurrection and of the whole life of Jesus. The *Gospel of Peter* is considered by scholars an important if controversial piece of evidence that raises serious questions about the early church.

The *Gospel of Thomas*, which is comprised entirely of sayings of Yahowshua, conveys a message that contrasts with the four canonical gospels. In the *Gospel of Thomas*, Yahowshua is not the only begotten son of God, but rather we can all become sons of God through a personal connection with the Divine. This teaching has been considered heretical and quickly buried with other so-called dangerous and blasphemous writings, even though the *Gospel of Thomas* had been mentioned by early orthodox Christian writers as early as 150 A.D.

The Gospels of *Mary Magdalene* and of *Judas Iscariot* were unearthed around the same time, creating a flurry of passionate debate amongst scholars.

These writings revealed another version of Yahowshua, as well as the reality that there had existed an alternative form of Christianity that was stamped out or buried with these scriptures. They leave a lot of questions in our minds about the role of Miriam Magdalene and of women in general in the early church, such as:

- Did women have more important roles in the church in those early days than they did later?
- Did Miriam author the Gospel that bears her name, and if so, what are the implications of that?

Fate of Israel's Levitical Priesthood

After considering all this, one might ask: What became of the old Levitical priesthood, and what are the different forms it has taken since the death of Yahowshua?

The alignment of the priesthood with Caesar, whom they recognized as their King, would have put the Levitical order out of alignment with the Divine force of their Messianic King. It would be safe to assume that, as time was leading the Romans from paganism toward a Roman Catholic empire, the Romans were also shaping the future of the Levitical priesthood and the lives of Jews under their control.

If we take a closer look at the Roman Empire during and after the time of Christ, it is not difficult to conclude that they always had a contemptuous attitude towards the Jews under their jurisdiction.[53] The Romans, as a rule, did not interfere with nor determine the religious precepts and customs of the Jews. The Romans allowed the Jews the liberty of living in their own communities as a subculture within the Roman state, and through their submission to the Caesars of the empire the Jewish priesthood and Pharisees enjoyed a particularly comfortable, pious life. These conditions led to the breakdown and decay of the morals and the national perspective of the Jews, who depended on their priests and elites for leadership.

The scriptures show how, after the crucifixion of Yahowshua, the Jewish priesthood exacted much persecution against His early witnesses, those who declared he was the Son of God, the Mashiakh. At first, these *Nazarenes* were not a threat to Rome, being small in number and not yet having gathered into a functioning church body. They were, however, a threat to the

---

53 Not all Jewish communities fell under their dominion. The Essene Jewish communities were beyond the rule of Rome, just as the Judaic empire of Ethiopia was.

colonized priestly order in Jerusalem, and many apostles would eventually be murdered by Rome on account of being condemned by the Jewish high priest.

The predicament that the house of Israel found itself in was one of an internal conflict. Internal, in that the followers of the Messiah were condemned as heretics by the clergy, who were merciless in their methods of extinguishing the fire of the gospel. The Jewish clergy were particularly concerned that, if the apostles rose to power, the blood of the murdered Messiah would be on their hands.

> And when they had brought them, they set them before the council: and the high priest asked them, saying, Did not we straitly command you that you should not teach in this name? And behold, ye have filled Jerusalem with your doctrine, and intend to bring this man's blood upon us.
>
> Acts ch. 5, vv. 27-28

The Pharisees and the Sadducees, along with the Scribes in Jerusalem, sat at the pinnacle of the Jewish hierarchy, and as such represented the nucleus of Jewish authority. This gave them power to judge amongst the Jews. For such were the laws of the state: the Romans allowed them to judge matters pertaining to their laws. Cases where death was the penalty, however, were to be brought to the higher authorities of Roman rule, although, as we saw, this rule was not always upheld. It could be said that there was more righteousness in the hands of Pontius Pilate than in the priestly body of the Jewish elite. After judging for himself this Jewish malefactor thrust upon him by the angry Jews, Pilate found no fault worthy of death in Him, and ordered that the Jews try Him themselves, by their own laws, if they wished to.

> In Judah is God known. His praise is great in Israel.
>
> Psalm 76, v. 1

Before Christ, Israel, as a people, become through their faithlessness two distinctly separate nations, Israel and Judah. But regardless of the transgression of the Israelites, there was to be, at some point in their evolution, a Divine manifestation through them that would affect the world around them and confirm them as the people of the living God. This would happen through countless trials, tribulations and warnings of prophets, ultimately leading them that *grope in darkness* the privilege to walk upright in light.[54] This light had to come from Judah — even if Judah had to be uprooted and replanted in another land. After becoming two nations, however, Israel divided even further, as they were broken like the rod of Aaron into three separate parts:

1. Israel (the people)
2. Levi (the priests)
3. Judah (the promised King)

As we stated, the members of the priesthood, in their unrighteousness, misled the people of Israel, who depended on them for proper guidance. Confusion increased, causing them to deeply infringe the covenant between the Jewish nation and their God. Judah was to be the promise and doorway to the Emmanuel; in order for this to happen, the Most High would first take Judah away captive, but only after the pearl was securely planted in the fertile soil of the ancient kingdom of Kush. Israel would then be smitten and break into factions (see Genesis ch. 49, v. 7), like dust to be blown to the four winds of the earth. After four hundred years of exile, their cries would come to the ears of their God, who would then rescue them from the hands of their oppressors.

---

54 According to Bible prophecy, the nations of Israel and Judah will one day reform themselves and reunite as one nation. But after the coming of Christ the Levitical priesthood would fall and was never reestablished. See, for instance, Job 12: 25, John 12:36.

Christianity and Egypt

The Egyptian (Coptic) Church based in Alexandria, according to tradition, received the gospel from the apostle St. Mark himself in the first century, during the reign of Roman emperor Nero. Christianity spread throughout Egypt within a half century of St. Mark's arrival in Alexandria. The Ethiopian Orthodox Church ultimately sprang out of the Egyptian Coptic Church based at St. Mark's church in Alexandria.

The founding of the See of Alexandria by St. Mark the Apostle is documented in the *Testament of St. John,* which was scribed in Coptic and can be dated to the early second century. This particular document is part of what became known as the *Nag Hammadi* manuscripts, which were found in Upper Egypt in 1945; like many of them, it raised important questions about the early development of Christianity. Questions like:

- Are there more gospels or writings pertaining to the life and works of *Christ* than the public has been made privy to, or are there only four Gospels? (We have seen there are).
- Was *Jesus* an Essene? (We have seen He was.)
- Did *Jesus* have a lover? (We have seen He did.)
- Was the father of *Jesus* Joseph?
- Was *Jesus* a vegetarian or a carnivore?
- What role did women play in the development of the early church?
- Is the King James Version the final authority on the word of God?

For many ages Egypt gave profound answers to many of the questions posed by theological and philosophical minds, and She continues to give forth new evidence illustrating her role in the

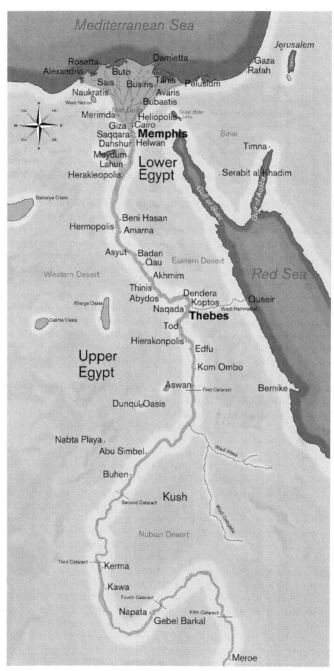

Map of Egypt and surrounding area

Egyptian Goddess

development of major religions. Without any doubt She ranks as a major contributor to Kabalistic[55] and esoteric societies.

The theological roots of Christianity can be seen in the religious and spiritual values of ancient Egypt. Egyptian mythology is the basis for Hebraic/Judaic theology and it is understood that Christianity sprang from Judaism. The Coptic Egyptian (Christian) Church, which is possibly the oldest church of all, is unique in many ways. For instance, the first important educational institution of Christian antiquity was the catechetical school of Alexandria, founded by the Christian scholar Pantanaeus in 180. This became the first and most important such institution in the early Christian world, teaching not just theological subjects, but also the sciences, mathematics and the (pagan Egyptian) humanities.

It was during and after the Christian controversies about the Creed, discussed below, while this school was flourishing in Alexandria, that the Romans launched their first direct attacks on the Alexandrian Christians. The famous library in Alexandria contained a rich treasure trove of information about this period of early Christianity, which was lost during one such attack by Rome.

It is fortunate that vital evidence about the origins of the Christian faith, and in particular about the age-old Coptic[56]. Christianity of Egypt, was preserved in the Nag Hammadi manuscripts discussed above. These manuscripts form a collection of twelve books of varying content written in Coptic, presenting themselves as a heritage of local Egyptian concepts and philosophies, ancient literature and occult mysteries. They include versions of the Old

---

[55] The word *Kabala* comes from the two important Kemetic concepts of *ka* = vital essence or life force and *ba* = the part of the soul that travels between the worlds of the living and the dead. These, along with the third entity *ankh* = (eternal) life, which was reserved for the select few, comprise the soul's trinity for the ancient Egyptians.

[56] *Coptic*, a word of Greek origin, refers to a group of ancient Egyptian languages, which survives today in the liturgical language of the Egyptian Coptic Church.

and New Testaments, the *Gospel of Thomas*, the Egyptian *Gospel of Philip*, (a compilation of sayings attributed to the Essenian master Yahowshua, and much more).

> And [his thought performed] a deed and she came forth, [namely] she who had [appeared] before him in [the shrine of] his light. This is the first [power which was] before all of them (and) [which came] forth from his mind, She [is the forethought of the All] — her light [shines like his] light — the [perfect] power which is [the] image of the invisible, virginal Spirit who is perfect.
>
> [The first power], the glory of Barbelo, the perfect glory in the aeons, the glory of the revelation, she glorified the virginal Spirit and it was she who praised him, because thanks to him she had come forth. This is the first thought, his image; she became the womb of everything for it is she who is prior to them all, the Mother-Father, the first man, the holy spirit, the thrice-male, the thrice-powerful, the thrice named androgynous one, and the eternal aeon among the invisible ones, and the first to come forth.
>
> *The Apocryphon of John* (II, 1; III, 1; IV; and BG 8502, 2, translated by Frederik Wisse, in the *Nag Hammadi Library* edited by James M. Robinson)

When the theological framework of Egyptian mythologies and teachings is closely examined, it becomes evident that they were taken and reshaped into the monotheistic laws and stories of the Hebrews. References to Egypt are plastered all over the Old and New Testaments. She plays an incredibly important role in the origins and evolution of the Jews, all the way through to the birth of Egypt's crown princess Ethiopia.

It is safe to say that while Christianity has its roots in the Mediterranean Levant, these roots are deepest in Egypt, and Egypt has contributed more than any culture to the incubation and early development of this major world religion. Like Judaism, Christianity has much to be grateful for in Egypt's contributions to her foundation and development.

Egyptian Monasticism

As an important example, the Christian monastic ideal began in Egypt, and it has been lived out there in many forms for centuries.

Amongst other contributions, Coptic Egypt is to be credited for Christian eremitism (hermits) and cenobitic (monastic) life as we presently understand them in the West. For over sixteen hundred years both forms of life have thrived uninterrupted in the deserts of Egypt, albeit under extreme difficulties at times when monasteries were sacked and monks massacred for their faith. As testimony to such difficulties, large stone walls and huge metal gates now protect many of these communes.

However, many of Egypt's fortress-monasteries have long been abandoned, and there is not much left to see for visitors to Aswan, Luxor and the Wadi Natroun region, where many holy shrines and monuments once stood. Wadi Natroun alone originally had 50 convents; 47 now stand in the entire region: evidence of the continuing presence of *angels amongst men*, as these ascetics were commonly called.

These ancient holy sites remain the first models of Christian ascetic life and the birthplace of a very significant part of Christian history. The desert-dwelling hermits of Coptic Egyptian monasticism, many of whom were Essenes and many Ethiopian, gave us many examples of holy men who went to extremes to live out their Christian conviction in solitude and silence.

Their lives in the caves and wildernesses of Egypt are the actual beginning of monasticism in the worldwide Christian movement. Only later was it brought to Europe with the renown of Saints Athanasius and Jerome. Religious leaders who followed the examples of the first cave-dwelling desert hermits and monks of Egypt include Athanasius, but also Pachomius, Anthony and Shenouda. They founded the movement that led to the founding of Europe's great monasteries, which became the centers of art and culture in medieval Europe for over six centuries.

Creeds and Definitions

The Ethiopian Coptic Church was created as a result of Egyptian Coptic missionary work[57] and so the Ethiopian church, like the Egyptian, is Monophysite, referring to the churches' particular theosophical philosophy, which we will examine shortly.[58]

Nicaea

The Nicene Creed, the bulk of which was adopted by the Council of Nicaea in 325 A.D., is the theological blueprint for all Orthodox churches and for most Christian churches of both East and West, including the Coptic Egyptians and Ethiopians. This creed, which was championed by Athanasius of Alexandria in Egypt, settled one contentious dispute by repudiating the beliefs of the Arians, who declared that there was a time that Jesus was not, and that he is a creature, not divine like God the Father.

---

[57] Though Frumentaus, the one larglely responsible for the Christian influence upon the 4th century Ethiopian Emperor Ezana, was a native Syrian, the credit goes to Egypt because Frumentaus had become an Egyptian Copt, whose supreme clerical head, Archbishop Athanasius, was based in Alexandria, Egypt. The church that Frumentaus established in Ethiopia had the unique flavor of the Church of Coptic Egypt.

[58] The Coptic and Ethiopian Churches are customarily called "Monophysite," although many theologians in this tradition prefer to use the term "Miaphysite" for their faith.

The Creed said:
> We believe in one God, the Father all-sovereign, maker of all things, both visible and invisible: and in one Lord Jesus Christ, the Son of God, begotten of the Father, and only begotten: that is, from the essence of the Father; being of the one essence with the Father; by whom all things were made, both things in heaven and things on earth; who for us men and for our salvation came down and was made flesh, was made man, suffered, and rose again the third day, ascended into heaven, and cometh to judge the quick and the dead: and in the Holy Spirit.

Chalcedon

Nicaea established that the Father and the Son were of one essence, but what about Christ's human nature? Although all sides agreed Christ was fully human as well as Divine, it was difficult to understand or explain how exactly he was both. Nestorius, Patriarch of Constantinople from 428 to 431, and educated at Antioch in Syria, emphasized the difference or distinction between Christ's Divine and human natures. Cyril, Patriarch of Alexandria from 412 to 444, led the opposition to Nestorius, and Nestorianism was repudiated at the Council of Ephesus in 431. Controversy continued to rage, however. The Council of Chalcedon in 451, with crucial input from Pope Leo of Rome, adopted a formula seen by some as a compromise, confessing:

> One and the same Christ, Son, Lord, ... to be acknowledged in two natures, without confusion, without change, without division, without separation; the distinction of natures being by no means taken away by the union.

The Monophysites, including the Egyptian Copts under Patriarch Alexander, denounced this formula as heretical, if not polytheistic. They affirmed that the Son of God combines humanity and Divinity in a single new nature.

So while the creed or definition of Chalcedon was accepted by the churches in Rome and Constantinople it was rejected outrightly by the Egyptian Copts and others. This affected how the Ethiopian Orthodox Church would evolve. The Monophysites clung to what they understood to be the teaching of Athanasius. That group, supported by the original line of archbishops of Alexandria, flourished in Egypt, and by the time of the reign of the Roman emperor Justinian (527-565), outnumbered those who accepted Chalcedon in Egypt, whom they called Melkites.

Over this issue, the Egyptian Church ceased to be in communion with what became the Roman Catholic and Eastern Orthodox Churches. The Melkites however appointed rival patriarchs and bishops who followed their Chalcedonian interpretation of the scriptures; and to this day, there are two lines of patriarchs of Alexandria, a Coptic line and a Greek-speaking Melkite line.

Therefore after the Council of Chalcedon, Roman citizens, following the Emperor, the Pope of Rome and the Patriarch of Constantinople, forsook Egypt as the recognized seat of the glory of Christianity, and looked instead to Palestine and Antioch for the Christian ascetic ideal, grossly depreciating and overlooking the Egyptian contribution to Christianity. After the Arabic conquest, first of Syria, and then of Egypt in 641, Christianity in those lands shrank into small pockets in the desert, while Muslim Arabs took control of the political and religious systems of Egypt.

Egypt Passes the Torch

The historical relationship between Egypt and Ethiopia is one of father and son, the father being Egypt, in the sense that Ethiopia received Her Christianity through the Coptic Christians of Egypt. The Patriarch of Alexandria in Egypt had jurisdiction over what was then the Ethiopian Coptic Church up until relatively recent times. This jurisdiction came with real power that Egypt and her ancient Christian faith had over Ethiopia.

When Egypt was unable to establish and maintain a Christian monarchy and became a predominately Islamic country after 641 Ethiopia, who had peacefully and wholeheartedly accepted the gospel in the fourth century and continued to cling to it, emerged as the Mother of Christianity.[59]

After the Arab conquest, Ethiopia emerged from the shadow of her religious parent as the new defender of the Monophysite Christian faith. There is ample archeological evidence that Gnostic and Essene communities are among those that sprang up in Ethiopia from Egyptian Christian monastic settlements, transmitting patterns which Ethiopia inherited and has protected up to the present.

Ethiopia is home of the Garden of Eden, the Throne of David and the Ark of the Covenant, and She gave birth to Yahowshua ha Mashiakh and Miriam of Magdala. Seamlessly adding Monophysite Christianity to Her glorious cultural and religious tapestry, She became the only Hebrew Christian Empire the world has ever known. In so doing She developed, preserved and defended a rich biblical pattern that is otherwise unknown.

---

[59] Later, Haile Sellassie I took pains to develop this crucial role of Ethiopia by developing the autonomy of the Ethiopian Church during His early years as Ras Tafari.

The seal and emblem of the Royal Apostles of Haile Sellassie I

CHAPTER 7

THE HEBREW CHRISTIAN EMPIRE

Existing records of ancient history suffer from a series of numerous gaps, virtually a perforated line, whose perforations must be filled if the whole entity is to hang together. Knowledge of Ethiopia fills the gaps, revealing an ancient and still living culture with parallels to Old Testament religion that are lost and forgotten in modern forms of worship.

This ancient culture makes Ethiopia's the foremost church in regard to authenticity. She exhibits the oldest, most authentic form of Christian worship in existence, which simultaneously crowns Her as the faithful Mother of Christianity and dethrones the Pope of Roman Catholicism to a mere infiltrator of the faith, though this claim could be seen as revolutionary, even sacrilegious, by most of the pious Christian world.

Ethiopia mystically embraced the gospel from a most strategic position, being that Her head and supreme authority, king Ezana, from whom Ethiopia anointed Herself in the oil and light of Christ, was himself a successor of David. Throughout biblical or literal history, no such event ever took place anywhere else. This makes Ethiopia's Christianity a continuous offshoot from the root of all that is sacred and pure in Judaism.

Judaism has had one and only one kingdom of its own since the 588 B.C. destruction of Jerusalem and dispersion of the Israelites, and that is the Jewish empire established in Ethiopia. When Ethiopia accepted Christianity as her sovereign faith she had been a Judaic nation for centuries before Christ, making her the only nation to have converted from Judaism to Christianity.

Her conversion is uniquely significant because her political seat is the Throne of David. For upon making a thorough study of the traditions of the Biblical Jewish nation one comes to understand that a Jewish nation cannot be established without the seed and throne of King David.

Ethiopia's Conversion

The Acts of the Apostles state that the Ethiopian eunuch whom Phillip baptized was an African who came to Jerusalem to worship in the manner of the Jews. Acts 2 explains that *devout men from all nations came to Jerusalem to worship*. A journey to Jerusalem to worship clearly implies devotion to Yahweh, the God of the Jews. One does not have to be a genius to realize that an Ethiopian would not make a pilgrimage from Ethiopia to Jerusalem to worship unless Judaism was already established in Ethiopia, as I said before.[60]

We do not know what became of the eunuch from Ethiopia, whether he preached the gospel to the royal court or became one of the early Christian monks of that land. The adoption of Christianity by the nation of Ethiopia as a whole seems to begin with a certain Frumentaus (300-380), a Greek-speaking Syrian, who not only preached the gospel but secured the wholehearted acceptance of the new faith at the Ethiopian royal court. The emperor sent him back to Egypt to ask Athanasius, by then the patriarch of Alexandria, to send a bishop to establish a church in Ethiopia. Athanasius schooled Frumentaus in the ways of the priesthood, ordained him a bishop, and then sent him back to Ethiopia. Frumentaus encouraged early believers to renounce material life and seek a life of austerity.

---

[60] One might ask, to what extent was Ethiopia Jewish? The answer is: to the extent that the empire was run from the Judaic seat of King David. From David's throne a thick fabric of Biblical religion always knit the people together.

Frumentaus became known as Saint Abba Selama, and is often depicted riding a lion, brandishing a maskal (cross). He is one of the first saints who, along with the nine Syrian Saints, helped to set up and execute the translation of the gospels and other scriptures into Ge'ez from Greek and Aramaic.

The *Kebra Negast* chronicles the turn of events by which Ethiopia became both the home of the Ark of the Covenant and the only Jewish state to accept the Gospel and Faith of the Christ.

Ethiopian Christians in Jerusalem

Many monks journeyed from Ethiopia, across the deserts of the Sudan and Egypt, and developed their own monastic communities in Palestine: in Jerusalem, Keranyo (Golgotha, where Christ is said to have been crucified), Bethlehem, and along the Jordan River. By so doing, they gained for Ethiopia patrimonial rights and privileges with regard to religious services in the holy places associated with the life of Jesus in and near Jerusalem. For example, the head of the Ethiopian community came to have the recognized prerogative of entering the Holy Sepulcher before anyone else every year and starting the celebration of the resurrection of Christ at Easter. These prerogatives were confirmed by the governor with jurisdiction in Jerusalem at the time, recognized by the other Christian communities, and continue to this day.

Anciency of Ethiopian Christianity

The Ethiopian Orthodox or Tawahedo[61] Church, has had a challenging history for nearly two thousand years. She is not alone in having had a challenging history; the early history of the developing Christian Church in general has not been easy. One

---

61 *Tawahedo* refers to the Miaphysite or Monophysite doctrine, according to which Christ has a single nature.

way in which she is fairly unique, however, is that She put down Her roots when the teachings that became so-called Christian doctrine were mere ideas in the minds of ambitious zealots like Saul of Tarsus, otherwise known as Paul, the patron saint and grand architect of most of Christianity.

This by no means devalues other churches, but we must attach great value to the antiquity of the Ethiopian Church as we delve into the soil from which Christianity emerged and seek to understand the many shapes it has taken. The fact that Ethiopian Christianity is not generally taken seriously by scholars and intellectuals greatly undermines whatever conclusions they might come to.

After Ethiopia converted Her Hebraic-Jewish state into a Christian kingdom in 333 A.D., She had a close relationship with Alexandria continuously for more than three centuries, but after Egypt succumbed to Islam in 641, Ethiopia was marooned from mainstream Christianity for more than 800 years. In her isolation, She developed a unique Hebraic-Judaic Christian church far beyond that found anywhere else in the ancient Christian world.

At a time when Europe was still largely pagan, an ancient type of Christianity thrived in Africa and was protected by the shedding of African blood through battle after battle with Arabs and outside Christian colonizers. For hundreds of years, Ethiopia remained the only Christian country in Africa and was aptly cited as *a Christian island in a sea of pagans.*[62]

By the fourth century, Ethiopia's fervent devotion to Her newly adopted Christian religion created a unique hybrid of indigenous cultures and influences from Egypt to Persia, visible in the church she birthed, faithful to the doctrine of Monophysitism — which

---

62 Taken from Menelik II's letter addressed to Rome.

supports the hope for a union of human nature with the Divine. Early Christian and then Mohammedan disciples too sought refuge in Ethiopia and the righteous rule of the sovereign of this ancient kingdom. Thus Ethiopia became a civilizational center in which Christians, Muslims and Jews enjoyed reciprocal peaceful interrelationships for centuries.

Egypt's Legacy of Monasticism in Ethiopia

The ancient history that Ethiopia shares with Egypt can be seen in their shared legacy of monasticism, a legacy which has survived virtually unbroken from the first century of Christianity until today.

Ethiopian monastic life, in particular, is founded upon Old Testament traditions of devotion, as was the wilderness life of the Essene John the Baptist. Many Gnostics perpetuated a similar tradition of life in the wilderness, the tradition which gave birth to such literary treasures as the *Dead Sea Scrolls* and the *Nag Hammadi Library*.

Monastic life is considered by Ethiopian laymen to be the calling to a life-long commitment unto God: they call it *the last life*.

Though it has long since disappeared in the West, the eremitical life is still widespread in Ethiopia. The cenobitical monks and indeed the ordinary people regard the hermitage as Man's highest abode on earth, though often monks seem fearful at the possibility of God calling them to it. In almost every monastery there are a number of monks — perhaps one tenth of the total — who confine themselves to their cells. They are described as *the monks who never see the sun*. They have no responsibilities within the community and do not attend the daily common prayers. Food is brought to their huts each day by a single monk permanently designated to the task;

the hermit only emerges for the Mass in church on Sundays and feast days. Usually their cells are within the monastery compound, though sometimes they are a short distance away: at Debre Damo, for instance, hermits can be seen in apparently inaccessible caves in the sheer cliff beneath the monastery. Other monks or lay people can visit them (if they can reach their cell), and even today many of the rulers of Ethiopia frequently seek the advice of these hermits on both spiritual and temporal matters, as indeed the Emperor Himself did.

Bahtawis

> Besides these monastic hermits, there are countless holy men (ba'atawi) living in remote forests and caves throughout Ethiopia. These men have totally rejected human contact, and if they ever visit a church they *come by night, crawling through the undergrowth so as not to be seen* as an admiring priest described it. They live only on the wild fruits and herbs which Nature provides. A few of these holy men are ordained monks who have left their communities, but mostly they are lay people — as another monk put it, *God has called them to holiness from nothing, as Christ called Peter and Paul.*
>
> Taken from: *The Monastic Community of Ethiopia*
> — By Robert Van de Weyer

Ethiopia preserves the oldest and most authentic example of the Essene way currently found, in the mystical traditions of the Bahtawi.[63] They are the Nazarites of Ethiopian Orthodox Christianity, consistent with the ancient Judaic laws and ordinances of the priesthood of Aaron and Zadok. Although these priests or monks are not associated with churches or chapels, they are considered by the Ethiopians to be the holiest of

---

63 *Bahtawi* is the Ethiopic word for hermit.

Bahtawi Priest

the holy. Historically, some have been radical breakaways from the ordinary church, going even deeper into the Christian faith, living with the discipline of a hermit. The Bahtawis are strict vegetarians, feeding on meager meals of herbs and sprouts.

Bahtawis are monks that live a life of renunciation through direct visions or revelations from God. The are mostly men, but many women have been known to disappear from their families or jobs to live this life of austerity, leaving the world behind. As a sign of their devotion to the spirit, they do not cut their nails nor shave, cut nor comb their hair, which is allowed to grow into matted tufts. As Nazarites, they live by vows. They do not aspire for spiritual heights for themselves, but bare their souls and sacrifice their bodies for the benefit of others.

Bahtawis live far from the metropolitan constructs of the cities and dwell in the remoter regions of Ethiopia, huddled, for instance, in caves in the rocky mountains of the northern highlands. They are known to perform various austerities, not unlike some of the practices of the Sadhus of India, and their discipline can be extreme in nature. Some of these hermits never leave their sanctuaries and eat very little; consequently their bodies become meager and frail from constant fasting. Some take vows that leave them standing, sleepless, or motionless in one spot for years; others take vows of silence leaving them literally speechless.

Others choose to eat a once-a-day meal, but only if it can fit in the palm of their hand. Some even vow to never eat, but live in meditation, with prayer as their food. Bahtawis are sustained mainly from the charity and goodwill of the faithful, who will leave them food in designated places. They are basically vegetarians or vegans whose physical existence is not dependent on daily bread, as it is written: *Man shall not live by bread alone, but by every word that proceedeth out of the mouth of God.*[64]

The Bahtawis serve as the oldest living manifestation of the ancient Essenes. The Nazarite vow of the Bahtawi is made unto the Priestly Mashiakh, Yahowshua, who is at the core of their teachings and devotion. Yet we find traces of this Bahtawi practice in all the mystical traditions of the world, including those of the Sadhus of India and the Sufis of the Middle East.

It is characteristic of the Bahtawis to retreat to the mountains for silent devotion, only emerging to break silence with prophetical warnings to the populations in the cities and towns. In 1974, during the coup against Haile Sellassie I's rule, the Bahtawis came forward in large numbers with just such warnings, dreadlocked, barefoot and clothed in white robes.

The Bahtawis are not unlike the Gnostics, who took their own interpretation of the scriptures as equally valid as the clergy's, not feeling the need to answer to any aspect of the church's authority. Their direct link to God give them insight and visions that they express with fierce authority to the church. They are not seen as parishioners, but rather as mystics reminiscent of the prophets of old. Living outside the jurisdiction of the church, at times they find themselves at odds with the church and the Abuna. The Bahtawis are known to pronounce their prophetical judgment upon the Church, the clergy, the house of nobles, and even the emperor. Their judgment is no respecter of persons, any more than were the many prophets before them who chastised the house of Israel for their misdeeds.

As hermits, the Bahtawis usually do not attend mass or any other church function, though they are known to sneak into churches in the deep of the night. By virtue of their ascetic discipline, they

---

64 Matthew ch. 4, v. 4

help to keep the church on the path; as mentioned before, they can be outright uncompromising and without reservation in their prophesying against the church. Consequently the church in return has been very harsh, even cruel, to the objective voice of the Bahtawis. Under the reign of the late Abuna Paulos, a number of Bahtawis were imprisoned, some even killed, sometimes on church grounds, for speaking out against the church's alignment with the Derg, the secular communist government that took over Ethiopia after the reign of Haile Sellassie I.

In Ethiopia the Bahtawis are associated with magic. They are known to perform miracles, and wild animals, it is said, do not attack them. They can appear and disappear at will, and can walk in the pouring rain without getting wet. Fable or no fable, the Bahtawis have a long history in Ethiopia and the church reveres their piety as that of saints.

Saint Tekle Haminot

Saint Tekle Haminot or Tekla Haymanot (*Plant of Faith*), circa 1215-1313, was an Ethiopian monk born in Zorare in the district of Selale to the priest Sagaz Ab (*Gift of Faith*) and his wife Egzi'e (*Choice of God*), who was considered barren. Thus Tekle Haminot was seen as a miracle child and was pledged over to the church in gratitude to God. He would later found one of Ethiopia's most important monasteries, the monastery of Debre Libanos.

Tekle Haminot lived for twenty-nine years after he built his monastery, dying in 1313, the year before the ruling Emperor Wedem Arad died. Haminot is said to have lost a leg through extended periods fulfilling a vow of prayerful standing devotion. He is the only Ethiopian saint venerated outside of Ethiopia, namely in Egypt and Rome, and is usually represented with two pairs of wings, standing on one leg with the amputated leg lying nearby. He was originally buried in the cave where he had lived as a hermit, but was later reinterred, almost sixty years later, at Debre Lebanos.

As a token of honor and reverence, Haile Sellassie I erected a church at Debre Lebanos over the shrine of the saint in the 1950s. The burial site of Tekle Haminot has become a favorite destination for pilgrims and a choice site for burials. In Ethiopia, the 24th day of every month is dedicated to this saint, while the 17th of August is his feast day.

Saint Gebre Menfes Kidus

Gebre Menfes Kidus, literally *the servant of the Holy Spirit*, is one of Ethiopia's most famous saints. His life was the perfect example of self-sacrifice. He is often depicted wearing a robe of hair girt with chains, with a long white beard and flowing locks, a couple pairs of lions and leopards at his feet, and a raven quenching its thirst from the water in his eyes. Abba Gebre Menfes Kidus, according to tradition, founded the Zeqwala monastery in 1370, and it is said that he lived there for 262 years, praying daily for centuries by the nearby Crater Lake.

Saint Gebre Menfes Kidus was born in Egypt of Egyptian parents, Simon and Aklisa, on the 28 of November 868 E.C.[65] Accounts of his life are filled with unbelievable tales; for instance, it is said that, having been set apart for the glory of God, he never in his life tasted earthly food, never even suckling at his mother's breast. At the age of three his parents, directed by a vision from God, obediently handed him over to a saintly monk named Gabre Berhan, *the relative of light*, to be schooled in the scriptures in a Coptic monastery in Egypt.

---

65 E.C. meaning the Ethiopian Calendar. This corresponds to 875 A.D.

When he was old enough to make deacon, God called him out of the monastery into the wilderness to pursue the life of an anchorite or hermit. According to one tradition, he lived in a place called Gebota in Egypt for 300 years, slowly withering in the desert cold and heat. His clothes disintegrated completely, and he remained naked until the Lord mercifully provided him with a garment of white fur. At last, after 300 years of suffering, he was visited in a vision by the holy Mother and the apostles and a host of heavenly angels, whereupon he gave his first covenant of forgiveness to the villagers of Gebota.

From there, according to legend, he obeyed the Lord's order and moved from Egypt back to Ethiopia, where he continued his devotion and his fight against the principalities of evil. Legend says, he arrived in Ethiopia during the reign of King Lalibela, accompanied by sixty lions and leopards who followed him everywhere. The king humbly bowed to the mystic several times in reverence and received him graciously, and the saint in return gave the king his blessings. The king and the saint then travelled together to Mount Zeqwala, where the Saint remained and eventually founded the Zeqwala monastery. When King Lalibela departed the mountain, he built a church in the name of Holy Miriam in a place called Adadi according to Gabre Menfes Kidus's advice. Many more fantastic stories are attached to this great saint's name.

Timkat

The twelfth-century French explorer spoken of by historian Graham Hancock (p. 23) witnessed a spectacle of exuberant popular worship in Ethiopia unlike anything he knew from Europe.

The men he saw carrying the Ark were indeed Ethiopians. They were carrying out the ancient rites and dances of David in

The Hebrew Christian Seal

the same way as they had done for centuries past, and as they continue to do today.

The explorer had witnessed the Hebraic-Christian tradition of the feast of Timkat, the Ethiopian celebration of the Epiphany or Baptism of Christ. This extraordinarily unique festival, a time of great jubilation, is indigenous to the African Christianity of which Ethiopia is the Mother. Timkat falls on January 19th or 20th (the 10th day of Terr in the Ge'ez calendar).[66]

The day before Timkat, men and women adorn themselves in white shammas (the national dress) trimmed with their national colors of red, gold and green, vibrating the nation with drumming and chanting. On the feast of Timkat, the Ark and its replicas in many churches are carried in procession on the heads of priests, out of the Holy of Holies and through the streets.

The various churchyards throughout Ethiopia are filled with the faithful, and the sacred liturgy is performed early in the morning near a body of water. Once blessed, the water is lavishly sprinkled over a jubilant and ecstatic crowd of believers, who never seem to get enough of its blessings. All over the country, bishops, priests and deacons, monks and nuns, and ordinary Christian men, women and children go in procession and dance, sing and ululate all day and into the night for three days, and engage in rites of bathing in lakes and rivers in memory of Christ's baptism in the River Jordan.

From the various churchyards they go marching with huge kettledrums and sistrums, with children in crowns carrying processional maskals, drumming women in groups swaying with the rhythm of ancient songs, to be joined by other neighboring chanters and celebrants from all walks of life. Under embroidered umbrellas, priests and deacons dressed in colorful silk brocades wave incense burners in procession through the overcrowded streets celebrating the Epiphany.

This is the most glorious day in Ethiopia, a day unmatched by any other for the glory with which it is celebrated. Hancock failed

---

66 The Ge'ez calendar is based on the old Coptic calendar of Alexandra. Like the Coptic calendar, the Ethiopian calendar has 12 months, each of 30 days, plus a period of 5 or sometimes 6 epagomenal days. In Ethiopia this period of time is called "Puaga'me" and is considered the 13th month. Like the Julian calendar, the Ge'ez and Coptic calendars add a leap day every four years. The Ethiopian calendar is 7 years behind the Gregorian calendar we use today, which was introduced by Pope Gregory XIII of Rome in 1582.

to give us the name of the twelfth-century French explorer, but he must have been bewildered thus to experience the glory of Zion in Kush. It must also have made him realize that Africans were living out the mysteries of the Bible and of faith much more richly, there in the heart of Ethiopia, than Europeans, who so vigorously claimed those mysteries as their own, had ever practiced them in Europe.

Stone Churches and Knights Templar

Places of worship in Ethiopia, especially the monolithic churches of Lalibela, where ten such churches were carved out of solid rock in the thirteenth century in the reign of King Lalibela, are more than remarkable monuments of the Christian conviction of those who built them. They are truly wonders of the world.

King Lalibela had a vision to build one of Christian antiquity's greatest monuments, which still stands alive and active to this day. This remote mountain village, known as Lalibela after the king, who founded her as his capital, became known as the New Jerusalem of Ethiopia. According to legend, the King spent all his wealth to finance the project, while he slept on rocks and ate herbs and roots. When the last church was completed two decades later, he gave up his throne to pursue a life of Christian contemplation. He is revered in Ethiopia as a true saint.

The extraordinary craftsmanship that went into the sculpted churches of Lalibela astounds and mystifies the minds of architects and historians alike. Kabalistic and Masonic symbols were carved and painted on volcanic rock inside the churches in a quite remarkable fashion. In various geometric forms, we find the seals of many secret orders that have existed through the centuries, such as the Templars and Essenes, and other mystical symbols from places like Persia and East Asia. A cross within the star of David, an Essene emblem, is a common motif both in these

A Window from St. George's Monolithic Church

churches and elsewhere in this ancient Judaeo-Christian empire. Windows were carved from the walls of the church of St. Mary in the form of a swastika, the sacred cross of numerous mystic orders, only later perverted by the Nazis.

The original guardians who created the church of St. George could very well have been Knights Templar. According to this theory, the Templars, an obscure group of phantom Christian knights, were descended from a mysterious Ethiopian sub-sect of Hebrew warrior priests, a veritable priest army. Once the Ark arrived in Ethiopia, their oath was understood to include the guardianship of the Ark of the Covenant. This mysterious sect of crusaders is said to have appeared in Ethiopia after the destruction of Jerusalem in 587 BC, around the time the Ark was taken to Ethiopia, and well before Templars appeared in Europe.

This is not far-fetched considering the rich but mysterious cloud in which history has enveloped Ethiopia, Her undying devotion to ancient Old Testament traditions and the principles of Monophysitism, and the ascesis of apotheosis She has preserved through countless acts of self-sacrifice.

The First Supper

CHAPTER 8

THE IMMACULATE CONCEPTION

When the religious or spiritual history of a people is written mostly by fanatics or devoted zealots, their convictions tend to distort it, sometimes completely changing its meaning. Thus, over-embellishment has reduced many of the histories in the Bible to mere myths and fables.

The stories in the New Testament about how Christ came to be born are an example of this. In conventional Christian theology, therefore, based on these stories, *Immaculate Conception* has come to mean birth without sex, generally referring to the birth of Jesus Christ.[67]

Immaculate conception is not a new concept. It has been found in the myths of the ancient Egyptians, Greeks and Romans. But philosophers from these cultures did not necessarily understand an immaculate conception literally as a sexless birth, but as a conception that arose from the sexual act of two enlightened beings, especially if the woman was a virgin. The fruit of such a union was considered to have been immaculately conceived.

According to the ancient Essenes, the purified virgin womb of Miriam of Nazareth was the ideal receptacle for the purified seed of Joseph, her espoused husband, in that the cycle of genealogical purifications of David's seed had been completed in her. On this basis, they said, it was given to Mary to become the Mother of God and to Joseph to become the father of God

---

[67] Some theologians insist that the Immaculate Conception refers also or primarily to the birth of Mary of Nazareth and/or Miriam of Magdala to *their* forebears, but then quibble about the definition of sex in the various cases. Essene scriptures would agree with the application of this concept to the Marys' origin, however, a broad consensus applies the Immaculate Conception particularly to the coming of Christ in the absence of sexual relations between Mary and Joseph. There is no other accepted name for this very important concept in Christian theology.

And they were both pure before God; and of them both was Iesu-Maria who is called the Christ. And the angel came in unto her and said, Hail Mary, thou that art highly favoured, for the Motherhood of God is with thee: blessed art thou among women and blessed be the fruit of thy womb... Fear not, Mary, for thou hast found favour with God and behold, thou shalt conceive in thy womb and bring forth a child, and He shall be great and shalt be called a Son of the Highest.

And the Lord God shall give unto him the throne of his father David: and he shall reign over the house of Iacob for ever; and of his kingdom there shall be no end.

...The Holy Spirit shall come upon Ioseph thy spouse, and the power of the Highest shall overshadow thee, O Mary, therefore also that holy thing which shall be born of thee shall be called the Christ, the Child of God, and his Name on earth shalt be called Iesu-Maria, for he shall save the people from their sins, whosoever shall repent and obey his Law.

Therefore ye shall eat no flesh, nor drink strong drink, for the child shall be consecrated unto God from its mother's womb, and neither flesh nor strong drink shall he take, nor shall razor touch his head.

...And the same day the angel Gabriel appeared unto Ioseph in a dream and said unto him. Hail Ioseph, thou that art highly favoured, for the Fatherhood of God is with thee. Blessed art thou among men and blessed be the fruit of thy loins.

Taken from the *Essene New Testament*[68]

---

[68] The *Essene New Testament*, also known as the Gospel of The Holy Twelve, is the New Testament translated from an even older, more authentic manuscript than what the King James Version was translated from. It gives us a contrasting view of the life and teachings of the Mashiakh and is considered by many scholars to contain the true teachings of Yahowshua the Jewish mystic. However, it remains to be a controversial document amongst some theological circles.

Understanding the Immaculate Conception

A comparative study of many ancient religious belief systems will show that sex was perceived as a Divine act by which Divinity manifests through the biology of human form. Goddess worship and devotion was at the foundation of this idea, in which the woman, as mother, becomes the embodiment and nurturer of God the Father. In reality, it is within the dark watery womb of the mother that the spirit of the seed of the father takes on form. This process has mystified the minds of men since the dawn of our existence, and has created a sense of deep mystery about the female body. Ancient cultures, such as those of the Sumerians, Canaanites and Assyrians were completely based on agriculture, tightly intertwined with the worship of the Earth Goddess and Her mystical rites and rituals. The symbol of a tree was Her usual insignia.

It could be said that the patriarchal roots of the Hebrews gave rise to a radical priesthood which was merciless to the worshippers of the Goddess. These priests claimed that their god, Yahweh, forbade the Goddess's paganistic rituals, and they invaded and utterly destroyed much of the Goddess-worshiping culture. Sacred groves and temples were burned and the land and people ravished by these Hebrews.

Their notion of Yahweh, the god of Abraham, who became the god of the Israelite nation, is the key element for understanding much of the decline of Goddess devotion. The god of the Israelites was the god of the sky, represented by the sun, which had no earthly counterpart. In the same way, Yahweh appears as a single male entity without a female counterpart, even though Sophia, or wisdom, sometimes seems to be the feminine aspect of Yahweh.

This theology of a solo male god, a celibate god in the heavens, eventually alienated the people of the earth. Also, this shift in the Israelites' belief to believe in an all-male god led to painful taboos and stigmas being associated with the female function and a denigration of woman's relationship to God. Throughout the history of the Jews, Babylon was seen as a whore and a menstruating woman, while backsliding Israel was often compared to an adulterous bride whose birth pains brought forth nothing more than "wind, for uncleanness" and scorn were pinned on the cyclical flow of the woman's blood, as well as on the process of childbirth. References in the biblical Book of Leviticus, ch. 12, depict the separate purification rites for the birth of a son, which took thirty-three days, versus those for a girl, whose uncleanness lasted twice as long. These and other laws show the Levitical superstitions attached to woman and her moon cycle. In many cases, because a menstruating woman was seen as unclean (as indeed she is still seen) she was banished to a nearby encampment constructed especially for the unclean.

I say all this to buttress the claim that the patriarchal Judaeo-Christian papacy contrived a conspiracy against sex and the Divine power in sex. The Immaculate Conception has come to be understood as an unnatural phenomenon, one that excludes human beings from the family of God. If the *Christ* was begotten of this type of Immaculate Conception, how can we as humans ever hope to emulate His ways and thereby develop His virtues in ourselves? Was it not He that said: *Greater works than these ye shall do...*? Yet this is only possible through us becoming one with the Divine I AM that He embodied. Indeed the acts of the early apostles did fulfill His words and are the best illustration of what unity in *Christ* can do.

At this point in history, a healthier approach to the metaphor of Immaculate Conception would be to view it as each and every one's birthright. By this I mean: self-realization through the second birth, the birth of the Divine within, requires everyone to have an Immaculate Conception. Everyone has this potential, but we do not necessarily fulfill our potential. If we are to be reborn,

She Gives Birth Unto Magic

The Immaculate Conception

we must take the initiative to activate this inner spiritual power. Only then can we truly say that God creates us and that God is our Mother and Father. Outside of this consciousness, one is merely born on the biological level. Rather, it is necessary for one to also experience a spiritual rebirth in order to claim their supreme birth, which ultimately is apart from a biological mother and father. No birth certificate can be given for this kind of self-rebirth, yet oftentimes the initiate takes on a new spiritual name. Taking a new name is also one's Divine right.

In all of this, however, what is significant about the Christ is His life, which happens to take form through a spiritually aligned, but very sexual, birth. This He maintained without mitigation, which means without corruption, throughout His lifetime. He proved His immaculate birth by overcoming the temptation of those thoughts, words and deeds that corrupt: first, the mind; then, the body; and ultimately, the soul of a man. During his brief ministry, He claimed direct descent from God, declaring that He, Himself, was God, the Father. He devoted His life to the cultivation of that conviction, and He was to prove that He proceeded directly from the center of the wheel to the periphery without interruption. Therefore, he affirmed: *I am the way, the truth and the life, no man cometh unto the father but by me.*[69]

His life was the doorway into a higher consciousness, the key, and the power over spiritual death in a mortal life. This was the key to everlasting life, through a spiritual rebirth manifesting physically. This is how one is born again. This is the power of Yahowshua's immaculate conception; this is also the key element in His resurrection. Believing is seeing, as He physically manifested Himself to those in whose spirits He resurrected.

After He died and resurrected, the power of the Holy Spirit was released upon an elect number of disciples, and these were

---

69 John ch. 14, v. 6

resurrected through His spirit, which gave them eyes of spirit to see Him. This opened up their understanding of the words He had left them. This spiritual empowerment made them one with Him in His life and now, in His death. Esoterically, the death, burial, and sealing up of Yahowshua in a sepulcher represent the conditions that most of humanity is born to. These conditions stifle the natural flow of life essence, through the fear of death. Nevertheless, through Yahowshua's example, one can be empowered to break the seven seals and roll away the stone, claiming the victory of life over death.

Woman/Ethiopia: The Cosmic Ark

On one level one can clearly see how the Ark of the Covenant became flesh when the stone tablet of the Law in the Ark is seen as the Mashiakh, and Mary is seen as the woman from whom the Law, the Mashiakh came forth. Therefore, symbolically, Zion, Ethiopia, Mary and the Ark are one and the same. Mary, accepted as the Mother of God in the Orthodox Christian faith, particularly symbolizes Zion.

As previously stated, this famous Ark of the Covenant is claimed by Ethiopia, the first and only Christian Empire ruled by Kings and Emperors sitting upon the Throne of David. Ethiopia therefore fulfills the prophecy in Revelation ch. 12, vv. 1, 2:

> And there appeared a great wonder in heaven; a woman clothed with the sun, and the moon under her feet, and upon her head a crown of twelve stars: And she being with child cried, travailing in birth, and pained to be delivered.

Ethiopia is the Woman, the chosen Habitation of the Godhead, and Mother of Yahowshua, the Son (Sun). She, the Tree of Life, a life which has Christ within the midst of Her, has been the protector and preserver of Her own independence.

The woman spoken of in Revelation ch. 12, v. 1 could not be the Virgin Mary of Nazareth, the woman who gave birth to Yahowshua. The Immaculate Conception had already taken place, and henceforth and forever the perfect Body of the Most High is on the earth, through the seed of King David as the Mashiakh resurrected.

Therefore, in the revelation of the Mashiakh in His Second Advent, His birth would not focus on His mother as a woman. It would focus on His Mother as a Place, which is Holy Mount Zion, where the glory of the twelve tribes of Israel is present as the crown of stars upon Her head.

These three things cannot be separated, the Mother, the Father and the Holy Spirit, which always agree in one, as the embodiment of the Godhead, the Holy Trinity.

Since Old Testament times, no country but Ethiopia has claimed possession of any of the following:

1. The Ark of the Covenant
2. The Throne of King David
3. Descent from King David through the Solomonic lineage
4. Rulers who rule as Head of Church and State, bestowed with titles like: King of Kings, Lion of the Tribe of Judah

These historical facts are just a few of many that demonstrate how Ethiopia stands apart from the rest of the world.

Elect of God, *King of Kings*, *Lion of the Tribe of Judah*, *King of Zion* and *Light of the World* are titles that have been characteristic of the Ethiopian sovereigns since they received the Glory

Revelation 12

The Immaculate Conception

of Zion centuries ago. Haile Sellassie I was the first of the Ethiopian kings to bear *Lord of Lords* attached to the title of King of Kings, as well as *Conquering* added to the traditional title of Lion of the Tribe of Judah. From the above facts, the reasoning mind will logically conclude that Ethiopia is the place called Zion, where Yahweh sits as King and Queen. These facts also confirm the position Ethiopia has played, is playing and will play in the very near future. By this, it is meant that everyone will have to look to Ethiopia, the Place, and to H.I.M., the Man, for the answers to many, if not all, of their questions pertaining to the Mashiakh in His Second Advent. John ch. 14, vv. 1-3 states:

> Let not your heart be troubled: Ye believe in God, believe also in me. In my Father's house there are many mansions: if it were not so, I would have told you. I go to prepare a place for you. And if I go and prepare a place for you, I will come again, and receive you unto myself; that where I am, there ye may be also.

> … Behold, I send the promise of my Father upon you.
>
> Luke ch. 24, v. 49

> As Jesus Christ has said: Where two or three are gathered together in my name, there I am in the midst of them. It is therefore our expressed hope that these words will be realized in their full significance in this great assembly.
>
> —H.I.M. Haile Sellassie I at the
World Evangelical Congress in Berlin

Sacred Geometry

When we look at the patriarchal trinity of Christianity, we should immediately realize that it is impossible for an all-masculine trio to produce anything but confusion, apart from the Divine feminine. The trinity of Father, Son and Holy Spirit is not realistically nor metaphorically complete in itself, lacking the feminine energy which is the catalyst for all emanation from the Divine. An all-masculine Divine trinity devalues the feminine or Shekinah glory, leading to distorted views of womanhood in general. To a psyche devoted to the Christian trinity, woman surfaces as a subordinate entity, who must bear the full brunt of the fall of man from the paradise of Eden.

This is the kind of mind that declares that, as long as woman has anything to do with the business of God, sex is inevitable, leading the soul of man into destruction. This is a false notion. In fact, an absence of the feminine prevents the true essence of any religion from being fully realized. We must study the Christian trinity objectively if we are to fully see the conditions that shape the psyche of the Christian masses. With the Father, Son and Holy Ghost trinity, the entire godhead is based upon masculine principles.

If the Father and the Son are indeed one, then the trinity is not a complete triune force, which would have to be three separate entities that culminate in one complete being. In the theology of Christianity, the Son is understood to be *of the one essence with the Father*, making one entity. The Holy Spirit is the other entity, representing the Father and Son on the spiritual level, kept continually in the realm of the unseen, yet the source of the parts of the Trinity that are seen.

In this line of reasoning, the Father, the Son and the Holy Spirit still do not constitute a triune force. This leads us to ask whether this concept was designed to illustrate the persons of the Divine trinity — or to oppress and deny the Divine powers of the mother. The latter seems the more appropriate answer. Once again, the denial of the mother aspect automatically reduces Christianity to a concept, out of alignment with the true trilateral energy that reproduces itself through the balance and flux of male and female polarities. By flux, I mean sex energy, the friction of the two opposite poles which, when balance is found, produces the archetypal form. Sex energy is at the core of all reproduction; hence sex energy is the means by which the Divine too emerges into form. To deny sex as a Divine act is to ultimately deny God as an organic structure, birthed from the ultimate power, the Mother.

The foundation of the trinity is found in zero, which is the fullness of the material world. All manifestation evolved out of the formless nothingness of zero. Zero can also be termed the Mother of all creation. From Her comes the number one, from the central point of Her essence. In separating from its point of origin, a point becomes a line, creating what is termed one dimension (stage 2 in the matrix opposite). The number one is unity, at the same time containing in its essence the number three. This is illustrated by the fact that when a point separates from itself, the point of origin becomes the first point, and two other points are naturally generated by the separation. Therefore, the number three becomes the key factor governing the one-dimensional world (stage 3).

As the number representing unity, one also symbolizes the platform upon which the unseen zero, as the foundation, created the multidimensional universe. Geometrically, the number two is a by-product of the numbers one and three. Yet two is fundamentally duality. This duality must be transcended through the return to oneness with itself. When two become one, the third, by Divine order, must emerge from this unity. Thus, two in its basic nature symbolizes friction and static, which, when

The Matrix of Planes and Dimensions

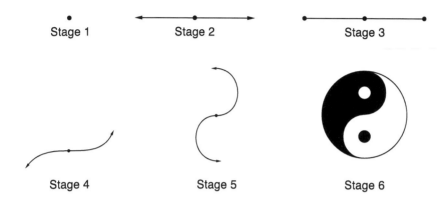

Movement arises from desire, from deep within the abyss of the primordial womb of consciousness of the androgynous Divine I. Within the Divine I, the feminine and masculine I's, out of their love and attraction to each other—a love based on their polar (opposite) natures—ignite a spark of light in the formerly cold darkness of the primordial wellspring, giving birth to infinite possibilities.

These opposing polar forces, because they are opposites, are destined at first to repel each other, create their own individualities, and develop their separate characteristics, before at last they unite. In their movement and process of repelling each other and then coming back together, they create the planes and dimensions of our universe. So in a sense all matter is a by-product of the yearning desire of point 2 and point 3, which are I and I (us), to return to point 1 (the Divine I) in oneness—at which point the third must manifest.

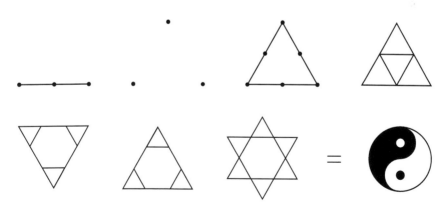

The Immaculate Conception

The Separation of the Trinity and the Creation of Dimensions

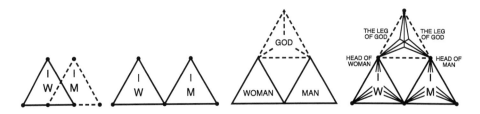

Thus we have the emergence of I and I from the separation of the Divine I from itself. The friction that is caused by this movement produces fire, heat and light and gives birth to the dimension of substance (matter). The balancing of the male and female energies establishes a flux of polar opposites in dynamic equilibrium; this balance is essential for creativity and the reproduction of matter. Every material thing has its governing intelligence, and it is this intelligence that determines the movement and destiny of all entities.

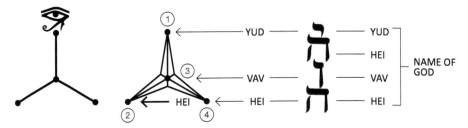

Haile Sellassie I's symbol of his name, which means the Trinity, and how it corresponds to the tetagramaton, the Old Testament name of the Hebrew God (YHVH).

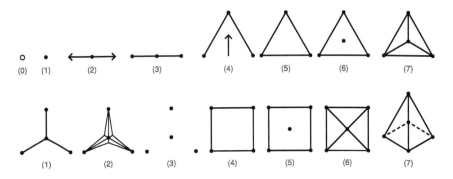

A Journey to the Roots of Rastafari

The Matrix of 7 in Conjunction with 3 and the Trinity

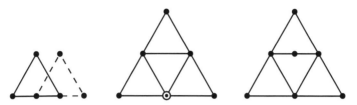

When the Trinity separates itself, an identical counterpart is revealed, making the 3 points now 6 points.

The 7th point comes naturally from the separation and is symbolic of the Holy Spirit or the Androgenous God-Head, the Crown and 7th Level.

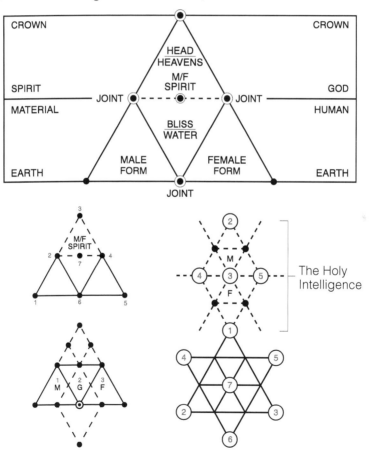

The Immaculate Conception

synchronized with their origin, produce Divine results. We call this Divine equilibrium the power of the Holy Trinity.

The fact that a line consists of at least three points, even though it represents the number one, makes the opening through which a plane or dimension is created. It manifests itself first as the equilateral triangle. This triangle is defined in just about every ancient culture, language and cosmology as the symbol of the Godhead or ultimate reality. Within this triangle of equal sides and angles are additional equilateral triangles manifesting the one-in-three and three-in-one phenomena. A triangle at the center is formed by the three surrounding triangles, representing the microcosm within the macrocosm.

The equilateral triangle therefore has hidden within it the potential and mystery of the number four. Contained within this triangle is the secret of the three-dimensional plane, which is the number seven.

For seven is created out of the separation of the trinity (equilateral triangle) from itself, creating an identical counterpart, making the three points now six points, joined by the central and seventh point. This seventh point completes a triad as the third part of the two, which becomes the common denominator. This seventh dimensional triangle is androgynous and functions on the spiritual level as the connecting force that governs the preceding pair of triangles as their intelligent counterpart, the Holy Trinity.

This is why seven is such a pivotal number in conjunction with the number three and the concept of the trinity

Super-Natural?

Let us then explore the concept of the trinity as the fundamental principle of existence. In so doing we will discuss this principle as the unseen aspect of all manifestations. Therefore, we will be forced to look at the trinity as a spiritual force, what is called the Holy Spirit. The Holy Spirit is the transcendental force that precedes all personalities and lineage. Christian theology declares the Holy Spirit to be the third part of the Holy Trinity and uses a dove as its symbol, but the element of fire is often used interchangeably with the dove.

It is the Holy Spirit in Christian theology that sanctifies and purifies all, without which there would be no divinity nor hope for carnal flesh. This is why to be born again means to be anointed with the Holy Spirit and only thus become a vessel for God's will. This, for the Christian mind, is the only way by which one can be saved. This train of thought implies that the Holy Spirit is not a natural part of human earthly life. According to Christian belief, one can only be complete as a human being by receiving the Holy Spirit as a gift, by accepting Jesus as the Son of God the Father.

The Holy Trinity as the spiritual executive power can be broken down into mind, soul and spirit, which is said to be the Law of God in action. Spirit and mind are synonymous with intelligence, from which the soul receives direct inspiration from within, while external influences create imprints and leave impressions, which also shape the direction of the body temple. The Holy Spirit does not constitute the entire concept of the trinity, but it is the part of the trinity which could be termed the intelligent or conscious aspect.

The Feminine

When I questioned an Ethiopian clergyman about the one-sided nature of the patriarchal trinity, which has no feminine counterpart, he rationalized that the feminine may be mysteriously hidden in the spiritual realm. This line of rationalization may be readily accepted by the biased minds of the dominant Christian zealots, but to objective seekers of the truth it certainly does not suffice.

Let us, for argument's sake, say it is so, in that the feminine god of the Christian trinity remains to be purely spiritual. This would then mean that Christ, as a personality, represents a deep suppression and denial of motherhood energy, because the scripture declares that Joseph was not His biological father, for the Holy Ghost united itself with Mary from within. But this father is something of a phantom, his identity a mystery. We do know that Christ's mother Mary added form and substance to the spirit of God in her virgin womb. Would this not mean that a feminine spirit impregnated an earthly woman, a fundamental impossibility?

> Some said Mary conceived by the Holy Spirit. They are in error. They do not know what they are saying. When was a woman ever conceived by a woman?
>
> *Nag Hammadi Library*, p. 143

The acceptance of this concept contradicts the notion that the feminine remains to be in the spirit. The very birth of the *Christ* from woman illustrates the literal presence of God, as Mother, giving birth to God, the Father, independent of man or male energy. Therefore, in my view, the Mother remains to be the first real manifested aspect of the trinity, in that She was before the Son. Even the idea of the trinity evolved out of her womb.

It is obvious that the Holy Trinity basically manifests itself to Western man as an active principle, one associated with masculine creative power, even though, as I expressed before, its feminine aspect known as *Sophia* has been coexistent with God since before creation. Fundamentally the Trinity is androgynous, combining both the masculine and feminine principles, representing the ultimate archetypal opposites. In the Genesis theory of creation we read that, after God created the earth and all of nature, God expressed, *Let us make man in our image after our likeness.... In the image of god created he him, male and female created he them* (Genesis ch. 1, vv. 26-27). Therefore, it is safe to say that a male-and-female ideal within the spirit made the decision to multiply itself, giving male and female archetypal form to energy.

> The masculinity of the spirit is meaningless until it enters into a feminine container, and ultimately no man can create anything without the equal participation of the woman without or the woman within. Even God could not transform Himself into man without the free consent of Mary.
>
> *Woman, Earth and Spirit* by Helen M. Luke, p. 7

Therefore, it is only natural that we perceive the *us* and the *our* in the Genesis creation of mankind as the combination of the Divine Mother and Father in a triune spiritual realm. Thus, a pragmatic and realistic view of the Holy Trinity would force us to declare the Earthly reality of the Father, whose potential, his seed, is nurtured into flesh and bones by the wisdom and power of the Mother.

This gives us as humans the primordial example of human origins, and makes perfect sense to us. Also, if the saying: *Be ye therefore perfect, even as your father which is in heaven is perfect* (Matthew ch. 5, v. 48) is of any pertinence, only by honoring our earthly Mother along with our heavenly Father will we give true honor to the Divine trinity from whence we came.

> Honor thy father and thy mother that thy days may be long upon the land which the Lord, thy god, giveth thee.
>
> Exodus ch. 20, v. 12

As long as Christian theology holds fast and continues to build upon a one-sided trinity as its foundation, Christianity will remain in the Dark Ages of human psychological evolution. This Father, Son and Holy Ghost theory is one of the fundamental snares that bind Christian minds to illusions and alienates them from the Divine Mother.

Some may point out that Mary, the mother of *Jesus,* is highly venerated, especially in the Catholic and Eastern Orthodox Churches. Some churches, not least the Ethiopian Orthodox, maintain many books and ancient manuscripts dedicated to devotion to the Mother of *Christ,* but this veneration, as I have observed it, is not equal to the worship given to Her Offspring. There is evidence that honor and worship in Her name began early in the development of the church. However, a true cult of the Virgin Mary was outlawed by the Holy Roman Empire; full worship of Mary Christ's mother has always been considered heretical, even though the flesh that came from Her womb is said to be one with the Father, equal to Almighty God. If one's acceptance of the Son does not naturally bring one into the bosom of the Mother, who leads the way to the Son, and the Son that leads to the way of the Holy Spirit, the *Comforter*, then one cannot say that they truly know the Almighty God, the *Father*.

For God so loved the world, that He gave His only begotten Son that whosoever believeth in Him should not perish but have everlasting life[70] is one of the most popular sayings of Christian evangelists and proselytizers. This would mean that God, the Father, a spirit, gave His only biological Son, *Jesus,* to the world as the savior from sin and the giver of eternal life, so that whosoever believes in Him shall escape the sting of death. The idea that a masculine spirit-God gave His offspring as ransom is a false mythology, based on patriarchal insecurities and rooted in fear of feminine power. The ability of the female body to transform potential into kinetic

---

70 John ch. 3, v. 16

energy signifies the power of God working practically through Her. If the *messiah* is the Son of God, then Mary, as His mother, is the Source of Light and the true Temple of God.

> Some said, "Mary conceived by the holy spirit." They are in error. They do not know what they are saying. When did a woman ever conceive by a woman? Mary is the virgin whom no power defiled. She is a great anathema to the Hebrews, who are the apostles and [the] apostolic men. This virgin whom no power defiled [...] "the [father who is in] heaven" unless [he] had had another father, but he would have said simply "[My father]."
>
> The Gospel of Philip (II 3), the *Nag Hammadi Library*

My father who art in heaven is an acknowledgement by Christ that he has an earthly father and mother. How could someone as significant as the Mother of Christ not be seen as the foundation of the Church? And since, according to the above scripture, His Mother could only have conceived through the balance of masculine and feminine energies, Joseph is therefore his earthly father. Can a body (temple) be complete if all the parts do not occupy their respective places and perform their respective functions? These are questions we must ask ourselves if we explore the meaning of the Christian trinity and the results of accepting it.

The Resurrection

CHAPTER 9

THE TWO MESSIAHS

Yahowshua ha Mashiakh: Archetypal Son

Let us not make any mistake about Yahowshua ha Mashiakh being man: he was man and will forever remain man in spirit and in form, an example of the *God-Man*.

The *God-Man* radiates from the power of the androgynous. He has found the inner Mother, which nurtures the inner child, and surrendered to Her illuminating glory, the Shekinah. In this, He is complete within Himself. This perfectly conscious human is the seventh and most total manifestation of God.

Humans have the highest capacity to process and transform untransformed energy into a practical, creative force. Every other life form manifests only a part of that fullness of God. Within humankind is the potential to emanate all levels of cosmic vibration. This is because only the human nervous system holds the seven levels of transformed and untransformed creative power. Still, the human being, in general, has only been able to radiate the vibrations on the level of which he or she has become conscious. When on the level of the unconscious, the corresponding nerve centers remain latent.

Within the capabilities of the *God-Man* is the Divine creative power, the consciousness of life of the eternal being. He is in At-One-Meant with the Ultimate Reality; therefore, He is able to radiate the Power of God-consciousness up to the seventh level as the Living Ark of the Covenant.

Within the Ark of the Covenant are the two stone tablets containing the Ten Commandments, a gold pot containing one measure of manna, and also the Rod of Aaron that was broken into three separate pieces but was originally one piece and one rod. We may also note that:

> ...There are three that bear record in heaven, the Father, the Word, and the Holy Ghost: and these three are one. And there are three that bear witness in the earth, the spirit, and the water, and the blood; and these three agree in one.
>
> 1 John ch. 5, vv. 7-8

In these verses of Scripture, you distinctly see the composition of the Godhead as a triune force combined in One Body, who is the Mashiakh. Therefore, the *Holy Bible* may also be dissected into three parts (note diagram), according to the manifestation of the triune Godhead. It was the appearance of the Mashiakh on the earth that turned time from B.C. (Before Christ) to A.D. (After Death).[71] Thus, we have the Old Testament, which is called B.C., and the New Testament, which is the fulfillment of the Old Testament, *In the Year of our Lord and Savior*.

At the end is the Book of Revelation, which is the fulfillment of the Old and New Testaments combined, known as *now* or *A.D.* Thus the three parts of the Godhead are manifested according to the three parts of time, as it is depicted in the *Holy Bible*.

---

[71] Some Christian historians give an unconvincing argument that A.D. comes from *anno Domini*, "in the Year of [Our] Lord." But why would A.D. stand for Latin words when B.C. admittedly stands for the English words *Before Christ*?

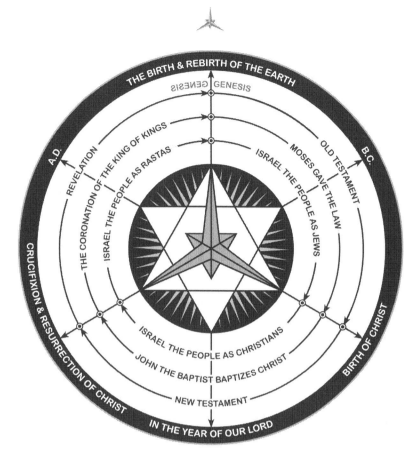

The Trilateral Time Wheel

The question that naturally comes to the surface for the curious mind after reading 1 John ch. 5, vv. 7-8 is: Who is the three in one that bears witness in the earth in this Revelation time? Who is the God that *is*, that *was*, and that *is to come*? Answering this question is the objective of the third and final Epoch of our *Journey*.

So far, the *Journey* has been one that deals specifically with some of the major historical and cultural facts of a people, those we know as Ethiopians. Therefore it should not be of any surprise that the man we will be talking about is also of Ethiopia. Psalm 87 tells us that:

> His foundation is in the holy mountains. The Lord loveth the gates of Zion more than all the dwellings of Jacob. Glorious things are spoken of thee, O City of God. Selah. I will make mention of Rahab and Babylon to them that know me: behold Philistia, and Tyre, with Ethiopia; this man was born there. And of Zion, it shall be said, This and That man was born in her: and the highest Himself shall establish her. The Lord shall count, when he writeth up the people, that this man was born there. Selah. As well as the singers as the players on instruments shall be there: all my springs are in thee.

To know Yahowshua ha Mashiakh as the Son of God is to know God the Mother and Father in your own time. *This* and *That* man, referred to in the above Psalm, speak of the ever living God, The Holy Trinity, which is Father (The Kingly Mashiakh/*This man*), and Son (The Priestly Mashiakh/*That man*), through the power of the Mother (The Shekinah or Holy Spirit).

Christian theology declares that the Father is ever present; He is the God that *is*. The Son, Yahowshua, remains to be the part of the Trinity that *was*. Therefore, it is impossible to *know* the Son of God as Yahowshua (His original name) in this Revelation time. He came so that humankind may be saved through their *belief* in Him as the Son of the Highest. Thus, it is one's belief in Yahowshua that will fuel the journey and transport one into the knowledge of the omnipotent God, the Almighty Mother and Father, in the consciousness of the *New Name*. We read in Isaiah ch. 43, vv. 15, 18, 19:

> I am the Lord, your Holy One, the creator of Israel, your King…remember ye not the former things, neither consider the things of old. Behold, I will do a new thing; now it shall spring forth; shall ye not know it?

Because of the inherent weakness of humanity, mankind grows from infancy to adulthood with a degree of uncertainty. This is the seed that sprouts the poison of unbelief, and is the vessel of ignorance and darkness. If you choose to believe nothing, you will never know anything. Therefore, *belief* can be the first step up the ladder to the path of knowledge and truth. The truth will be revealed unto you according to your faith in your belief, thus giving birth to something more tangible and substantial than mere belief. Belief is the unseen held together by faith, and needs to be confirmed by the substance of material; therefore the need to know in fullness is manifested in that which is seen (as in Yahowshua ha Mashiakh).

When Yahowshua walked the earth as the Second Adam, He *called all people unto Him* because they could not come of their own will. Darkness was still upon the face of the depths, and so He came as the *Light of the World* to bear witness to the Father, the Spiritual King of Kings. Therefore, He was surrounded by thick darkness from both the Jews and the ruling Roman Empire, which led to His crucifixion. It also prevented them from knowing Him during His life, Him who Himself is/was the *Way* by which they would eventually know the Almighty Mother and Father. He preached to all men to *believe in Him* who came from God, that they might receive salvation through His living example.

It was only after the shedding of His blood and His triumph over death through resurrection that the Spirit of Truth made Her abode with men. Thereafter, humanity entered into the era of knowledge of God, the Father, through belief in God, the Son, who came forth from the wisdom of God, the Mother.
The Gospel of Luke ch. 1, vv. 31-33, reads:

> And behold thou shall conceive in thy womb, and bring forth a son...And he shall be great and shall be called the son of the highest, and the Lord God shall give unto him the

throne of his father David: and he shall reign over the house of Israel forever: and of his kingdom there shall be no end.

This prophecy was fulfilled, in part, upon the birth of Yahowshua. However, the latter part was left unfulfilled until His Second Advent as King of Kings and Lord of Lords, which would be the third manifestation of the Holy Trinity in the flesh as the Father on the Throne of King David: revealing also the Mother on both the spiritual and material levels. Once we take the time to reason and ponder the words quoted from the Gospel of Luke, a realization soon manifests itself in the words, which brings us closer to the living God.

This train of thought is: If Yahowshua is the Son of the Highest, then God, the Almighty, is His Father and Mother: which would mean that David is symbolic of the Almighty, the Highest. It was his Throne that was promised unto Yahowshua. This explains why Yahowshua was often referred to as the *Son of David*. When Yahowshua finally ascends the Throne, the world will behold the Son, glorified as the Father, with His beloved Bride, Holy Mother Miriam, the Embodiment of the Divine Feminine.

Yahowshua: The Faithful Witness to Haile Sellassie I

> I can of mine own self do nothing: as I hear, I judge: and my judgment is just; because I seek not mine own will, but the will of the Father, which hath sent me. If I bear witness of myself, my witness is not true. There is another that beareth witness of me; and I know that the witness which he witnesseth of me is true.
>
> Ye sent unto John, and he bare witness unto the truth. But I receive not testimony from man: but these things I say, that ye might be saved. He was a burning and a

Haile Sellassie I

shining light: and ye were willing for a season to rejoice in his light.

But I have greater witness than that of John: for the works which the Father hath given me to finish, the same works that I do, bear witness of me, that the Father hath sent me. And the Father himself, which hath sent me, hath borne witness of me. Ye have neither heard his voice at any time, nor seen his shape. And ye have not his word abiding in you: for whom he hath sent, him ye believe not.

St. John ch. 5, vv. 30-38

That which Yahowshua bore witness to was unknown to those who walked in His days. It was not yet revealed, but was visible in Him in His witnessing of His Father. His expression: *I can of my own self do nothing* shows His surrender to a commanding power which He refers to as His Father, who is also His Teacher. He says, *I seek not my own will, but the will of the Father which hath sent me*. Yahowshua was sent. Being born of a woman in organic flesh made Him the son of man. As such, He bore witness to the Almighty, the First Power of the Holy Trinity.

This principle was shrouded in mystery and the ancient Hebrews gave it many names, but in time the true name will be revealed, through the power of the *I AM*, in the flesh of the elect. To the ancient Hebrews, the power of the Holy Trinity was not fully revealed, but Yahowshua revealed it unto them in the witness that He bore. This is the great mystery about Yahowshua in His advent. He knew something in the spirit that could only be revealed over a process of time through the occurrence of numerous events which had previously been prophesied. The Son, in His First Advent, bore witness to that which will eventually bear witness to Him through a Second Advent. Therefore, He says:

> If I bare witness of myself, my witness is not true. There is another that bare witness of me; and I know that the witness which He witnesseth of me is true.

In this we see that the Son's true witness had not yet come; He knew that He first had to lay a foundation and set a standard in such a way that His true witness would come through the work he would do after his resurrection. His work was to establish a *New World Order*, a *New Way* and a *New Faith*, which became known as the Way of the Nazarenes. Through this Faith, the ascended Son, who is esoterically the Father, shall come as a King on David's Throne. This King will confirm and validate the reality of the Son, who by now has become a mythological figure.

Who then was John the Baptist? He was a witness unto Yahowshua and a preparer of the Way, to introduce the Light of the World to the people, in His words: *That which came after me is greater than me, for He was before me.* In the same manner Yahowshua was a witness, and indeed the true witness, to Haile Sellassie I, though during Yahowshua's life on earth, Haile Sellassie I was yet unborn.

Yahowshua prepared the Way by which a people were made conscious of *Christ* as a principle to be lived out in their lives. Hence Haile Sellassie I, the Comforter who came after the Son, came, through the Way the Son prepared, to become a greater witness than John the Baptist.

> And the Father Himself, which hath sent me, hath borne witness of me. Ye have neither heard his voice at anytime nor seen his shape...

They had neither heard nor seen the Father Himself because he had taken the form of the flesh of the Son and borne witness in the Son, but the total manifestation of the Father as King in Glory was not yet revealed. Therefore He said:

> It is expedient for you that I go away, if I go not away, the Father will not come to you.
>
> John ch. 16, v. 7

Thus, the Father must be accepted in the form of the Son, as well as the Son accepted in the form of the Father. But still greater, yet to be revealed, is the ascendance of the Daughter to the Throne of the Mother, which is on the Right Hand of God the Father, who is the Mother's Son. The Book of Revelation points to Yahowshua ha Mashiakh as the faithful witness, the first begotten of the dead and the Prince of the Kings of the Earth:

> John to the seven churches which are in Asia: Grace be unto you, and peace, from him which is, and which was, and which is to come; and from the seven Spirits which are before his throne; and from Jesus Christ, who is the faithful witness, and the first begotten of the dead, and the prince of the kings of the earth. Unto him that loved us, and washed us from our sins in his own blood, and hath made us kings and priests unto God and his Father; to him be glory and dominion for ever and ever. Amen.
>
> Rev. ch. 1, vv. 4-6

If Yahowshua, the Son, is the Prince of the Kings of the Earth, then His Father, by virtue of that fact, is naturally the King of the Kings of the Earth. In accordance with Ethiopian-Egyptian tradition, the Son is Prince of Kings through His Divine Priesthood and consecrated lineage, rising head and shoulders above the carnal Kings and rulers of the earth. In the realms of metaphysics, His Father as well, through Divine Kingship and the natural moral order, would have ascended above the rulers and kings of the earth as the Hebraic-Christian King of Kings.

In Rastafarian thinking, if the titles *King of Kings*, *Lords of Lords*, *Conquering Lion of Judah*, and *Elect of God* are ascribed to the Christ, then Haile Sellassie I, who is also the *Defender of the Faith*, is, in His witnessing of Yahowshua, truly the one that the Son spoke of in the dialogue from the Gospel of John given above. In His own words, Haile Sellassie I confirms that:

> When Jesus Christ was born from the Virgin Mary, from that time on, He lived an exemplary life, a life which men everywhere must emulate. This life and the faith that He has taught us assures us of salvation, and assures us also of harmony and good life upon earth. Because of the exemplary character of the life of Jesus Christ, it is necessary that all men do their maximum in their human efforts to approximate the good example he set. It is quite true that there is no perfection in humanity. From time to time we make mistakes and commit sins, but even as we do that, deep in our heart Christians know they have a chance of forgiveness from the Almighty. Christ taught that all men are equal regardless of sex, national origin or tribe, and also that all who seek Him shall find Him. I want to follow Jesus Christ precisely to the degree that a Christian life is a healthy life.
>
> *Speeches Delivered by H.I.M. Haile Sellassie I on Various Occasions*

In the Book of Revelation, Yahowshua, as Faithful Witness to the King of Kings, was the precursor to the One the *Two Witnesses* of Revelation are presently confirming, namely, the God who is, who was, and who now has come, the Almighty. Esoterically, these *Two Witnesses* represent the multiplication of the Faithful Witness

The Two Messiahs

Yahowshua, the first fruits of the dead and the giver of life. As the first to overcome death, he conceived new life and became pregnant with the Two Witnesses in a Divine multiplication of self. And when the Two Witnesses of Revelation become one, their union must produce a third, in this case a She, representing the purified Church body, a *New Way*, defending the life of the New Name in *Christ*. This Church is to be built in the name of The Divine Mother Zion, upon the principle of Haile Sellassie I, the ascended Son.

In the theology of the Eastern Orthodox Church, each person of the Holy Trinity is distinguished by the gifts He is given or gives. This distinction is founded upon the words spoken by Yahowshua ha Mashiakh. In the Gospel of John ch. 16, v. 14-16 we read:

> He shall glorify me: For he shall take of mine, and declare it unto you. All things whatsoever the Father hath are mine: Therefore said I, that he shall take of mine, and shall show it unto you. A little while, and ye shall not see me: and again, a little while, and ye shall see me, because I go to the Father.

THIRD EPOCH

A.D.

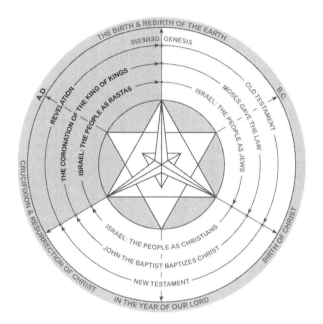

Third Epoch A.D.

Lij Tafari

CHAPTER 10

THE MAN HAILE SELLASSIE I

The Rising

On July 23, 1892, Haile Sellassie I was born Lij[72] Tafari Makonnen in the Hills of Ejersa Goro near the famous medieval city of Harar in Ethiopia. His father was His Highness Ras Makonnen. His mother was Woizero[73] Yeshimebet (Lady of a Thousand), who passed away when Tafari was only eighteen months old, during childbirth when she was thirty.

This Child was the 225th descendant of the union of King Solomon and Queen Makeda of Sheba, otherwise known as the Queen of the South.

> The queen of the south shall rise up in judgment with the men of this generation, and condemn them: for she came from the uttermost parts of the earth to hear the Wisdom of Solomon; and, behold, a greater than Solomon is here.
>
> St. Luke ch. 11, v. 31

The birth of Lij Tafari marked the end of a long drought in the Ethiopian plains and brought showers as blessings to water the parched and thirsty land. The royal chaplains and astrologers of Ras Makonnen's court had foretold the infant's conception and birth. They explained that the planets Neptune and Pluto were slowly moving towards each other as they radiated from the zodiacal constellation of Leo, which corresponds to the Biblical House of Judah, Jacob's fourth son.

---

72 *Lij* — literally *child* is a title given to children of nobility, like *Prince*.

73 *Woizero* is a honorific title of Ethiopian aristocracy that is bestowed upon the wives of nobles.

Under Emperor Menelik II, it had been Ras Makonnen's duty to carry out the nation's foreign relations, a position we know today as Minister of Foreign Affairs or Secretary of State. As such, he traveled to Europe twice and developed an appreciation of education and modern medicine. He developed a strong desire to see the Ethiopian people develop technologically like the societies he observed in Europe. It was in his Son, Tafari, however, that many of his dreams and aspirations were fully realized.

His Highness Ras Makonnen raised his Son at the age of thirteen from the rank of Lij to that of Dejazmatch (Commander of the Door) and appointed Him Governor of the province of Gara Mulata. But shortly thereafter Ras Makonnen fell gravely ill on his way to the capital Addis Ababa, having been summoned by the Emperor, and he passed from this life on March 21, 1906, when Tafari was still thirteen years young. Thus the youthful Tafari Makonnen was, first, without mother, and now, without father. From the age of thirteen however, although His physical strength may not have been great, His spiritual powers began to increase steadily, and He began His ascent to the Imperial dignity.

After the passing of His Highness Ras Makonnen, Emperor Menelik II granted Dejazmatch Tafari the Governorship of Selale, and by 1908, when He was only sixteen, appointed Him partial Governor of the rich province of Sidamo. By this time He was old enough to execute judgment and justice at court, which He did on Wednesdays and Fridays. By 1910, He was advanced in rank and granted His heart's desire, the Governorship of His home city of Harar, a position His late father had held before Him.

On July 23, 1911, on His nineteenth birthday, Dejazmatch Tafari married Woizero Menen, the granddaughter of King Mikael of Wollo, who bore Him three sons and three daughters. Of the Empress, His Imperial Majesty says:

She is a kind woman; in Her nature, She is a total stranger to cruelty and offensiveness… beside from good, there is no evil or malice in Her.

In 1916, after the passing of Emperor Menelik II, Lij Iyassu, the Emperor's grandnephew and an uncle to Woizero Menen, was named the new Emperor. Lij Iyassu, however, converted to Mohammedanism while emperor, causing a serious breach of Ethiopian Law, and He then drew his sword in the name of Islam to spill the blood of fellow Christian brothers and overthrow the Christian nature of the Throne he occupied, bringing Ethiopia to the verge of civil war. For Ethiopia for some 1600 years has had a tradition of Christianity of the strictest Orthodoxy, and as such, all Her Emperors vow solemnly to uphold and defend the Christian Faith.

In defense of the Christian Faith, Dejazmatch Tafari led an army of over 60,000 soldiers against Iyassu and his father Ras Mikael. In a great battle fought at Segalle, Tafari emerged victorious, and the Christian sovereignty of Ethiopia was saved. Lij Iyassu was dethroned and exiled. On February 11, 1917, the Council of State appointed Princess Zawditu, the daughter of Menelik II, to the position of Empress, while the Regency, with the title of Ras and the right of succession to the Throne, were bestowed upon Dejazmatch Tafari Makonnen. As decided by the Council of State, Empress Zawditu would be the Head of State, but Ras Tafari, as Regent Plenipotentiary, was the Head of Government.

As stated before, Ras Tafari[74] developed and executed strategies by which the Ethiopian Orthodox Church gained Her independence from the Coptic Egyptian Church in Alexandria, making Ethiopia, a powerful island of Christianity in the horn of Africa, fully free. As Regent and Heir to the Imperial Throne, He instigated

---

[74] *Ras Tafari* is Amharic for *Head Creator* or *Fearful Ruler*, *Ras* being a title of nobility meaning *Head* or *Ruler*, and *Tafari*, meaning *fearful* or *creator*.

and directed Ethiopia's admission to the prestigious League of Nations, which took place in 1923. The wisdom of this move was to prevent the European colonialists from threatening Ethiopia's independence under the Covenant of the League, which states that there should be no more wars of conquest. This historic and momentous occasion marked the birth of a new era, not only in Ethiopian, but also African, and on a larger scale, world history.

Five years later, in 1928, Ras Tafari became Negus (King), and two years later, after the passing of Empress Zawditu, He ascended the ancient Throne of King David, being crowned Emperor on November 2, 1930. He took the throne name Haile Sellassie I (First Power of the Trinity), along with the Titles *Elect of God, King of Kings, Lord of Lords, Conquering Lion of the Tribe of Judah, King of Zion* and *Light of the World.*

In the June 1931 issue of National Geographic Magazine, we get this intimate illustrated view of the coronation of H.I.M.

The Coronation

> We are ready to start officially for the coronation of His Imperial Majesty Haile Sellassie the First, King of Kings of Ethiopia, Conquering Lion of the Tribe of Judah. A typically sharp, blue Ethiopian morning has just dawned... From the American Legation in Addis Ababa to the Cathedral of St. George is five minutes by motorcar. The journey ended, I take my official seat in the great Cathedral hall between two gaunt and venerable feudal chieftains. I know these bearded "greats" to be from the more remote parts of the Empire because they wear the ancient style of lion's-mane regalia...
>
> I look immediately over the head of Italy's Prince of Udine. Facing me across the open space before the twin

Coronation portrait of their Imperial Majesties, Addis Ababa 1930. Photo. Photo used by permission courtesy of the National Geographic.

thrones is a row of imposingly large and gilded chairs. The first seat holds a prince of England, more than resplendent in his guardsman's uniform. Next to him sits a prince of the ancient and royal line of Solomon; then a marshal of France, using his knee as a rest for his gold baton; a king of Tigre, an ambassador of Belgium, and so on. Great and representative men from the Occident and from the Orient; bearded feudal chieftains from the north, the south, the east, and the west of this ancient Empire of Ethiopia — Christians and Moslems and many others are all gathered for the coronation of a new Emperor on this second day of November, A.D. 1930 (the Ethiopian date of Takemt 23d, 1923) — modern civilization cheek by jowl with medievalism.

The studded doors of the Holy of Holies open ponderously. Through them rolls, in giant and stirring hum, the seemingly far-off chant of hundreds of priests, probably exactly as it would have sounded on an Ethiopian coronation day a thousand and more years ago. The Conquering Lion of the Tribe of Judah and His Empress have just completed a night of prayer and devotion at the most holy altar within. Preceded by waving incense-burners, His Majesty enters now the main part of the Cathedral and takes His throne. The thrilling but solemn silence gently breaks to the throaty voice of His Holiness Abuna Kyrillos: "Ye princes and ministers, ye nobles and chiefs of the army, ye soldiers and people of Ethiopia, and ye doctors and chiefs of the clergy, ye professors and priests, look ye upon our Emperor Haile Sellassie the First, descended from the dynasty of Menelik the First, who was born of Solomon and the Queen of Sheba, a dynasty perpetuated without interruption from that time to King Sehale Sellassie and to our times."

> Taken from the June 1931 issue of the *National Geographic*, article entitled "Haile Sellassie the First, Formerly Ras Tafari, Succeeds to the World's Oldest Continuously Sovereign Throne," by Addison E. Southard, US Minister to Ethiopia.

The coronation ceremony of Ethiopian Emperors as described above was unique in the world for its faithfulness to the Hebraic traditions Ethiopia inherited from ancient Israel and authentically combined with her indigenous Christian culture, making it rich with the legacy of the Bible and thousands of years of Her own tradition. That legacy of hundreds of coronations prepared Ethiopia to be the stage and gateway for the coming of the Messiah in the Second Advent.

Yet the coronation of their Imperial Majesties in 1930 was the greatest coronation ever held in Ethiopia. No other coronation in Her history was ever of this magnitude. For the first time, the entire Ethiopian Empire was invited and tens of thousands of their subjects attended, along with as many representatives of European nations.

From the description in the above article, after completing a night of prayer and devotion in the Holy of Holies, the most sacred chamber (otherwise reserved for the Archbishop), the Emperor and His Empress entered the main hall of the cathedral in a cloud of frankincense smoke and ascended David's Throne. *Behold he cometh with clouds; and every eye shall see him, and they also which pierced him* (Rev. ch. 1, v. 7), and so He did. Yet many who were privileged to be present didn't have eyes to see the mystery revealed in that moment — as many Christians misinterpret clouds in the quote to mean the clouds in the sky, which the Messiah ascends beyond, leaving them preoccupied with supernatural expectations, gazing up at the clouds above for the return of the Messiah.

Yet the scriptures were fulfilled according to the metaphysical and esoteric mystique of the prophecies. For those who had eyes to see did see indeed as the mystery of God set forth in the *Book of Revelation* was revealed. Therefore, Rastafarians rejoice in the day of their Imperial Majesties' coronation, awaited for centuries even up to the day of their immediate predecessors, the Garveyites and Howellites. Though they may not have been present at the coronation, they were true witnesses to H.I.M.'s prophetical fulfillment of the text: *Beloved, we are God's children now, and what we shall be has not yet appeared; but we know that when He appears we shall be like Him, because we shall see Him as He is* (1 John ch. 3, v. 2).

Seven Symbols of Awe and Majesty are Bestowed

> For five hours then we witness the unfolding of the ancient and traditional Hebraic-Christian ceremony of the crowning of a ruler of the Empire of Ethiopia. Forty-nine bishops and priests of this ancient Christian country, in groups of seven have held place for seven days and nights in the seven, corners of this national Cathedral to chant without ceasing nine Psalms of David. They are now joined by hundreds more. The Established Coptic Church is revered and all-powerful in Ethiopia. This is a day when it may, and does, show its impressive might and splendor.
>
> The Emperor, whose name may be Anglicized as Power of the Trinity, is vested first with his sword of gold studded with precious stones. Chanting and prayers to the God of Gods rise from a multitude of priestly throats and reverberate from the lofty ceilings of the Cathedral. Bestowals of the imperial scepter of ivory and gold and a golden globe of the earth follow. The diamond-

encrusted ring, the two traditional lances filigreed in gold, and the imperial vestments are all bestowed in turn with appropriate and lengthy ceremony. Seventh and last comes the magnificent crown. Seven differently scented ointments of ancient prescription are received on the imperial head, brow, and shoulders — one with each of the seven ornaments of the coronation.

After the completion of the coronation ceremonies for the Emperor, the Empress enters and takes Her throne. She is crowned with less elaborate but always impressive rites, conducted also by the archbishop, his bishops, and his priests.

The final ceremony is a grand tour of the Cathedral by Their Imperial Majesties. They are escorted by the bishops and priests, the princes and high dignitaries, assistants, and others, carrying palm branches and chanting in mighty volume, "Blessed be the King of Israel." Shortly after noon the cannons boom. There is the fanfare of a thousand trumpets. The triumphant ululation of tens of thousands of waiting women is released in waves over the city of the "New Flower." We go forth in proud procession, which escorts to His "Hill of the Palace," across the city, the three hundred and thirty-fourth of all the kings of Ethiopia and the one hundredth and thirty-fourth of the Christian kings of the Empire.

The Ethiopians list their kings from Ori, of 4478 B.C., to Haile Sellassie the First, of A.D. 1930 — with time out, naturally, from the date of the Deluge until the Fall of the Tower of Babel. What matters time in a country which can reach with such apparent certainty directly back into the dim mists of the past!…

Taken from the June 1931 issue of the *National Geographic,* article entitled "Haile Sellassie the First, Formerly Ras Tafari, Succeeds to the World's Oldest Continuously Sovereign Throne," by Addison E. Southard, US Minister to Ethiopia.

The title of this section of the coronation begins with the number seven, and the first paragraph beneath it starts (almost) with the number five. It is intriguing to observe that the passage proceeds to describe the Bestowal Ceremony with a series of numbers divisible by seven or by three, and ending with nine, another mystic number. These numbers are highly significant, as discussed on p. 139 in the *Matrix of 7 in Conjunction with 3 and the Trinity.*

(1) 7 x 7 = 49 bishops and priests
(2) in groups of seven
(3) held place for seven days and nights
(4) in the seven corners of the Cathedral
(5) chanting without ceasing nine Psalms of David. The number nine (3 x 3), in this case, esoterically symbolizes infinity, completeness, and perfection — as in 360 = 3 + 6 + 0 = 9, encompassing the whole cycle of life.

The *Hebraic-Christian* ceremony continues — as the Emperor is vested, first with

(1) a golden sword studded with precious stones, then
(2) the imperial scepter of ivory and gold,
(3) a golden globe representing the earth,
(4) the diamond-encrusted ring,
(5) two gold filigreed lances,
(6) the imperial vestments and
(7) the magnificent golden crown.

Finally, Haile Sellassie I is anointed with "seven differently scented ointments of ancient prescription," concluding His Coronation Ceremony with a mystical biblical trope, when the priest, dignitaries, and high officials carry palm branches and chant in mighty volume, Blessed be the King of Israel.

Yes! You heard right. Haile Sellassie I was the Emperor of Ethiopia, but He was also the King of Israel by Ethiopian tradition. How is this possible, unless Ethiopia is the land of Judah and the Rastafarians, the scattered people of the lost Tribes of Israel?

Rastafarians assert that the Seven Symbols bestowed on H.I.M. correspond to, and are symbolic of the Seven Gifts spoken about in the Book of Isaiah, ch. 11, vv. 2-3: (1) wisdom, (2) understanding, (3) counsel, (4) fortitude, (5) knowledge, (6) piety and (7) fear of the Lord, which are likewise given by the Holy Spirit unto the ascended Son, who is ordained to take the book (Bible) and break the Seven Seals, a breaking of Seals through which the mystery of God shall be fully unveiled.

The Throne Room is a Scene of Splendor

> Through the early morning the chanting of praises continued, accompanied by the dancing of the priests with their great pulsating drums, the whole suggestive of the ancient Jewish rites which were in use at the time when King David danced before the Ark of the Covenant.
>
> The ritualistic ceremonies of the coronation were performed in a large auditorium, immediately adjacent to the west side of the Cathedral, which had been especially constructed for the occasion to provide adequately for the seating of the 700 officials and guests. The side walls of the building were of white cloth, decorated only at the pillars with clusters of small flags; a lofty ceilings was formed of orange-yellow cloth caught in several drapes, and across the entire front rich, gold-shot, red curtains

fell in loose folds to separate the inner sanctuary from the main portion of the hall.

Some distance apart, and about one third of the length of the room from the sanctuary, stood the wide thrones of the Emperor and Empress, beneath gold-posted canopies surmounted by large golden crowns. The throne at the left, designated for the Emperor, was decorated in scarlet and gold, while that at the right, for Her Majesty, was covered in blue and gold...

Long shafts of early morning sunlight streaming through the tall windows and diffusing through the white side walls lifted out the rich colors of the hangings, the thick floor rugs, and the resplendent costumes, converting the scene into a spectacle of unmatched prismatic beauty. The inner sanctuary, behind the draped red curtains, was suffused with a golden-red light.

Shortly after 7:30 o'clock, His Imperial Majesty, attired in white silk communion robes, entered the ceremonial hall from the church, with an escort of aides and the clergy, and took his place upon the throne. Thereupon the ceremony began... Following ancient custom, as when Samuel anointed David, and Zadok and Nathan anointed Solomon, so the Abuna anointed His Majesty's head with oil, and then placed thereon the crown, made from pure native gold, encrusted with diamonds and emeralds. He then concluded with the words, *That God may make this crown a crown of sanctity and glory. That, by the grace and the blessings which we have given, you may have an unshaken faith and a pure heart, in order that you may inherit the crown eternal. So be it.* Throughout the whole ritual and the chanting of Psalms, nothing disturbed the impressive solemnity save the staccato exhaust of low-flying airplanes which circled above. Otherwise the centuries seemed to have slipped suddenly backward into Biblical ritual.

> Taken from the June 1931 issue of *National Geographic* article entitled "Coronation Days in Addis Ababa" by W. Robert Moore

The stage having been set, Robert Moore through his words in his article above, paints vivid images of that glorious and fateful morning of the Coronation of Haile Sellassie I. He describes the majesty, pomp and beauty of the atmosphere so skillfully that you can almost smell the incense and feel the warm shafts of sunlight, the sunbeams that fall upon your skin. In his detailed recording of this historical occasion, Moore gave the world an intimate and upfront view of the coronation — and made us co-witnesses to one of history's most significant events.

There are those who have eyes and see not, and after reading this article repeatedly over the years, I often wonder: how much of what they witnessed registered as life transforming for the Europeans who were present? considering they had front row seats to the greatest spectacle on earth. These colonialists of the 1930s, attending the coronation of an African who ascended the Throne of David as the sovereign of one of the world's oldest countries, could only have been present through Divine will. How bizarre that, of the seventy-two nations said to have been represented at the coronation ceremony of Haile Sellassie I, the overwhelming majority were in Europe, and this because those nations had conquered the African Continent. The only free African nation represented, in fact the Host — Ethiopia. Thus the paradox, that while Europeans held Africans in captive oppression, and dominated all Africans elsewhere, they answered the call and were present at the crowning ceremony of an African king in Ethiopia, in effect giving homage to him.

Empress Menen

A Journey to the Roots of Rastafari

From a biblical viewpoint, the paradox of the European presence at the coronation of Haile Sellassie I fulfilled the prophetical verses: *And the glory of the Lord shall be revealed, and all flesh shall see it together, for the mouth of the Lord has spoken* (Isaiah ch. 40, v. 5); also Isaiah ch. 43, v. 23, states: *By myself I have sworn; from my mouth has gone out in righteousness a word that shall not return: to me every knee shall bow, every tongue shall swear allegiance.*

Crowning the Empress

In a brief ceremony the Crown Prince pledged to serve and support his father, the Emperor. The princes then made obeisance on bended knee before the Emperor, and the assembly applauded their greeting, and the visiting naval band played the national anthem, while outside cannon roared a salute of 101 guns, and cheer after cheer came from thousands of subjects massed in the vicinity of the Cathedral.

As soon as the ceremonies for the Emperor had ended, the Empress, accompanied by her ladies of honor, entered from the right side of the sanctuary and took Her throne. After the chanting of the Psalms, she was presented with a ring encrusted with diamonds, as a symbol of the faith, and then assumed the scarlet and gold coronation robes. Taking the Empress's crown from the hands of the Emperor, the Abuna offered the prayer, *"O our Lord, place this crown of glory and joy on the brow of thy servant the Empress Menen. Make it a crown of charity, piety, wisdom, and of intelligence. O Heavenly Father, make this crown to be a crown of honor and glory. So be it."*

He then placed the crown on Her head, after which the Empress advanced toward the throne of the Emperor, bowed, and returned again to Her throne. Again the national anthem was played, the cannons voiced their salute, and the multitude cheered, following the obeisance of the nobles and the applauded greeting of the assembly. Thereafter Their Majesties removed their crowns and coronation robes and again, in white communion dress, they retired to the inner sanctuary of the Cathedral to attend the sacred mass and communion.

Taken from the June 1931 issue of *National Geographic*,
article entitled "Coronation Days in Addis Ababa"
by W. Robert Moore

For thousands of years, Ethiopian tradition dictated that the Empress be crowned three days after the Emperor, and it was only at the 1930 coronation of Haile Sellassie I that that tradition was broken. The example Haile Sellassie I established remains a radical shift for Ethiopians in the realm of gender equality. Although Ethiopia has had a long standing tradition of gender equality (in a sense), there is also a long standing tradition of women, and even female animals, being banned from setting foot on certain holy grounds, monasteries and other such places. In the past no exceptions were made even for the Empresses that ruled the kingdom.

Her Imperial Majesty Empress Menen was the first and the last Ethiopian Empress to be crowned on the same day as the Emperor — and in Her case even immediately after Her Emperor, albeit with less elaborate ceremonies. The taking of the Empress's crown by the bishop from the hands of the Emperor symbolized the Emperor's sharing of the glory, bestowed upon Him by the Almighty, equally with His Empress. Empress Menen is usually pictured on the right-hand side of Haile Sellassie I, since in Eastern Orthodox Christian tradition the Empress always sits at the right (hand) of the Emperor, and in many pictures of the imperial couple she can be seen at the Emperor's right even when they are not seated, although there are exceptions.

Another intriguing aspect of the coronation is the twin thrones, understood by inherited tradition to be the seat of God. Historically, the Throne of David is perceived and accepted as a singular entity. However, on this particular occasion, the Throne of David represented the Male-Female/Mother-Father God-Principle, recorded and perfectly illustrated in the 1930 coronation portrait of Haile Sellassie I and Empress Menen.

Thus, the Power of the Holy Trinity was revealed in reality as a principle that encompassed the male and female polar energies synchronized in dynamic equilibrium. The Throne of David is symbolic of the *Mercy Seat* that Moses was instructed by YHWH to make between the cherubim as the habitation of the Godhead. After all, from the beginning humanity was created in the image of God as male and female (Genesis ch. 1, vv. 26-27). *I am the Alpha and the Omega, the beginning and the end* (Rev. ch. 22, v. 13). Hence: as it was in the beginning, so shall it be in the end.

The Giving of the Law

Shortly after His Coronation, in 1931, Haile Sellassie I gave Ethiopia Her first written Constitution and began a process of steady modernization, joyfully and with a light yoke. In Rasta theology, the fact that He gave the Law from the Throne of David is significant, in that prophecy, in Jeremiah ch. 23, vv. 5, 6, was fulfilled, automatically sealing Him. He was the first and only Emperor to open such a door in the history of the people of Israel.

As the giver of the Law Haile Sellassie I was the repairer of the breach. It is He who purged the sacred seed, restoring the true nobility of David. As the Emperor on the Throne, with absolute power, only He could give back to the people the power that they had ignorantly handed over to a man to rule as King over them in the days of Saul. The single most empowering aspect of the Law of 1931 is that it ends absolute rule according to hereditary succession and sets up a Constitutional Monarchy, making the Emperor, who was the first Emperor to do so, the Last King. In the law, the citizens received the right to elect their own leaders, the power of the electoral vote, even allowing a peasant, after a process of education, to ascend to the noble office of Prime Minister, as the leader of the country. All of this was made clear in the Essene prophecies contained in the passage below, taken from *The Holy Megillah: Nasarean Bible of the Essene Way:*

> Then, toward the end of the age inaugurated by the Priestly Mashiakh, the second stage begins: A Kingly Mashiakh, the seed of David through Solomon and the Ethiopian woman comes forth. Yea, and not only the seed of David in body, but the very soul of David; for this is David returned and transformed; for it is fitting that the first of the line should be the last, and that He should rectify what He put amiss. And He shall be a Conquering Lion; for He shall conquer Himself and lay His throne at the feet of the Priestly Mashiakh, the Lion shall be truly enthroned; lo: He shall manifest the blazing crown of light. And then the Priestly Mashiakh shall return to the Lion even His earthly crown, the crown of David through Solomon.

It is not customary for kings to voluntarily give over or share their power with the people, especially with the poor, the underclass. Thus history will judge Haile Sellassie I to be among the truly wise and righteous kings. It takes a different kind of human being, an extremely rare individual, to fulfill such a role, one in whom the carnal instincts give way for the Divine will or higher self to manifest.

The Cosmic Man or Grand Architect of the universe, often referred to by religious mystics, is the Mashiakh, the God-Man. He is the embodiment of all Divine ideas, such as intelligence, life, love, substance and strength. This Mashiakh or so-called perfect man, in its external existence in the Divine mind, is the true, spiritual, higher self of every individual. We must endeavor to manifest this internal potential we each have in order to experience true kinship to our Divine origin. Through the process of devotion, discipline and self-discovery, the God-Man becomes the supreme principle, with dominion and mastery over the carnal, animal self. Therefore, for Rastafarians, Haile Sellassie I is understood not only as a historical personality, but also as a most potent principle of reality to be reckoned with.

It was the age-old tradition of the Solomonic Kings of Ethiopia, the Rulers of the State, to also be the Head of the Church. However, the overwhelming workload and responsibility of these offices were too much for one individual, and therefore an *Abun* or Archbishop was appointed to take charge of the affairs of the Church. Subsequently, the Emperor was not seen without the Abun. This historic development of the Abun or bishop of Ethiopia, who was formerly appointed by the Coptic Egyptian Pope, into an independent Archbishop with bishops of his own, took place under the reign of Haile Sellassie I.

The fact that the Emperors of Ethiopia were Head of both Church and State gave us a unique and rare opportunity to glimpse theocratic government at work, which is the office of Melkizadek. This was taken to new dimensions when Haile Sellassie I gave the Law, in the form of a Constitution, from the Throne of David, which is the seat of *God*, to Ethiopia, the world's oldest sovereign Christian state. Theocracy took on its truest meaning from the blueprint that was given to the world in this mystical move by His Imperial Majesty.

The Calamity

In 1935, Italy under the Fascist dictator Benito Mussolini interrupted the progress of the King of Kings and brought Divine judgment down upon the heads of the nations.

> I will also gather all nations and will bring them down into the valley of Jehoshaphat, and will plead with them there for my people, and for my heritage Israel, whom they have scattered among the nations, and parted my land.
>
> Joel ch. 2, v. 2

As a result of Italy's invasion of Ethiopia, Haile Sellassie I was placed in a unique position. Never before in its history had the League of Nations ever been addressed by a King or Head of State, and when He appeared he put the League of Nations to the ultimate test. After many requests by His Imperial Majesty for the League to resolve a threat to peace, as it was designed to do, the League imposed sanctions on both countries. This was the extent of their action, and it paralyzed Ethiopia, preventing Her from receiving any assistance to defend Her independence. All of Haile Sellassie I's requests for assistance were denied, and thus, Ethiopia's fate was left to the will of the Divine.

Italy's mission was to totally exterminate the Ethiopian population. The words of the fascist General Graziani: *Il Duce will have Abyssinia with or without the Ethiopians,* illustrated the Italian determination to crush the Ethiopian people. They breached the International Laws of War numerous times. An example of this is the spraying of a deadly rain of mustard gas over the Ethiopian landscape, poisoning the water supply, killing innocent civilians, cattle and plants, causing a Holocaust of the Ethiopian people, with over 200,000 dead.

It was the tradition of the Ethiopians to take the Ark of the Covenant out on the battlefield to go before them in battle. In 1896, when Italian invaders violated the Ethiopian borders, such had been the case. There are numerous paintings in the unique Ethiopic style depicting the priest and emperor with the Ark in the midst of battle. This time, however, the Ark did not accompany the army in the fashion of centuries past; it was replaced by the

Unto Us A Child Is Born

living Ark, as is written in the scriptures. We read in Isaiah ch. 37, v. 35 and Zechariah ch. 14, v. 3:

> No longer of itself will the Ark of the Covenant go out and defend for my people. But I myself will go out and fight for my people.

Rastafarians interpret this to mean that the Ark of the Covenant was replaced by the form of Haile Sellassie I, who led his troops in the Battle of Maichu, the battle that more or less determined his fate and Ethiopia's.

Ethiopia will soon stretch forth Her hands unto God … (Psalm 68, v. 31). This verse was used by Emperor Menelik in the 1896 crisis[75] and again by Haile Sellassie I forty years later. Its true meaning is experienced every time Ethiopia's independence is threatened. She looks to Her God, which happens to be Christ, for Her deliverance from the clutches of colonialism.

---

75 Read below about the Battle of Adowa, in which the Italians were defeated.

In 1936, such was the case, when Haile Sellassie I pleaded with all the powers that be, and as if that were not enough, with the World Council of Churches as well, to no avail. It seemed as though there were no God in the world of imperial Europe nor in colonial Africa that had Ethiopia's interests at heart. Therefore Haile Sellassie I had an uphill battle liberating his country from the fascist penetration, using whatever power was within Him and the minimal external assistance provided. It was sheer willpower and confidence in Divine law and justice that brought the Conquering Lion and His people out of the jaws of the beast. As the whole world was watching, the only god that ever pled for a nation's cause came and pled for Ethiopia's, taking the form of the man who bears the titles of the Blessed Anointed King of the *Book of Revelation*. Haile Sellassie I Himself bore the weight and pain of His nation after having done everything to prevent war from breaking out. But the nations would ultimately come to bear their fair share of pain and misery after they failed to heed the prophecies of H.I.M.

> Aggressions have taken place in increasing number. The contagion has been propagated. Certain States are now engaged in full struggle, others are threatened. Fear reigns over the world. The present and forthcoming victims tremble for the future, and they think they may improve their situation by flattering those whose aggression they dread. International morality has disappeared. The excuse of these weak peoples is their very weakness, the certainty that they would be abandoned as Ethiopia has been, and between two evils they have chosen the one which the fear of the aggressor leads them to consider the lesser. May God forgive them!
>
> H.I.M. Haile Sellassie I, taken from: *Appeal to the League* — *An Anthology of Some of The Public Utterances of His Imperial Majesty, Haile Selassie I.*

After fighting as Commander in Chief of His army to repel the Italian onslaught, Haile Sellassie I went into exile. After being denied a request to stay in Switzerland where He would have been conveniently close to the League Assembly, His lonely mission took Him to Bath, England, where He continued the battle for justice through the spoken word. He did not give up hope that the League would honor the Covenant the member States had made to protect each other's independence; He persisted in His appeal for justice. But in His farsightedness, the Conquering Lion realized that the League would in fact fail to uphold the Covenant, and so He spent much of His time in exile organizing His *Gideon*[76] Troops located in the Ethiopian highlands to maintain the resistance through guerrilla warfare.

Return of the Conquering Lion

He did not cease His constant efforts to keep the rape of His country in the minds of the world. Haile Sellassie I rebuked by means of letters every country that broke the Covenant by accepting the Italian occupation of His country: Austria and Hungary received such letters.

With the expertise of Major Orde Wingate of the British army, Haile Sellassie I organized the 2,000 strong Gideon Force of Ethiopian patriots, whom He commanded personally with the assistance of British officers. On January 18, 1941, the Gideon Forces reached the tiny Ethiopian frontier village of Um Iddla. Within two days Haile Sellassie I joined Major Wingate, and the banner of the Lion of Judah was raised in Ethiopia once again. In less than three months, a vast number of patriots joined the Gideon Forces, and the advance towards total liberation from the Fascist invaders began. The King of Kings rode triumphantly

---

76 *Gideon* — The name of the troops that were organized by H.I.M. while in exile, that fought the Italian invasion by means of guerrilla warefare.

The King of Kings Slays the Beast

back into His capital on May 5, 1941, almost five years to the day since He departed into exile.

History records this victorious day when the Conquering Lion of Judah prevailed. The King of Kings had returned to His Kingdom, and the first words he addressed to the people that gathered to welcome Him were:

> My people, this is a great day in the history of Ethiopia; since this is so, do not repay evil with evil… Do not stain your souls by avenging yourselves on your enemy…

By November 1941, all Italian resistance in Ethiopia came to an end. The Empire of Mussolini — which had been an empire in name only, an idea whose time had come and gone before it could achieve its desired end — perished with Mussolini. He had imagined a thing that he could not perform and his failure led to his death at the hand of his own people. On April 28, 1945, Mussolini was captured and killed by a hostile and disappointed crowd of Italian peasants. His body was then hung upside down, along with those of his wife and other officials, in the same public square where thousands of dedicated followers had once looked up to him.

The Rastafarians assert that the fate of Mussolini was prophesied in the *Holy Bible,* in Isaiah ch. 14, vv. 12-16:

> How art thou fallen from heaven, O Lucifer, son of the morning! How art thou cut down to the ground, which didest weaken the nations! For thou has said in thine heart, I will ascend into heaven, I will exalt my throne above the stars of God: I will sit also upon the mount of the congregation (Zion), in the sides of the north: I will ascend above the heights of the clouds; I will be like the Most High. Yet thou shall be brought down to hell, to

the side of the pit. They that see thee shall narrowly look upon thee, and consider thee, saying, Is this the man that made the earth to tremble, that did shake kingdoms?

For its failed attempt to colonize Ethiopia, Italy paid with the lives of 5,000 Italians and 10,000 Askaris (Eritrean soldiers loyal to Italian colonial rule). By June 1936 Italy had spent about twelve billion lire (£12,000,000,000), that is about seven million pounds sterling (£7,000,000) or seventeen million dollars ($17,000,000) at the time, on her effort to conquer Ethiopia. Mussolini had squandered his country's treasury on the war, and Italy was now bankrupt, with no empire to show for it. On February 10th, 1947, Ethiopia and Italy signed a peace treaty, although they did not resume diplomatic relations until 1952.

Shortly after the peace treaty was negotiated, Ethiopia slapped Italy with a bill for damages and losses inflicted on her during the war years. The memorandum is as follows:

Persons lost:
(1) Killed in action 275,000
(2) Patriots killed in battle
    (i.e. men killed during the occupation 1936-1941) 78,500
(3) Women, children and others killed by bombing 17,800
(4) Massacre of February 1937 30,000
(5) Persons who died in concentration camps 35,000
(6) Patriots executed by sentence of summary court 24,000
(7) Persons who died from privations due to the
    destruction of their villages 300,000
    Total: 760,300

Other losses recorded:
(1) Churches 2,000
(2) Houses 525,000
(3) Slaughter and confiscation of beef cattle 5,000,000

(4) Sheep and goats 7,000,000
(5) Horses and mules 1,000,000
(6) Camels 700, 000

For these losses, the Economic Commission for Italy was presented with a bill for reparations totaling £184,746,023 (lire) — over 100,000 pounds or 200,000 dollars.

The Battle of Adowa

This war was not the first time Italy and Ethiopia came to blows. In 1889, Italy expanded the territory they then occupied in East Africa. Their advance went unobstructed and they were able to gain a foothold in the outskirts of the northern highlands of Ethiopia, officially consolidating it as a colony, calling it Eritrea, from the Latin for *Erythraeum Mare* (Red Sea). This was Italy's way of saying that they were here to stay. It was also the beginning of the rift, which has lasted now for over a hundred years, between Ethiopia and her one-time Province of Eritrea.

Ethiopia's Emperor Menelik II eyed the Italian advance for some time, realizing that further movement into the interior of his empire would lead to conflict between Ethiopia and Italy. I believe that this is why he continued a tradition of making treaties of friendship with Italy, to secure diplomatic relations with Italy, but more importantly to safeguard border agreements that had been made in previous treaties.

On May 2, 1889, Ethiopia and Italy signed a groundbreaking treaty which called itself an agreement of *perpetual Peace and Friendship* between the two countries. It was called the Wechale Treaty (sometimes Wychale or Wichale) after the village where it was concluded. The Wechale Treaty was written in Amharic and Italian, and was to be the occasion for further dispute between the two countries, that led to the Battle of Adowa. The agreement was

Menelik II

advantageous for both parties, but Article 17 created an issue. The Amharic text stated, like previous treaties, that the emperor, Menelik in this case, should have the power to avail himself of the government of the King of Italy for any communications he might have with other powers or governments. The Italian version, however, unlike the previous Italo-Shewan Treaty of 1883, made it mandatory for Ethiopia to use Italy as her protector in international affairs.

Italy claimed that the agreement gave them the right to internationally represent Ethiopia as Her protectorate, but Menelik declared that, in accordance with the Amharic version of the agreement, he was not obligated, but entitled, to ask Italy for protection. Thus, on September 17, 1890, he sent two pieces of correspondence in protest to Italy's King Unberto I, one dealing with the Wechale Treaty dispute and the other with the continuous Italian encroachment upon Ethiopian soil. He made himself clear in this statement: "When I made that treaty of friendship with Italy, in order that our secrets be guarded and that our understanding be not spoiled, I said that because of our friendship, our affairs may be carried on with the aid of the Sovereign of Italy, but I have not made any treaty which obliged me to do so, and, today, I am not the man to accept it. That one independent power does not seek the aid of another to carry on its affairs Your Majesty understands very well." Based upon these issues, the two countries came head to head in a border dispute, as Italian and Askari troops commenced an advance upon Ethiopian territory. The infamous Battle of Adowa had begun.

In 1896, when the Ethiopian frontier was invaded by Italian forces, the Italians devised a strategy to divide and conquer, hoping to take advantage of the regional, ethnic, and religious differences among Ethiopians; but Ethiopia gathered Her troops, over 100,000 strong, to counter the invasion, succeeding in uniting the diverse population for the common goal of defending and maintaining Her sovereignty. Ethiopia's victory in the Battle of Adowa will long be remembered, a feat at which the whole world marveled.

Italy's shame at her crushing defeat hung over her for the next forty years, until she invaded again in 1935-1936.

As previously stated, the Battle of Adowa, where the Ethiopians defeated the Italian army, was a victory not only for Ethiopians, but also for Africans scattered all over the earth who found themselves in bondage to those who would systematically colonize them. It was a victory of independent Africa over European colonial ambition, fought with blood and the sword. As written in the Holy Bible: *Blow the trumpets in Zion . . . Beat your plowshares into swords, and your pruning hook into spears: let the weak say, I am strong.*[77]

Esoterically as well as literally, the victory at Adowa preserved the Sovereign of Zion in order to prepare a place on earth that was fit for the Kingly Christ to spring out of, the One who later, in 1936, would come plead the cause of Ethiopia in person before the League of Nations and the world. This battle of words was the *sword which cometh from the mouth of the Lord, with which he smites the nations.*[78] He appealed to the conscience of the world, being the moral standard when there seemed to be no standard of righteousness or of justice among the nations.

In this war of words the victory was less concrete, and is thus less celebrated than the victory at Adowa. The irony of the victory at Adowa is that, out of this one crisis in 1896 came the vengeful ambition that Italy displayed in 1936. But Ethiopia's great moral victory came when an independent African state agitated, and not for the first time, for a moral standard to judge the hypocritical value system of the Eurocentric world, which was void of morals and justice, even though moral standards appear on paper in the Covenant of the League.

---

77 Joel ch. 2, v. 15, (Joel ch. 3, v. 10)

78 Revelation ch. 19, vv. 12-16 Verses 15-16 state: "...and out of his mouth goeth a sharp sword, that with it he should smite the nations: and he treadeth the winepress of the fierceness and wrath of Almighty God. And he hath on his vesture and on his thigh a name written, KING OF KINGS, AND LORD OF LORDS." Note that W-O-R-D-S becomes S-W-O-R-D when the letter S is moved to the front.

No Country but Ethiopia

By Divine will, Ethiopia has managed to maintain Her independence and sovereignty for thousands of years, while the rest of Africa and the world was swallowed up by the colonial powers of Europe. There was a time in history when these powers were conquering lands and seas in the four corners of the earth, during which time the African people on the Mother continent and those in the Western hemisphere were held captive under the bonds of the colonial yoke. Ethiopia alone, firmly rooted in Her age-old independence, stood as the hope and voice for a people deprived and downtrodden.

During this time, Ethiopia was viewed as an impenetrable hermit kingdom, because all attempts to colonialize Her had failed, even while She was denigrated by Europe as the most backward of countries. Yet She was the only African sovereign that had to be reckoned with, and would soon become the voice and symbol of redemption and independence for all colonialized states, within and without Africa.

This distinguishes Ethiopia from every other country. The prophet Isaiah had seen Zion in his visions and prophesied saying:

> Look upon Zion, the city of our solemnities: thine eyes shall see Jerusalem a quiet habitation, a tabernacle that shall not be taken down; not one of the stakes thereof shall ever be removed, neither shall any of the cords thereof be broken. But there the glorious Lord will be unto us a place of broad rivers and streams; wherein shall go no galley with oars, neither shall gallant ship pass thereby!
>
> Isaiah ch. 33, vv. 20-21

Egypt usually comes mind when people think of ancient kingdoms and civilizations. However, as we plunge deeper into the truth about our beginnings, new data keep being unearthed in the land of Kush, unlocking the mysteries and secrets of Her true identity. Contrary to the histories written by many past and present scholars and historians, Ethiopia's kingdom was established long before Egypt was born. It was the Ethiopians that migrated down the Nile and constructed what we now know as Egyptian civilization.

Egypt and Ethiopia have always enjoyed an intimate relationship, one that has brought forth many monarchs who contributed greatly to the richness of Egyptian civilization.

> The traditions with respect to Memnon serve very closely to connect Egypt and Ethiopia with the country at the head of the Persian Gulf [Persia]. Memnon, King of Ethiopia, according to Hesiod and Pindar, is regarded by Æschylus as the son of a Cissian woman, and by Herodotus and others as the son of Susa. He leads an army of combined Susianians and Ethiopians to the assistance of Priam, his father's brother, and, after greatly distinguishing himself, perishes in one of the battles before Troy.

> At the same time he is claimed as one of their monarchs by the Ethiopians upon the Nile, and identified by the Egyptians with their king, Amunoph III, whose statue became known as *the vocal Memnon*. Sometimes his expedition is supposed to have started from the African Ethiopia, and to have proceeded by way of Egypt to its destination. There were palaces called "Memnonia," and supposed to have been built by him, both in Egypt and in Susa; and there was a tribe, called Memnones, near Meroë. Memnon thus unites the Eastern with the Western Ethiopians; and the less we regard him as an historical

personage, the more must we view him as personifying the ethnic identity of the two races.

> *The Five Great Monarchies of the Ancient Eastern World*
> ch. 3, p. 48 by George Rawlinson

As previously stated Kush, the son of Ham, the son of Noah (see I Chronicles ch. 1, vv. 8-10) is said to be the founder of Ethiopia, and to have founded Her in 6280 B.C., which is three times the length of time from the birth of the Mashiakh to our times, a total of 8,200 years. In its earliest history, Ethiopia included not only Africa, but also Southern Asia as far as India.

The present system of government and religion, especially the Christian faith and doctrine, of Ethiopia came down through various cultures across the ages, from foundations laid by the Atlantean civilization, which gave birth to ancient Ethiopian/Kushitic civilization.

Two Questions

Two questions are raised in the preface of a book entitled *Greater Ethiopia* by Donald L. Levine. Because of their pertinence here, I would like to to take this opportunity to quote and then answer them.

> 1. The usual question regarding the Italian invasion is: what weakness in the international system permitted this aggression?

> 2. One also may ask, why Ethiopia? What was it that enabled Ethiopia alone among traditional African societies to retain its sovereignty until the Italians chose to exercise their anachronistic appetite for empire in the 1930s?

Weakness in the International System

The first question is of great importance because, to answer, one is compelled to take a very close look at world politics from as early as the 1600s up until World War I. The attitude of the European governments towards the continent of Africa has long been one of contempt and covetousness. Africa was seen as a wealth of untapped natural resources, Her non-industrialized peoples the uncivilized savages of a *Dark Continent*. The whole objective of the European governments was to colonize the entire continent, subdue the people, and use Her natural resources to build up Europe.

All of this was done under the guise of Christianity, or rather, of Western Christianity. The forces of the colonialists were greater by far than those of Africa's valiant chiefs and warriors, and although the natives fought for their freedom and their lands, the countries of Mother Africa fell one by one under the sway of such colonial powers as Britain, France, Spain, Belgium, Italy and Portugal. By the 1800s the whole continent of Africa was submerged in darkness under the so-called *civilizing mission* of the Church of Rome, except for Ethiopia, the mountainous Christian stronghold, the oldest continuously sovereign kingdom in the world.

The League of Nations is on trial; God and history will be your judge. These were the words of Haile Sellassie I as He addressed the League of Nations in 1936, after they failed to apply the stipulations of the covenant protecting members of the League from wars of conquest. History has proven the accuracy of the Emperor's words, and shortly thereafter it became clear that the League's failure had planted the seeds of World War II.

After World War I (1914-1918), the *war to end all wars*, a group of fifty-three independent nations (none of them African) established the League of Nations to ensure that a catastrophic war of conquest would never again threaten the peace of humankind. *Collective security* was the post-war watchword.

Each member nation swore under oath to defend and uphold the solemn Covenant of the League and respect the territorial integrity and political independence of the other member states. No recognition was to be given to any acquisition of territory gained by force.

For some time after World War I, Italy, however, nurtured the idea of avenging the shame that covered them after the Battle of Adowa, and the dictator Benito Mussolini set his evil eye against Ethiopia. For years he secretly sought out allies and manipulated events to support his malicious intent against Ethiopia. After rising to power on October 28, 1922, in an Italy suffering tremendous economic strains, Mussolini set as his Fascist regime's primary goal preparing for a war against Ethiopia. This despite the fact that Italy, along with France, helped push for Ethiopia's membership in the League of Nations in 1923, and even though his war of conquest required him to break his country's covenant as a League member.

Finally, on October 3, 1935, Mussolini was able to stand on his balcony on the Piazza and announce the invasion of Ethiopia by his Fascist army. In a show of contempt for Haile Sellassie I's Ethiopia, he made no formal declaration of war. On the eve of the invasion, above a cheering multitude of Italians, Mussolini proclaimed:

> Not only is an army marching, but forty million Italians are marching in unison with this army, because an attempt is being made to commit against them [the Italians] the blackest of all injustices, to rob them of a place in the sun.

The attempt he was referring to was the League's feeble effort to impose sanctions on both Italy and Ethiopia, which turned out to hurt Ethiopia while helping to unite Italy under the Fascist regime. Mussolini felt the European powers cheated Italy out of her fair share of the spoils of World War I. Therefore, he would

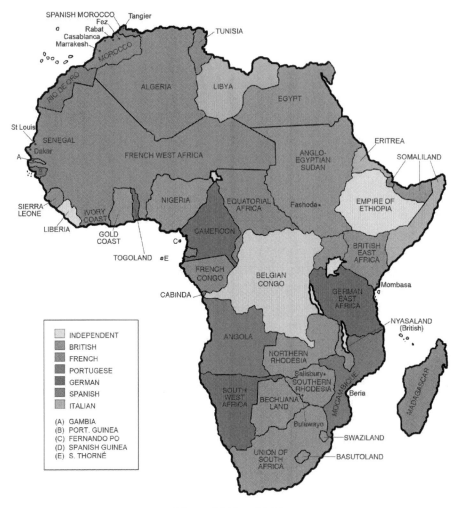

Map of Africa 1914

be the one to gain for Italy what he believed to be her fair share of glory on the *Continent of the Sun* — the same place so often referred to as the *Dark Continent*.

To say that Italy's actions were gluttonous would be a gross understatement. By this I mean to point out that Italy already occupied vast stretches of territory in the Horn of Africa, in what was called Italian Somaliland. Eritrea as well as Libya were also under Italian rule.

A 1914 map of Africa shows Ethiopia as the only independent realm on the continent. All other countries except Liberia, a republic founded by freed African Americans in 1847, were under one or another colonial flag. Nevertheless, when the time came to stand up for this sole surviving African state, the League of Nations was bound hand and foot by its own hypocrisy and stood in silence and fear while Mussolini raped and brutalized a fellow League member.

There are many important reasons why the League did not stand up for Ethiopia. One is that Ethiopia was the only African nation ever to have elevated Herself to such a prestigious position in a world where white supremacy dominated. Only the ancient kingdom of Ethiopia was able to stand on equal footing with them. The defense of a black man and his nation would be too much for the colonial League, whose members were guilty of enslaving and exterminating Africans under their control from east to west. This hypocritical folly soon led to the dismantling of the so-called *peacekeeping* League of Nations. They defeated themselves by turning their backs on the King of King's plea for justice; they could not stand in judgment, so the useless League dissolved, all the while fulfilling a number of prophetic verses in the *Holy Bible:*

> Why do the heathen rage, and the people imagine a vain thing? The kings of the earth set themselves, and the rulers take counsel together against the Lord, and against his anointed, saying, Let us break their bands asunder and cast away their cords from us.
>
> Psalm 2

Likewise, in the Book of the Prophet Isaiah, ch. 2, v. 4, we read:

> And he shall judge among the nations, and shall rebuke many people; and they shall beat their sword into plowshares, and their spears into pruning hooks: nation shall not lift up sword against nation, neither shall they learn war anymore.

The last quote could easily have been the motto of the League of Nations, but they failed to live up to it, as they failed to live up to the solemn promises they made under oath just after the first Great War. This was all prophesied thousands of years before, for *Ethiopia to stretch forth Her hands unto God* (Psalm 68, v. 31), and for God to *bow down the heavens* (Psalm 18, v. 9) and make His glorious presence known to the sons of men by the judgment He executed upon the nations.

To the mind of the Rastafarian, Revelation ch. 19, vv. 13-16, clearly depicts the world situation when Haile Sellassie I appeared before representatives of the world at the League of Nations in Geneva, Switzerland on June 30, 1936:

> He was clothed in a vesture dipped in blood; and his name is called the Word of God. And the armies which were in heaven followed him upon white horses, clothed in fine linen white and clean: and out of his mouth goeth a sharp sword, that with it he should smite the nations: And he shall rule them with a rod of iron: and he treadeth the winepress of the fierceness and wrath of Almighty God. And he has on his vesture and on his thigh a name written, King of Kings, and Lord of Lords. Amen.

Rastafarians are convinced that Haile Sellassie I fulfilled this prophecy in 1936, in a fulfillment too significant to be ignored. The judgment pronounced by the Conquering Lion of Judah was fiercely accurate. His appearance and His words are well-documented in the pages of the historical chronicles.[79]

> "I Haile Selassie I, Emperor of Ethiopia, am here today to claim that justice which is due to my people, and the assistance promised to it eight months ago, when fifty nations asserted than aggression had been committed in violation of international treaties.
>
> None other than the Emperor can address the appeal of the Ethiopian people to these fifty nations.
>
> There is no precedent for a head of State himself speaking in this assembly. But there is also no precedent for a people being victim of such injustice and being at present threatened by abandonment to its aggressor. Also, there has never before been an example of any government proceeding to the systematic extermination of a nation by barbarous means, in violation of the most solemn promises made to all the nations of the earth that there should be no resort to a war of conquest, and that there should not be used against innocent humans the terrible poison of harmful gases. It is to defend a people struggling for its age-old independence that the Head of the Ethiopian Empire has come to Geneva to fulfill this supreme duty after having Himself fought at the head of His armies.
>
> I pray almighty God that He may spare nations the terrible sufferings that have just been inflicted on my people, and of which the chiefs who accompany me here have been horrified witnesses.

---

[79] In 1977 Time-Life Books published a volume entitled: "Prelude to War": *World War II*. In CH. 5, entitled *"Downfall of a Feeble League* gives us some insights to His impassionate appeal to the nations.

It is my duty to inform the governments assembled in Geneva, responsible as they are for the lives of millions of men, women, and children, of the deadly peril which threatens them, by describing to them the fate which has been suffered by Ethiopia...

....None other than myself and my brave companions in arms could bring the League of Nations the undeniable proof. The appeals of my delegates...has remained without any answer; my delegates had not been witnesses. That is why I decided to come myself to bear witness against the crime perpetuated against my people and give Europe a warning of the doom that awaits it if it should bow before the accomplished fact.

...Should it happen that a strong Government finds it may, with impunity, destroy a weak people, then the hour strikes for that weak people to appeal to the League of Nations to give its judgement in all freedom. God and history will remember your judgement....it is us today, it will be you tomorrow."

"H.I.M. Haile Sellassie I, taken from: *Appeal to the League – An Anthology of Some of The Public Utterances of His Imperial Majesty, Haile Selassie I."*

I conclude that hypocrisy and racism were the basic vices that caused the weakness in the international system that permitted Italy's aggression against Ethiopia. These were the two main factors leading to the breakdown of international security, in answer to the first question raised by Levine in *Greater Ethiopia*.

Why Ethiopia?

At this point, answering the second part of Donald Levine's question: *Why Ethiopia? What was it that enabled Ethiopia alone among traditional African societies to retain its sovereignty?* let it suffice to say that its strategic location and Orthodox Christianity, and the love and mercy of the Almighty, together have kept Ethiopia's sovereignty secure from external domination.

The most obvious and popular answer looks to the Ethiopian realm's geographic situation on the mountainous eastern side of the Horn of Africa. Because Her homeland was an isolated plateau, She remained an island of Christianity, suspended in time, safeguarded by Her fiercely independent and patriotic people. In describing Ethiopia, the historian and author of *Inside Africa*, John Gunther, states:

> We reach now a country utterly unlike any we have seen in Africa so far. Ethiopia, sometimes called Abyssinia, is a mountain fastness, a fortress cut off, to a large extent, from the adjacent world; by the mere fact of its altitude, an impregnable feudal kingdom lost in space.

Geography however, is not the only reason, and may even rank beneath the next reason we will consider. After careful observation and extensive study of the other countries in Africa, Ethiopia stands out as unique for one very important reason, namely, Oriental Orthodox Christianity, that She was not Christianized by Western missionaries, but is indigenously Christian through the acceptance of the faith as early as the fourth century. And that, starting long before its conversion to Christ, the Ethiopian Kingdom was ruled by Hebraic-Jewish kings from the lineage of King Solomon who sat on the Throne of David.

The Christian rulers who came beginning in the fourth century A.D. were of Solomon as well, but they sat on his Throne as Hebraic-Christian messianic Kings, with titles including *Elect of*

God, and *Defender of the Faith,* as well as *King of Kings* and *Lion of the Tribe of Judah.* Their conversion followed a natural progression from Judaism to Christianity, with the sovereign Hebraic lineage of King David maintained intact. The true Jews did indeed accept the promise and substance of the Christ, as we see clearly in the development of Christianity in Ethiopia from Judaic roots.

As the possessor of such precious religious relics as the Ark of the Covenant and the ancient Throne of King David, one does not have to look through a microscope to see why Ethiopia has been the target of Italian aggression for centuries past. Rome, the chief city of Italy, was the dominant force and influence in world politics for centuries; there was a time in history when the Jews were severely persecuted by colonial Roman rulers. Under the dictatorship of Julius Caesar, Jews that rebelled were imprisoned or murdered, and not much change came under his successor Octavius (who changed his name to Augustus), who also ruled with the iron fist of a tyrant.

In the days when Yahowshua ha Mashiakh was active in His ministry, Israel found themselves under the authority of Octavianus Augustus. When the fame of Yahowshua spread, the Jews delivered Him up to Pontius Pilate, Roman Governor over Judea, the province of the Jews, that He might be condemned to death. After His crucifixion and reported Resurrection, His faithful followers experienced extreme and increasing tribulation under the Caesars of Rome. Like the Jews before them, early Christians were subjected to cruel hardships and savage atrocities from the Romans; many had to flee to more tolerant cities in neighboring countries.

For over 300 years, the Roman government sought to halt the spread of Christianity, but their efforts were in vain. Finally, in 313 A.D., the Emperor Constantine (306-337 A.D.) issued a decree, the Edict of Milan, which ended the official persecution of Christians and granted them religious toleration. By the first half of the fifth century, the Roman Empire had not only adopted Christianity as its official religion but also actively suppressed other faiths. Rome contrived Catholicism, the form of Christianity centered in Rome, which could be said to have completely overrun Western Europe by the end of the eleventh century.

The *Dum Diveras* ("Until Different") was a papal bull issued by Pope Nicholas V on the 8th of June 1452. This document is credited with giving birth to the West African slave trade, as it authorized Alfonso V of Portugal, for one, to subdue and hold his non-Christian subjects in *perpetual slavery*. *Dum Dimeras* states:

> We grant you (Kings of Spain and Portugal) by these present documents, with our Apostolic Authority, full and free permission to invade, search out, capture, and subjugate the Saracens and pagans and any other unbelievers and enemies of Christ wherever they may be, as well as their kingdoms, duchies, countries, principalities, and other property (…) and to reduce their persons into perpetual slavery.

With this document the Roman Catholic Church embarked on the expansion of her empire through what she called her *civilizing mission*, an agenda to spread her form of Christianity to as many countries as possible through force and bloody violence. Through those missionary activities, Rome spread its influence and its doctrine around the world. All the different branches of Christianity that have been established in Europe since the Reformation, including Anglicanism (Church of England), Lutheranism, and Calvinism or Presbyterianism, are offshoots of the Catholic Church of Rome; though they fall under the name *Protestant*, meaning, exactly as the name implies: protesting. Thus Protestant missionary activity may be considered an offshoot of this Catholic mission.

Rastafarians reason that, had the Italians succeeded in blinding the eye of truth by conquering the ancient Christian Empire of

Ethiopia, they would have succeeded in spreading their blanket of darkness over the entire world, even Zion — giving ultimate power to evil over good. The world must thank Haile Sellassie I, the Kingly Mashiakh of Ethiopia, for being the Redeemer of mankind from the vain imagination of the Dragon and the Beast. Psalm 46, vv. 4-10 reads:

> There is a river, the streams whereof shall make glad the city of God, the Holy place of the tabernacle of the Most High. God is in the midst of her; she shall not be moved; God shall help her, and that right early. The heathens raged, the kingdoms were moved: He uttered His voice, the earth melted. The Lord of hosts is with us; the God of Jacob is our refuge. Selah.

> Come, behold the works of the Lord, what desolations he hath made in the earth. He maketh wars to cease unto the end of the earth; He breaketh the bow, and cutteth the spear in sunder; He burneth the chariot in the fire. Be still, and know that I am God; I will be exalted among the heathen, I will be exalted in the earth.

His Imperial Majesty Haile Sellassie I confirmed:

> Even in the 20th century, with faith, courage and a just cause, David will still beat Goliath.

> > H.I.M., Jubilee Palace, Addis Ababa 1971

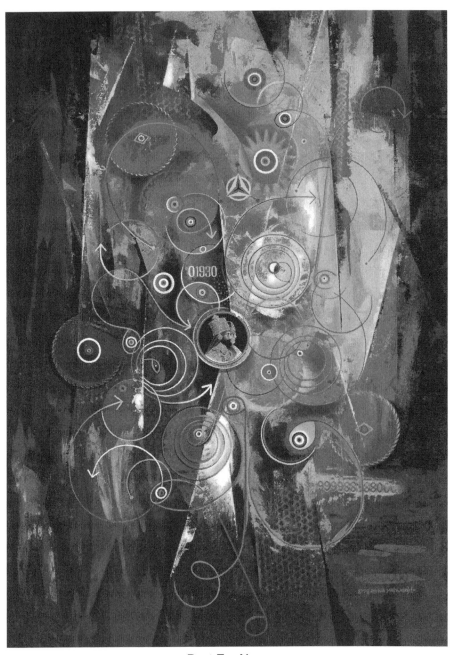

Past For Now

CHAPTER 11

RASTAFARIAN FOUNDERS

The Birth of African Zionism in Jamaica

> The humble shall see this, and be glad: and your heart shall live that seek God. For the Lord heareth the poor, and despiseth not his prisoners. Let the heaven and earth praise him, the seas, and every thing that moveth therein. For God will save Zion, and will build the cities of Judah: that they may dwell there, and have it in possession. The seed also of his servants shall inherit it: and they that love his name shall dwell therein.
>
> Psalm 69, vv. 32-36

Zion is a Hebrew word meaning *sunny, unobstructed, very dry, established, constituted landmark,* and *fortress.* These words, in and of themselves, conjure images of Ethiopia, which has preserved historical traditions of the Biblical landmark fortress erected in King David's reign. As previously stated, the true Biblical Zion is the resting place of the Ark of the Covenant, as well as of the Holy Mother Mary and Her Christ Child, who is David come again.

On a metaphysical level, Zion represents spiritual consciousness. This Divine energy of spiritual consciousness is the intergalactic chamber in which Zionism has its roots. Revivalism and in particular Zionism (as I define it in this book) are at the core of all messianic movements from the time of ancient Judaism to Rastafari today.

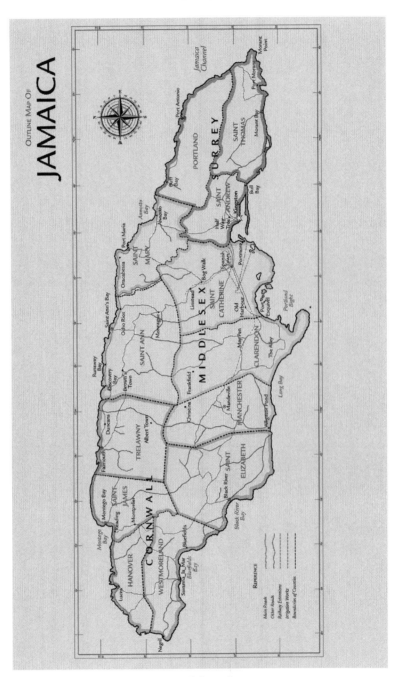

Map of Jamaica

Few historians or other scholars are aware of the Caribbean *(Carry Beyond)*[80] Jamaican origins of African Zionism, which was taking shape in the minds of newly emancipated Africans as early as the late 1800s. This form of Zionism gave birth to what is termed Ethiopianism, a patriotic identification with Africa, which flourished after Ethiopia's victorious battle to secure Her independence and repel the 1896 Italian invasion. It is important to note, however, that Ethiopianism did not start with the victory at Adowa, but it gained momentum then, at a time when Africans abroad needed to identify with an African sovereign, one that even the colonial forces had to reckon with. It is in this atmosphere that a unique indigenous Zionism metamorphized into a people there in Jamaica who called themselves Israelites.

Jamaican Zionism gave birth to the back-to-Africa movement of *Marcus Garvey* in the 1920s, which is the basis of repatriation for the Rastafarian Zionist.

It is stated by some historians that what is termed African Zionism was introduced into South Africa at the turn of the century, circa 1902, through the missionary ministry of P. L. Le Roux, an Afrikaaner. Le Roux began his missionary work with the Zulus, who took his Zionist form of Christianity and firmly established a unique African form of it in Zululand. But the fact that Le Roux and his missionary colleagues introduced the idea of Zion to some African tribal groups absolutely does not mean he introduced the concept of Zion to Africa as such. On the contrary, the metaphysical concept of Zion originated among African people, as found in the traditions of the Hebrews in Egypt and Ethiopia.

In looking at the situation of Africans in the Diaspora, we see them having a desperate need for a link with their ancestral homeland and heritage. Native Africans such as the Zulus had

---

80 *Carry Beyond* is Rastafarian jargon for the Caribbean, which to them is a part of Babylon's kingdom. The Rastafarians are very conscious that — the Africans were carried by force beyond their borders into the Western hemisphere. Hence the term *Carry-Beyond* refers to the Caribbean, and the West in general.

no such need. For natives of the Diaspora, though, Ethiopianism was established more and more firmly over time, until there developed a Zionist consciousness in Jamaica that brought forth the revivalist enthusiasm which was first labeled *African Zionism*.

Individuals such as Bedward, preaching African Zionism and the Divinity of the Ethiopian Lineage, emerged only from a resolute colonial resistance. In fact, the Rastafarians of today and their predecessors arose from a political and religious backdrop similar to that which gave rise to the early *Christians* almost two thousand years ago.

Jamaica's Port Royal, in Her heyday of colonial glory, when pirates such as Blackbeard and Captain Henry Morgan roamed the high seas, was the capital of the whole West Indies. Jamaica, a colony within the British Empire, carved out for Herself an epic history of slave rebellions, then developed a resistance to colonial rule stronger than that which developed in any of the other colonies except for Haiti. *Black Zionism* emerged in the late 1800s, especially after Ethiopia's victory over Italy's attempt at colonizaton. This African Revival gained so much momentum that the rise of the individuals you are about to read about was inevitable.

A fiercely independent-minded island, Jamaica has played a central role in the revolution of Pan-African consciousness. She has helped lift the spirits of millions of individuals around the world to identify with the African within them. Even Africans on the African Continent itself are persuaded to this conclusion. Renowned leaders on the mainland of North America, such as the Hon. Elijah Mohammed, Malcolm X, Angela Davis, and Luis Farrakhan, to name a few, were directly influenced by the character, ideals, concepts and achievements of the Jamaican-born Marcus Mosiah Garvey, who was still a young man when Pan-African Zionists such as Bedward were active.

If Ethiopia is viewed as the Mother, *Zion*, as per the Holy Scriptures, and as aligns with the archeological evidence, then the tiny island of Jamaica reveals Herself to be the *Daughter of Zion* spoken of in the same scriptures. We read in Psalm 9, vv. 11, 13, 14:

> Sing praises to the Lord, which dwelleth in Zion: declare among the people His doings…Have mercy upon me, O Lord; consider my trouble which I suffer of them that hate me, thou that liftest me up from the gates of death: that I may shew forth all thy praise in the gates of the Daughter of Zion.

This is the voice of a people taken away captive, sold into bondage, enslaved and persecuted. This is also the voice of the children of the Daughter who found their salvation in the Glory of the Mother. This salvation is manifest through one particular individual, who comes to symbolize redemption from the yoke that has befallen the children. For the Rastafarians, it is Haile Sellassie I who represents the gift of Divine intervention coming to them from Mother Zion, Ethiopia. In the consciousness of the Divine, Zion is a sacred space within. Nevertheless, Jamaica manifests Herself as the Daughter of Zion in an outward or geographical location.

Out of the womb of this colonial island came such vibrant lights as Nanny of the Maroons, Cujoe, Sam Sharpe, J. A. Rogers, Louise Bennett, Marcus Garvey and Bob Marley, all from the grass roots of Jamaican society. Out of the injustices of colonial Jamaica came one of the most significant anti-colonial forces the planet would ever reckon with. The sublime vibration of the Rastafarians emerged as the dominant force in the struggle against Roman Catholic and other Eurocentric colonial value systems.

In 1936, in answer to the invasion of fascist Italy, Ethiopia gave us first principles in the lessons of dignity and morality. Through sacrifice, Ethiopia, in Haile Sellassie I, has given unto all a chance for redemption through the principles of *Christ*. Of all the nations of the world, it took the tiny island of Jamaica to give birth to a people who would recognize, accept and embrace Ethiopia's potent example.

Alexander Bedward

Jamaica Native Baptist Free Church was founded and developed in Augustown, St. Andrew, Jamaica, by H. E. S. Woods, commonly known as *Shakespeare*. Shakespeare spearheaded the revivalist movement that came to be known as Bedwardism after his handpicked and appointed successor Alexander Bedward, because of Bedward's devotion in service of the Church. Shakespeare and the legacy he left behind fit perfectly into biblical context, and give us eerie glimpses into a world of prophetical visions and public proclamations of imminent destruction upon the surrounding towns and cities.

For in 1891, Alexander Bedward, commonly known as *Bedward*, a Mayalist[81] *spirit-man* (and Baptist), arose to lead a group of Jamaican black nationalists, who became known as Bedwardites. Based on Psalm 68, Bedward proclaimed the coming of the King of Kings from Ethiopia as the returned *Christ*. Wearing white robes, this revivalist called for immediate repatriation of people of African descent to Africa, which for him was the *Blackman's Zion*.

Alexander Bedward was born an only son in 1859 in the parish of St. Andrew in Jamaica, and grew to become an uneducated youth laboring on the Hope Plantation. According to *The History of Bedwardism* he had become a vile character by his early manhood years, indulging in various lasciviousnesses, which created a certain unpleasantness in his marriage.

---

79 See the explanation of Mayalists and Mayal men on p. 224.

So much the more signal therefore had to be and was his transformation from the natural to the spiritual. The transforming wonders of Divine Grace are gloriously manifested in A. Bedward, who once so vile, now seems to combine in himself the faith of Abraham, the meekness of Moses, the patience of Job, and the love of St. John.

> A. A. Brooks, *The History of Bedwardism*, ch. 2, p. 6

Like a prophet of old, Bedward was plagued by numerous visions, which became the directing force of his life. From early on in his life, furthermore, he was haunted by poor health, being particularly afflicted for a period of thirteen years; in order to change his ailing condition, he took it upon himself to migrate to Colón (I want to suggest up front that his migration was against, not in response to, the voice of God), Gran Colombia (now Panama) in 1883 for a change of climate. However, the visions persisted and his health continued to fail. Like Jonah, Bedward found himself in the belly of the beast as a result of disobeying the voice of God, which had given him specific commandments to follow. So prompted by a series of visions that instructed him to return to Jamaica, he went back after being in Colón for only two years.

> He saw the appearance of a man who stood before him and said, "Go back to Jamaica. If you stay here, you will die and lose your soul, but if you go back to Jamaica, you will save your soul and be the means of saving many others." Bedward said, "But, I cannot go, for having recently come here, I have no money to pay my passage." "I will provide the means," he was answered. "Go to John Renford, Jos. Waters, Wm. Waters, and Robert Law, and ask them for the help you need."
>
> At this Bedward slept and saw another vision, or dream, in which he found himself in Jamaica, and going up

the Constant Spring Road. Arriving at a certain place here was a wide gate ajar; a man passing in just before him hindered his getting through before the gate was shut. The gate-keeper was on the other side, and asked Bedward for his Passport. He showed him what he thought was it, upon which the gatekeeper said in a very impressive tone, "But you are lost."

This so confounded Bedward with mortifying grief and anguish of soul, that with his hand upon his head, he turned back crying at the top of his voice, "I am lost. I am lost." He soon met another man standing by the road side, who said to him, "Come here, I do send you to Augustown." "To Augustown?" said Bedward. "Why that is the Place I am fleeing from." The man so stamped his foot upon the ground that the earth shook dreadfully, and with an authority which was awe inspiring said, "Go to Augustown, submit yourself to Mr. Raderford for instruction, with fastings on Mondays, Wednesdays and Fridays. Then be baptized: for I have a special work for you to do." Bedward awoke to find it was a dream, and that he was still in Colón.

Brooks, ch. 2, pp. 7-8

Alexander Bedward's obedience to the voice in his visions would have life-altering effects on him. He arrived in Jamaica from Colón on the 10th of August 1885 and was eventually baptized by Mr. Raderford on January 1886.

On the 10th of October 1891, Alexander Bedward officially started his ministry, and two months later, on December 22, he gave his first public address at the Mona River, where he baptized, and *dispensed the water as medicine*. He ordered a fasting vigil, and he declared the water of the Mona River as blessed and potent for healing, based on revelations that he received. Hundreds of people were recorded as coming to the healing river of Bedward and seven people who took the water medicine were immediately cured of their illnesses. These seven cured were some of the first devotees who took up Bedward's tri-weekly fasting vigil. Great excitement was stirred among the people upon hearing of the healing waters of the Mona River and Alexander Bedward's evangelical works upon its banks. But the attention and curiosity of the civil authorities was aroused, and Bedward became their public enemy number one.

> At one time the feelings of many in high circles were indignantly aroused, and Bedward was threateningly watched by Agents of the Civil Authority. Undauntedly, the devoted servant of God conducted his work until in God's own time they took him.
>
> On Monday 21st Jan., 1895 about 7 p.m. Bedward said, "They are coming for me to-night." Only a few hours later, during the stillness of the night a company of about forty-five men with arms were at his house, Union Camp, Augustown. Bedward meekly said, "Why so many of you have come for me? If you had sent a child for me I would have come." So they placed him in a carriage between two officers. On either side of the carriage, there rode a horseman. Thus was Bedward arrested by night on the charge of sedition.
>
> Brooks, ch. 2, p. 10

After spending four months in the Spanish Town Jail awaiting trial, one of the witnesses, an unnamed constable sent by the authorities to spy and report on the doings of Bedward, refused to bear false witness against that innocent man and the charges were dropped. Alexander however, now a branded man because of this fiasco, was placed in the Lunatic Asylum for no less than a month. Instead of pacifying him however, his arrest and institutionalization strengthened his faith in the works he knew he was ordained to do. Thereafter, Bedward embarked on his mission with even more devotion than before. As his fame grew, so did his followers, whom the locals now began to call Bedwardites.

Some fundamental features of Bedwardism are: (1) Fasting and Prayer, (2) Initiation by Vow, (3) Sabbatarianism, (4) the Lighted Candle Emblem of the Trinity, (5) Apocalyptic, (6) Jesus as Perfect Man and God, (7) Baptism, (8) the Single Law of Love, (9) Zionism, and (10) Ceremonial White Robe and Turban Dress.

Bedwardism grew into pan-African Zionism, a religious movement that was to become a thorn in the sides of the corrupt, the unruly, and the unrighteous masses of those days. The Bedwardites believed that they were the inheritors of the legacy of Christ's Gospel, calling the faithful to their holy fete of righteousness through a rigorous routine of fasting on Mondays, Wednesdays and Fridays. They practiced a form of revivalist Christianity that was steeped in Jewish principles similar to those of the ancient Essenes. The Bedwardites believed that Jamaica was a special place reserved to fulfill the Lord's work in the latter days.

> It has pleased the Supreme Disposer of events to choose the land of Palestine or Canaan for the Jews, and for His special purpose. So is He pleased to choose Jamaica in the Western World. Augustown compares to Jerusalem. Union Camp to Mount Zion.
>
> Brooks, ch. 6, p. 27

The Bedwardites were convinced that they were the fulfillment of the divine prophecies revealed in Jamaica to bring to fruition the word and works of the living God. They declared:

> As Judaism was succeeded by Christianity, so Christianity is being succeeded by Bedwardism. With all

humble boldness is it declared that Judaism, Christianity, and Bedwardism, are in the order of the Father, Son, and Holy Ghost, for the retrieve of fallen man. Judaism has done its part, Christianity has had and is having its triumph: And one of its chief and latest triumphs will be its handing over from various Denomination[s], Creeds and Persuasions, the children of God unto Bedwardism.

Brooks, ch. 3, p. 17

The Right Honorable Marcus Mosiah Garvey: Father of Black Nationalism

Look to Africa where a Black King shall be crowned and He shall be the redeemer of the African people.

With the words above, Marcus Mosiah Garvey was to spearhead a further revival in African awareness, leading a people to their redemption through seeing clearly their own identity. It is said that no leader has, in their own lifetime, influenced so many Africans so profoundly as has Marcus Garvey. Though most of his specific proposals and projects were not realized, he stimulated a revolution in African consciousness that is unparalleled in history.

Marcus Garvey was born in Jamaica, in the parish of St. Ann, on August 17, 1887. His father was a brilliant intellectual and his mother a sober and soft-spoken conscientious Christian woman. As a boy growing up in Jamaica, his playmates were a mixture of white Jamaicans, East Indians and Africans. When he was young, Marcus did not experience any difference between his white friends and himself. He received his education from many sources, including private tutors and public school, two high schools and two colleges. He developed a strong and forceful character and was well liked and respected by his peers.

Garvey became a printer's apprentice while still very young and learned the trade of publishing and about the affairs of business. But during his teenage years, Marcus began to experience the prejudice of the Jamaican white upper class and petty bourgeoisie. After getting his first lesson in racial discrimination, he resolved to develop a deeper African pride in himself and to assist others to the same end.

> I prefer to die at this moment rather than not to work for the freedom of Africa. If liberty is good for certain sets of humanity it is good for all. Black men, Colored men, Negroes have as much right to be free as any other race that God Almighty ever created, and we desire freedom that is unfettered, freedom that is unlimited, freedom that will give us a chance and opportunity to rise to the fullest of our ambition and that we cannot get in countries where other men rule and dominate.

> We have reached the time when every minute, every second must count for something done, something achieved in the cause of Africa. We need the freedom of Africa now, therefore, we desire the kind of leadership that will give it to us as quickly as possible. You will realize that not only individuals, but governments are using their influence against us. But what do we care about the unrighteous influence of any government? Our cause is based upon righteousness. And anything that is not righteous we have no respect for, because God Almighty is our leader and Jesus Christ our standard bearer. We rely on them for that kind of leadership that will make us free, for it is the same God who inspired the Psalmists to write *Princes shall come out of Egypt and Ethiopia shall stretch out Her hands unto God.* At this moment me thinks (I think) I see Ethiopia stretching forth Her hands unto God and me thinks (I think) I see the Angel of God taking up the standard of the Red, the Black

Marcus Mosiah Garvey

and the Green, and saying, *Men of the Negro Race, Men of Ethiopia, follow me.*

Philosophy and Opinions of Marcus Garvey, Or, Africa for the Africans — By Marcus Garvey

After returning from a tour of Europe on July 15, 1914, Marcus Garvey founded and organized the Universal Negro Improvement Association, or U.N.I.A, with the aim of *organizing and centralizing* Africans into a governmental organ, through education and self-reliance, to repatriate to Africa. Thus to the world a name was born, a movement created and a man became known.

Embarking on this mission, Garvey was exposed to tremendous trials and tribulations, which shed a whole new light on inter-race prejudice. *Garvey is crazy. He has lost his head. Is that the use he is going to make of his experience and his intelligence?* were some of the remarks made by the Jamaican petty bourgeois. Garvey had to decide: Would he be an Uncle Tom and please his friends or would he defend and help improve the condition of the suffering black millions? He chose the latter course and became the champion of African rights and sovereignty, its leading light, until Haile Sellassie I entered the world arena in 1936.

By forming the U.N.I.A., Marcus Garvey consciously brought to light, as a new dawn, a revolution, an African solidarity. Garvey made the U.N.I.A. a machine for mobilization, laying the infrastructure for chapters all across the Americas. This organization was the first of its kind and remains the standard which Pan-Africanists and Black Nationalists around the globe proudly build upon.

The author Booker T. Washington, just before dying that same year, invited Marcus Garvey to visit the United States in 1916. Upon arrival in the U.S., Garvey traveled to thirty-eight states, where he found the same problems afflicting the African race that he had seen in the Caribbean, caused by exploitation and injustice served out to them by the colonial policies in place in the U.S. He also found a new problem, certain *so-called negro leaders*, after studying them closely, he found that:

> they had no program, but were mere opportunists who were living off their so-called leadership while the poor people were groping in the dark… I ask where is the black man's government, where is his King and his kingdom, his President, his country, and his ambassadors, his army, his navy, his men of big affairs? I could not find them, and then I declared, I will help to make them.

The Black Star Line was Marcus Garvey's idea of a fleet of merchant ships owned and operated by *Negroes*. It soon collapsed, a victim of undercapitalization, conspiracy, mismanagement and inexperience. Garvey was unable to meet the heavy costs of maintenance and the project folded, losing thousands of Garveyites the investments they had made in this enterprise.

> The temporary ruin of the Black Star Line in no way affected the larger work of the Universal Negro Improvement Association, which now has 900 branches with an approximate membership of 6,000,000. This organization has succeeded in organizing the Negroes all over the world and we now look forward to a renaissance that will create a new people and bring about the restoration of Ethiopia's ancient glory…My work is just begun and as I lay down my life for the cause of my people, so do I feel that succeeding generations shall be inspired by the sacrifice that I made for the rehabilitation of our race. Christ died to make men free. I shall die to give courage and inspiration to my race. I shall live in the physical or the spiritual to see the day of Africa's glory…Look for

me in the whirlwind or the storm, look for me all around you, for with God's grace, I will come and bring with me countless millions to aid you in the fight for liberty, freedom and life…After my enemies are satisfied, in life or death, I shall come back to you to serve even as I have served before. In life I shall be the same, in death I shall be a terror to the foes of Negro liberty. If death has power, then count on me in death to be the real Marcus Garvey I would like to be…Be assured that I shall never desert you and make your enemies triumph over you.

— Rt. Hon. Marcus Garvey

It is Marcus Garvey who took on the task of amplifying the voice of the Africans in their struggles with injustice. He intensified and made concrete the consciousness of Ethiopia in the psyches of Jamaican and other African people around the world. Marcus Garvey's specifically Ethiopic perspective was crucial for a number of Pan-Africanist Movements that followed him, from Jamaica's Howellites to the Black Panthers of Oakland, California.

The philosophies and teachings of the Right Honourable Marcus Mosiah Garvey are the primary building blocks and the cornerstone of the Rastafari Movement. Above all others he is responsible for the African orientation and African awareness that continue to shape Rastafari perspectives and agendas. His teachings addressed all aspects of African development, starting with the re-education of African people around the world: championing an educational system founded on the Sovereign and Divine identity of the African, seeing God through the spectacles of an Ethiopian, and knowing yourself, as an African, to have no less worth than any man.

Marcus Garvey gave birth to a nation by spearheading a radical mission to organize and mobilize the oppressed African Diaspora.

He gave strength and hope to a people *groping in darkness* under a yoke of colonialism, at a time when the odds were stacked so high against him that his task must have seemed impossible. Yet he left his mark, a highly visible mark, a scar and more than a scar on the soft underbelly of the colonial beast. Marcus left us a rich legacy, a treasure trove of wisdom, and a prime example of what is possible if we *organize and centralize* our resources, starting with our selves. Self-development was essential to Garvey, who believed that to cultivate good character was a sign of civilized intelligence.

> *Look for me in the whirlwind...*
>
> — Rt. Hon. Marcus Garvey

It awaited the next generation to reckon with the spirit, teachings and prophecies of Marcus Garvey, to live out many aspects of his vision — a generation that was psychologically and emotionally ready to take that awakened African consciousness to the next level of spiritual development. The patriarch Leonard Percival Howell found himself in such a generation. The Howellites, as the immediate predecessors to the Rastafarians, became the vanguards of a new way for Africans to identify themselves. On the ground level of Pan-Africanism that Marcus built up in the early nineteen-twenties, the Howellites erected the platform of a Messianic Movement.

Brother Leonard Percival Howell: First Patriarch of Rastafari

> Thus said Ras Tafari the Living God of Creation, vast Rome has deceived the race of man, and has killed the mortal supreme monarch. Ethiopia's glory is no guesser. Long before this world was, Ethiopia's glory has been running cotrillions of centuries ago.
>
> — Leonard P. Howell *The Gong*

Brother Leonard Percival Howell was a well-read seaman who traveled to Africa, Japan and throughout the Americas. He believed salvation was a communal and international reality, not an individual matter. Inspired by King Tafari's 1930 coronation and enthronement on the Throne of David, Howell ushered in a new Afro-Jamaican Revivalist Faith, whose followers became known as Howellites. This movement gave birth to Rastafari as a people. Howell was to build the first Rastafarian community, which he named the Ethiopian Salvation Union, in 1932. He renamed it the Ethiopian Benevolent Society in 1939, and then the Ethiopian Salvation Society, and finally in 1940 the Pinnacle Community.

The Pinnacle Community

Wearying of constant harassment by the Jamaican police force, Leonard P. Howell, or the Gong, as he was commonly called, retreated with his followers to the hills. It is said that he purchased a piece of land near the town of Sligoville in the parish of St. Catherine. There, in 1940, he established his community based on the African traditions that the maroons[82] had preserved. It was called Pinnacle, and was the first community to call upon the Name of Haile Sellassie I.

Leonard Howell's Pinnacle was a self-sufficient agricultural community that is said to have housed from 500 to as many as 1500 followers. Amongst the crops they planted was *Cannabis sativa*,

---

82 The *Maroons* of Jamaica, whom Nanny and many others, such as Sam Sharpe and Cujoe, are associated with, are historically escaped slaves who became anti-slavery freedom fighters, creating some of the first free African communities in the Americas. In 1655, when the British captured Jamaica from the Spanish, many, rather than continue in slavery under the British, escaped into the rocky mountainous regions of the island. The free communities created by the maroons in the mountains became reservoirs of African culture, retaining strong African traditions. They fought many bloody battles with the new colonists, but on March 1, 1739, the British governor in Jamaica signed a treaty with the maroons promising 2,500 acres in two regions of the island. The stipulations of this treaty, known as articles of pacification, caused great tension between the enslaved population and the maroons, as the maroons, now allied with British, agreed to return any further runaways who sought refuge with them for a set fee from the government.

Patriarch Leonard Percival Howell

locally called ganja. After about a year, in 1941, residents of the area complained to the police that the Howellites were demanding taxes be paid to them, in the name of Haile Sellassie I, instead of to the Jamaican government. The police raided the community and arrested over seventy Howellite Rastafarians on charges of possession of dangerous drugs and violence. The Gong managed to escape during the raid, but was later apprehended and imprisoned for two years.

Upon his release from prison, Howell returned to rebuild Pinnacle. He moved it deeper into the countryside, and increased its security. Pinnacle thrived thereafter for over a decade, uninterrupted by any external force. It is said that during this time its members started wearing their hair in locks and referring to themselves as *Ethiopian warriors*. The years of peace enabled the community to establish its specific ceremonies and rituals, which laid the foundation and the first structure in the spirit of this new gospel.

Love Feasts of the Howellites

Like the Bedwardites, the Howellites also became a thorn in the side of the Jamaican colonial system under King George V and his Queen (Victoria) Mary. They declared that colonial rule must come to an end, and that Ras Tafari was the earth's rightful King and Redeemer. Needless to say, the government persecuted and crushed their communities; they imprisoned Howell in Bellevue Insane Asylum, calling him mad for declaring Haile Sellassie I *the Returned Messiah*.

> Dear inhabitants of this world, King Ras Tafari and Queen Omega are the foundation stones of the resurrection of the Kingdom of Ethiopia.
>
> Their prayer and labour for our resurrection is past finding out; no library in this world is able to contain the work of their hands for us, for they work both day and night for our deliverance.

As for this generation of the 20th century you and I have no knowledge how worlds are built and upon what trigger Kingdoms are set.

In King Alpha's Encyclopedia, He will explain to us all, how worlds are being built and upon what trigger Kingdoms are set on. He will also explain to us the capacities of generations.

Speaking for the Universe and the womanhood of man, Queen Omega, the Ethiopian Woman is the crown woman of this world. She hands us Her Rule-Book from the poles of Supreme Authority. She is the [Canon] Mistress of Creation.

King Alpha and Queen Omega are the Pay Masters of the world, Bible owners and money mint. Do not forget they are Black People if you please.

Owing to the Universal [trend] of our ancient and modern [Kingdoms], we are at this juncture of our history scattered over the globe into little sectional groups.

All our local bands throughout the globe are bent towards King Alpha's Royal Repository. The Royal Authority is to admit all Bands, Mission Camps, and Denominations into the supreme Royal Repository.

Queen Omega being the balming mistress of many worlds, she charges the powerhouse right now.

Ethiopia is the succeeding Kingdom of the Anglo-Saxon kingdom. A man of greater learning and a better Christian soul than King Alpha is not to be found on the face of the Globe. He makes the nation's hearts rejoice with raging joy, we give Him the glory. Ethiopia rulebook leads us into different departments of the kingdom; the records of the kingdom are with us unto this day. The Regulations point us to the basis of the kingdom.

Many will not see the truth, because they are spiritually blind. See Matthew 3:13. The woman of Samaria first refused to obey the request of our Lord because she was spiritually blind. But when the great Physician opened up her eyes and healed her infirmities concerning her many husbands in the city of Samaria, she found out that her first teachers of denominations throughout the state or country of Samaria were false. Then she cried aloud unto the inhabitants of the city and said, "Come see a man that told me all that I ever did and is not a native of Samaria but an Hebrew; is not this man the very Christ?." Our cities of today are inhabited with the same qualities of people as it was in the days of Jesus and the woman of Samaria.

Taken from Howell's The Promise Key,
"Ethiopia's Kingdom"

Leonard P. Howell wrote *The Promise Key*, the first literary work of Rastafari as a Faith, under his spiritual name, GangunGuru Maregh, which means *Teacher of Wisdom* in Sanskrit. *The Promise Key* clearly outlines the fundamental principles and perspectives from which the Rastafarians of today emerged, making it a most significant work of what can be called *Rastheology* or *Rastology*. *The Promise Key* clearly demonstrates that the accession of Ras Tafari, an African, to the Throne of King David manifests the Divinity of the Black Race; in doing so, *The Promise Key* gave birth to the philosophy of *Black Supremacy*. This was a fundamental tenet of early Rastafarians and is still very evident in the philosophies of some of the present houses of the movement. Father Howell can be called the first Rastafarian, and for his concept of Black Supremacy through African Divinity in the name of Ras Tafari he was persecuted more than almost any person. He spoke outrightly against the colonial government of Jamaica, declaring that Ras Tafari was the earth's rightful ruler and the King of all mankind.

In 1933, Howell was charged by the Jamaican government for making seditious remarks against His Majesty King George V of England, to the effect of blatant abuse, and contempt for the King who was sovereign over England and Jamaica. Howell was also charged with creating disaffection amongst the subjects of His Majesty by poisoning their minds against colonial rule. This was in reference to a speech Howell made at Seaforth, St. Thomas, Jamaica.

To the charge, he pleaded *Not guilty*, and he eventually appeared before the court of appeals. On cross-examination by H. M. Radcliff, assistant to the then-prosecuting Attorney General, Leonard Howell was asked: *Did you say anything about Ras Tafari?* To which he replied: *Yes, I told them to think of their King as Ras Tafari, King of Kings, Lord of Lords, Conquering Lion of the Tribe of Judah, Elect of God and Messiah of Love.*

In his address to the jury, Leonard Howell declared: *I know I am innocent. I was born a hero, and beyond a shadow of a doubt would die a hero defending my Race.* But the jury found him guilty and sentenced him to two years in prison.

Throughout his trials, and they were many, Father Howell and his followers stayed unshaken in their convictions about Haile Sellassie I as the second coming of *Christ* and fulfillment of the Promise. The very blueprint for Rastafari theology is therefore to be seen in *The Promise Key*, the theology of Howell, which he received, not through his private inspiration only, but as revealed in the Coronation of an Ethiopian Emperor and Empress in the Biblical line of David. This is what divided the *Howellites* from the *Christians* of their day, as it divides Rastafarians from Christians today.

Howell was released from prison in August 1936, and the Gong gathered his flock in Kingston, where he planned what he called a *love feast* celebrating his emancipation. As soon as he hoisted the red, gold and green Ethiopic banner, however, a brutal attack by the Jamaican constabulary (police force) brought the feast to an abrupt end. The flag and its pole were burnt to the ground. Food provisions and other goods of the group were confiscated. Participants were beaten and arrested. This was typical of the government's treatment of the early Rastafarians.

The *love feast* or *holy feast* was a common and customary practice of this unique group, especially for breaking their holy fasts. *The Promise Key* gives us this in the chapter on *How to Fast*:

> The King of Kings of Creation, the First and the Last, said: "Blessed are they that searcheth the deep things on the Tree of Life, for his wisdom is deep and is past all finding out." Thus said the living God and owner of life, to overcome white bondage and filth and black hypocrisy amongst your own black skin, you have to fast hard... Always have a basin of fine or coarse salt on your fast table as long as God is your ruler. When you break your fast...the elder will ask "Is it all well with thee?," everybody shall say together "All is well with me." Then the elder shall ask again "Who will bear a true witness for the Tree of Life?" All shall say, "By the living God I will."...
>
> Then everybody [shall] walk quietly and respectfully throw away the water, then come in and wash your hands and face in a basin of salt and water. Then break your real fast and be happy, feeling satisfied and revived and lovely. House to house fasting is very powerful; it

lifts the work and removes devils from homes of those in distress. Once a week for the general assembly is all right. A love feast every three or six months is needed... the misery of the land is healed by fasting.

This is very consistent with the tradition of the ancient Essenes, and specifically the *Therapeutae* of Egypt, who had a communal bread-breaking ceremony, which they also called the *holy feast*.

There is reason to see Leonard Howell, like Alexander Bedward, as a *mayalman*, a term which has come to be applied to devotees of any number of African-derived religions that developed among the slaves in Jamaica. *Mayalman* has its roots in the Asante word *myal* meaning *spirit*, so *mayalman* translates literally as *spirit-man*. *Obeahman* and *obeah worker* are additional terms used in Jamaica to describe the religious or quasi-religious roles played by herbalists, bush doctors and witch doctors, also known as sorcerers.

Europeans coined the term *black magic* to stigmatize this African spirituality. In fact, African people in the Diaspora were invoking the power of their ancestral spirits not for evil but to liberate themselves from the yoke of colonial slavery. In fear, the white man outlawed all forms of African spirituality, with the result that Africans up to the present live in slavish deference to taboos against such spiritual forms, especially forms that cut against the grain of colonial Christianity, into which most black people have been assimilated.

Obeah is the name for the tradition that calls forth the strongest taboos amongst the Jamaican population. Its roots are in the Asante word *obayifo*, which means *sorcerer*. The individuals called *obeah workers* were usually African-born slaves, who had the greatest knowledge of African rituals and rites of passage. With this knowledge, newly arrived slaves became *obeah* practitioners and a significant influence on their Creole brothers and sisters, both religiously and politically, since they agitated for many slave rebellions. Unrest among slaves led to the passage of oppressive legislation, such as a law in South Carolina in 1696 outlawing the assembling of large numbers of Africans on Sundays and holidays. This law required slave-owners to prevent *any drumming or meeting of any slave, not belonging to their own plantations, to rendezvous, feast, revel, beat drum, or cause any disturbance.*

From then on, Africans had to practice their religion under the guise of Christianity, in secret, as is evident in Pocomania, Voodoo, Santería, and other religious expressions of the African Diaspora.

Brother Joseph Natiel Hibbert: Patriarch of Rastafari

Another vanguard and founding father of the Rastafarians was *Brother Joseph Natiel Hibbert*, a Jamaican, who lived in Costa Rica for 20 years but returned to the island in 1931 to propagate his new convictions about Ras Tafari. During his years in Costa Rica, he became a devoted Garveyite, eventually becoming the president of the local branch of the U.N.I.A. Hibbert introduced African Freemasonry (most likely an affiliate of Prince Hall's[83] branch of Freemasonry) into Jamaica, overwhelming the European form of Freemasonry, which had outlawed such African writs and rites as voodoo, witchcraft and obeah. In 1924, he formed the *Ethiopian Mystic Masons*, aligning them with the *Ethiopian World Federation*, turning it into a Masonic movement that in turn gave birth to

---

[83] Prince Hall is known as the father of Black Masonry in the West. He was born free on one of the British Caribbean islands circa 1748. His father was an Englishman and his mother a free woman of color, of French Creole background. He educated himself and became quite literate, taking a deep interest in the abolitionist movement, and would later be one of the few blacks that fought at Bunker Hill. Based on racist attitudes towards people of color, the already established white Freemasonry Lodges were not prepared to become brothers with blacks by vowing any obligation to them as lodge members. In 1784 therefore Prince Hall developed a branch of Freemasons in North America, bearing his name, made up primarily of Blacks. The laws and principles drafted by Hall became some of the first laws of government for freed Africans. Some of these principles were obviously influential on progressive thinkers of the time like Garvey, Howell, Hibbert and other founding fathers of the Rastafarian movement.

the *African Descendants United Association*. Hibbert incorporated an Ethiopic influence into Freemasonry, drawing on the literary sources of the Ethiopic Masonic traditions of old, and spurring the development of a parallel Judaic Kabalistic movement among Africans. He became one of the founding fathers of Rastafari. Hibbert too, was eventually arrested and declared insane as other vanguards of the Faith were.

The connection between the Essenes and the Rastafarians can be seen in the allegiance and alignment of both groups with *Christ*. Ancient Essenism was essentially mystic Christianity, as is Rastafari. As previously stated, the Essenes emerged at a time when one age was giving way to another, when the old dispensation was being replaced and replenished by the new, and Essenes and Rastas alike were a part of both, being strict observers of the esoteric teachings of Moses living in the love of *Christ*.

Brother Henry Archibald Dunkley: Patriarch of Rastafari

Brother Henry Archibald Dunkley was, like Garvey and Howell, a seaman, who, like Garvey, worked on the boats of the United Fruit Company. He left the sea in 1930 and returned to Jamaica, convicted of Haile Sellassie I as the *Black Christ*, the King of Kings, the Returned Anointed. He preached a form of Christianity that was highly influenced by Judaism, becoming the third inaugurator and cultivator of the Ethiopic Messianic conviction in Jamaica.

He studied the Bible and interpreted its message to conclude that Haile Sellassie I was truly the redeemer of the downtrodden black masses. A whole new value system evolved out of this conviction, with a new perspective and a better hope for African redemption. Although from early days he saw Ras Tafari as the *Christ*, it was later in his life that he came to accept Him as the Almighty God. It is this view that truly distinguishes full-fledged conviction in the new Faith of Rastafari.

King Emmanuel

To the imperial and colonial government, these three revolutionists had one threatening thing in common, and that is a complete surrender to another sovereign, who was Biblical and African in origin. Imagine the threat that a *Black Messiah* posed to colonial minds. The magnitude of the threat was matched by the magnitude of the persecution meted out to these first pioneers of the Rastafari Faith. They should rightly be called saints, because many, too numerous to count, have been martyred for their devotion to this *New Way*.

King Emmanuel: The High Priest

One of the most prominent Rastafarian leaders in the shantytown, Back-O-Wall[84] days, was known as (Prince or King Emmanuel) Charles Edwards. In 1958, he organized a twenty-one-day convention known as a *Groundation* in an effort to *organize and centralize* Rastafari as a body. This gathering was the first of its kind. The scope of this Groundation gave the Jamaican public a taste of what had been quietly brewing under the oppressive vise of the British colonial system. He was able during his lifetime to build the strongest of the Rasta "tabernacles" ("houses" or "mansions" — sects), and he is the patriarch who is currently most influential among the many up-and-coming young Rastafarians.

Emmanuel was severely persecuted and prosecuted by the Jamaican government for his twenty-one-day Groundation vigil. The police raided his compound shortly after the gathering ended. He was arrested and the camp burned to the ground. After his highly publicized trial, however, he was released, and returned victorious to reconstruct his community. In 1966,

---

84 Back-O-Wall, later renamed Tivoli Gardens, is a shanty town in rural West Kingston where the poor have-nots make a life for themselves in abject poverty and foment political unrest. Constant persecution and destruction of their camps by the Jamaican Police Force caused many early Rastafarian brethrens to seek refuge in Back-O-Wall, which became more or less a central rallying point for them. However, the government got weary of the goings on at the Back-O-Wall settlement, and on the morning of July 12, 1966 the order was given for "Operation Bulldoze and Burn," a government clean-up program, to be put in effect. Several bulldozers and a regiment of 250 police officers assembled, and destroyed Back-O-Wall.

however, the Jamaican government destroyed the Back-O-Wall shanty communities of rural Kingston, leaving many Rastafarian families homeless. Many returned to the countryside, but most assimilated into the general population of Kingston and tried hard to survive in the very system they so opposed. Emmanuel soon founded a new center of operations at Bull Bay (see below). King Emmanuel developed the first established priesthood community in Rastafari according to the theological blueprint of *The Promise Key*. His efforts to *organize and centralize* the spiritual nation of the Rastafarians into a physical organ led to his higher vocation working for the repatriation and restoration of African victims of the European slave trade, whom, he said, the British held captive in the Diaspora.

He founded his Church upon the principles of the *Church Triumphant*, Howell's archetypal church, which was based upon the supremacy of blackness revealed in the Divinity of Haile Sellassie I. For him, the Church Triumphant was the *right* and *true* Church for black people worldwide, and the Roman Catholic Church was the seat of the devil. He was a strong and devout believer in salvation through Yahowshua ha Mashiakh, but his theology embraced a Mosaic interpretation of the teachings of *Christ*. In his lifetime, he lived out the *Christ* life, defending the poor and the fatherless, in a communal *livity* based in part on the New Testament, but even more on the Old Testament. The Sabbath, for example, was observed with the strictest discipline. Absolutely no work in any form was done, except for the chanting of praises and all that that entails. White robe and turban were mandatory for all priests and priestesses within the camp.

In 1966, when Haile Sellassie I came to Jamaica, He found Himself face to face with the High Priest of the people that bore witness to Him. Dressed in a long red robe with the Bobo Shanti trademark head wrap, arrayed with medals and brooches; a long red, gold, and green sash dangling over his shoulders; and wearing white gloves, he bowed and shook the Emperor's hand. One can only imagine what Haile Sellassie I's impression may have been of this remarkable character who worshipped Him as *Christ*. There is something very significant about those two individuals being in the same place at the same time, a mystery that can be unraveled only by grasping his life's work, a work he accomplished in the years from 1960 to 1981, after which he left this dimension of life.

Nine miles outside the city of Kingston, in the parish of St. Thomas, at a place called Bull Bay, the small monastic community of Rastafarians founded by Emmanuel, known as Bobo Shanti or Bobo Ashanti, sits today, nestled against the rocky mountainside.

King Emmanuel accomplished far more in his lifetime than most men ever do. He did this with no formal education and without ever leaving the shores of Jamaica, having declared he would never take flight on the *iron bird* invented by *Babylon*. With little education and no wealth, he carved out a unique space in the history of Jamaica and the Rastafarians.

It is written that *a prophet is never honored* in his own time, or *in his own country*, by his peers. This cliché, however, could not be applied to King Emmanuel, later to be known as Melkizadek, and the Living Black *Christ*, sent, some Bobos asserted, by Haile Sellassie I to establish His Church in Jamaica. The Bobo Shanti know him as the Living God, a functioning part of the Godhead inseparable from Haile Sellassie I.

This People

CHAPTER 12

THE RASTAFARIANS: THE ESSENES REINCARNATED

Rastafarians as the Essenes Reincarnated

> For Zion's sake will I not hold my peace, and for Jerusalem's sake I will not rest, until the righteousness thereof go forth as brightness, and the salvation thereof as a lamp that burneth. And the Gentiles shall see thy righteousness, and all kings thy glory; and thou shalt be called by a new name, which the mouth of the Lord shall name... Behold, the Lord hath proclaimed unto the end of the world, Say ye to the daughter of Zion, Behold, thy salvation cometh; behold, his reward is with him, and his work before him. And they shall call them, The holy people, The redeemed of the Lord: and thou shalt be called Sought out, A city not forsaken.
>
> Isaiah ch. 62

> ...This people have I formed for myself; they shall show forth my praise.
>
> Isaiah ch. 43, v. 21

The Rastafarian movement is an eccentric indigenous Jamaican sub-sect within the multicultural but generally Christian population of Jamaica. The conviction that Haile Sellassie I, the last Ethiopian Emperor, is the manifest second coming of Christ, is the single most distinctive mark of a Rastafarian. The second most distinctive mark, and the most obvious sign of conviction, is the matted tufts of hair called dreadlocks (which, as discussed above, have been and remain distinctive of Nazarites generally).

Just about any Rastafarian will refer to his/her locks as their "covenant," a holy seal between the individual and Haile Sellassie I. In this chapter, our discussion of Rastafari as a people, we will look closely at the fundamental belief system planted by the early pioneers of this Faith, and into how Rastafarians from the beginning have aligned with the ancient Essenes. Exploring and expounding on the traditions and ideals of the early vanguards, discussed in the previous chapter, will give us a clearer perspective of where Rastafari came from and how it has progressed, helping us to understand the essence of this movement. Once this is established, one will be able to see without obstruction the past, present and future function of this mystic group. The journey will take us on the paths of bygone sages to identify the Rastafarians, through their ascetic lifestyle, and in the name of Haile Sellassie I, as the reincarnated souls and body of the ancient Essenes. The present writings are the first of their kind. They glean world history to put the mundane into a new perspective; by so doing they will trigger deeper insights into Rastafarian beginnings.

Beliefs are fundamental identifiers of any group. Religions and other organizations throughout the ages have evolved out of specific belief systems. In looking at the ancient Essenes and at their origins, evolution and beliefs, one can see definite parallels to those of the Rastafarian Faith. It may be discerned from the evidence available that the Rastafarians are indeed the reincarnated souls of the ancient Essenes, manifesting as the fulfillment of Essene prophecy in the present dispensation.

A brief outline of the twelve fundamental distinguishing characteristics of the ancient Essenes points to:

1. Messianism
2. The Doctrine of the Two Mashiakhs

3. The Nazarite Vow
4. Vegetarianism
5. Water Baptism
6. Fasting
7. Sabbatarianism
8. Melkizadek Order
9. Mother-Father God
10. Tree of Life consciousness
11. The Apocalypse
12. White Robe and Turban priest- and priestess-hood

These words of the Essene Prophet Malachi, taken from *The Holy Megillah,* illustrate the parallel between the first-century Essenes and the Rastafarians of today:

> ...The Davidic bloodline, corrupted by the influence of the animal sacrifice cult, shall be returned to righteousness. For the Conquering Lion will conquer Himself; yea, for the first time ever, a temporal king will dethrone himself in favor of the Spiritual King. And all the accomplishments of his temporal life will be as nothing compared to this one act; for the self-dethronement of the last King of the Davidic bloodline will bring to an end the legitimate authority of any temporal kings or rulers on earth who do not do likewise, and will establish a New Way: self-chosen submission to the Kingship and Queenship of Yahowshua and Miriam, our Lord and Lady.
>
> All people, the rulers and the ruled, the rich and the poor, shall be called to that New Way. And many of the ruled will accept the New Way, but few of the rulers. And the ruled who accept the New Way shall nonviolently withdraw their allegiance from the rulers who accept not the New Way; yea, their allegiances shall be given over to Yahowshua and Miriam and the Church founded on their gospel. And that

New Way will be planted like a mustard seed when the words of this prophecy are declared unto the people who have gathered in the name of the Conquering Lion.

The Rastafarians are the only people to date who have gathered in the name of the Conquering Lion of Judah, the biological specimen of the seed of David called by the name of Haile Sellassie I. The true nature of the New Way spoken of by Malachi, in the light of the New Gospel, is manifest in the Rastafarians, and most especially in the Essene Nazarite Monastic Order of Melkizadek.

Our power of recognition, formed by our culture and training, enables us to identify the precise fulfillment of specific prophecies. This is not to say that Divine apparitions are known only through one's philosophies and beliefs — *I know the blasphemy of them which say they are Jews, and are not, but are the synagogue of Satan* (Rev. ch. 2, v. 9) — but one's faith is born in a definite belief system, and prophecies and fulfillment are known from this faith.

Prophetical fulfillment is a Divine phenomenon arising from the spirit of foresight, and is the energy that shapes the ages. The prophet represents the voice of God as the herald of events to come known from past records and present happenings. Every prophet is a mystic, judge, priest or priestess of the Order that is, that was and that is to come; therefore the mystics of all ages are always present through the power of reincarnation. Within the incarnated soul of the mystic lies the power of purification, of change, which is manifest in a process specific to one's system of beliefs. This change introduces a new faculty of interpretation. The power of purification is the agent of transformation, which is what is needed to reform and reconstruct the present system. Every prophet to date has illustrated this fact, especially such significant figures as Yahowshua ha Mashiakh and Haile Sellassie I.

> So through many changes must ye be made perfect, as it is written in the Book of Job: I am a wanderer, changing

place after place and house after house, until I come unto the city and mansion which is eternal.

> Yahowshua ha Mashiakh in
> *The Essene New Testament*

Where are we to look for our survival, for the answers to the questions, which have never before been posed? We must look, first, to the Almighty God who has raised man above the animals and endowed him with intelligence and reason. We must put our faith in Him, that He will not desert us or permit us to destroy humanity, which He created in His image. We must look into ourselves, into the depths of our soul. We must become something we have never been, and for which our education and experience and environment have ill-prepared us. We must become bigger than we have been, more courageous, greater in spirit, larger in outlook. We must become members of a new race, owing our ultimate allegiance not to nations, but to our fellow men within the human community.

— Haile Sellassie I

Messianic Consciousness: The Uprising

In Enid Smith's article about the Rosicrucians, she states:

> *The Freemasons find pure Christianity in Essenism and consider the "Brethrens of the White Clothing", or the Mystic Order of Essenes, to be the most important fraternity the world has ever seen.*

This statement is also true for *the Essene Nazarite Monastic Order of Melkizadek,* who are the truest example of the Rastafarians today. Although the Order functions from no visible, organized physical center, and has no organized system of initiation, it is nevertheless the most important Order in this dispensation.

As we have made clear ever since Chapter 2, the concept of a Messiah did not originate with the Jews. It was the Hebrews however who first established themselves as a messianic order, a people awaiting a Messiah. The Messiah fulfills Divine prophecy and confirms the order as a Divine theocratic manifestation. Thus a Messianic monotheistic culture was cultivated in Hebraic-Judaic theology, which always awaits a Messiah.

Messianic movements are often seen as millenarian, in that the cycle of prophetical fulfillment expresses itself in a thousand-year period. Christianity, by acknowledging Yahowshua as this Divine manifestation of the Godhead, fulfills the criteria for a messianic order, which sprang out of Judaism and took on the substance of Judaic theology. In the present time, the Rastafarians appear to be the fulfillment of the tradition inherited by the Christian messianic order, with their conviction that Haile Sellassie I is the Messiah. This means that the Rastafarians represent a mystical vibration in total alignment with the messianic prophecies of the ancient Essenes.

A messianic group is built upon its faith in the God of prophecy and the principle of Divine incarnation. In this context, the Rastafarians, like the ancient Essenes, are in their morphogenesis the truest examples of a messianic movement. By studying the beliefs and dogmas of the ancient Essenes, we see a clear though mystical parallel with the Rastafarians of Jamaica. When the beliefs of the two groups are juxtaposed, it becomes apparent they are a single body, the substance of the prophetical Universal Messianic Church.

Nazarites Today

The Nazarites, (as we discussed beginning on p. 42) can be broken down into two basic groups. The first is what we term the

Birthright Nazarites, who took their vows through their mothers via Divine intervention. Samson, Samuel, John the Baptist, and Yahowshua were Nazarites consecrated in this way.

> And the angel of the Lord appeared unto the woman, and said unto her, Behold now, thou art barren, and bearest not: but thou shall conceive and bear a son. Now therefore beware, I pray thee and drink not wine nor strong drink, and eat not any unclean thing: for, lo, thou shalt conceive, and bear a son; and no razor shall come on his head: for the child shall be a Nazarite unto God from the womb: and he shall begin to deliver Israel from out of the hands of the Philistine…And the woman bare a son and called his name Samson: and the child grew, and the Lord blessed him. And the spirit of the Lord began to move him at times in the camp of Dan between Zorah and Eshtaol.
>
> Judges ch. 13

> And it came to pass, when she pressed him daily with her words, and urged him, so that his soul was vexed unto death; that he told her all his heart, and said unto her, There hath not come a razor upon mine head; for I have been a Nazarite unto God from my mother's womb: if I be shaven, then my strength will go from me, and I shall become weak and become like any other man… And she made him sleep upon her knees; and she called for a man, and she caused him to shave off the seven locks of his head; and she began to afflict him, and his strength went from him…

> But the Philistines took him, and put out his eyes, and brought him down to Gaza, and bound him with fetters of brass; and he did grind in the prison house.

However the hair of his head began to grow again after he was shaven...And Samson called unto the Lord, and said, O Lord God, remember me, I pray thee, and strengthen me, I pray thee, only this once, O God, that I may be once avenged for the Philistines for my two eyes...And Samson said Let me die with the Philistines. And he bowed himself with all his might; and the house fell upon all the people that were therein. So the dead which he slew at his death were more than that which he slew in his life.

Judges ch. 16

The second group of Nazarites is those who consecrate themselves by virtue of personal tribulation or direct revelation from the Spirit. A period of at least forty days of fasting and abstinence in the wilderness was standard procedure for this type of Nazarite. These could be called *Temple Nazarites,* due to the fact that their initiation into Nazariteship came with all the basic ordinances stated in Numbers ch. 6: *And the Lord spake unto Moses saying, Speak unto the children of Israel, and say unto them, when either men or women shall separate themselves to vow a vow of a Nazarite, to separate themselves unto the Lord ... all the days of the vow of his separation there shall no razor come upon his head: until the days be fulfilled, in the which he separated himself unto the Lord, he shall be holy, and shall let the locks of the hair of his head grow.*

This type of covenant was traditionally made before a priest and in the presence of a witness. It was also necessary to sacrifice animals as a trespass offering as stipulated by the laws governing the vow. If for any reason he defiled himself by exposing himself to anything dead, the Mosaic law of the Nazarite required that his head be shaved.

To say that Nazarites can be broken down into two basic groups is not to disclaim that within these two groups variations exist.

The Rastaman

In the Bible, many different vows were made and there were numerous reasons why they were made the way they were. To have *a vow*, as the scriptures sometimes put it, as in Acts ch. 18, v. 18, oftentimes means that the individual is a Nazarite. Not all vows make one a Nazarite, but all Nazarites carry the vow of the covenant; and this covenant always takes the form of coils of matted hair, which distinguished the Nazarite vow from the many other vows of the ancient Hebrews.

> And he put forth the form and of a hand, and took me by a lock of my head; and the spirit lifted me up between the earth and the heaven, and brought me in the visions of God to Jerusalem.
>
> Ezekiel ch. 8, v. 3

In the days when judges ruled the people of Israel, a covenant of locks was the outstanding sign of every judge, setting them apart from every other man. This tradition was mimicked by Europeans and is evident in British governmental bodies, where the magistrates wear wigs of judgment as a symbol of their official rank as judges. The term *bigwig* has its roots in the wig-wearing practice of European imperial authorities. For the judges of Israel, the covenant of locks was an insignia of high moral and spiritual conduct. The prophet and mystic Samuel, who was the last to judge Israel under Mosaic Law, handed Israel over to a new era of judgment, in which the judge rules as king under the covenant of a crown. Henceforth, all the judges of Israel who sat on the royal Throne wore the new covenant, the crown. Since Haile Sellassie I wears a crown, he does not wear the covenant of locks, but those who bear witness to Him do, in a spiritual covenant called livity by Rastas. After the accession of kings in Israel, the Nazarites, however, continued to exist, their locks a judgment and a reminder of the Law, especially to the corrupt kings that were to rule over Israel. Elijah was a prophet of this type, the forerunner of many others that were to come.

The Re-emergence of the Mystics

What we know of *Jesus Christ* is from the scriptures; outside of scripture, not much has been written about Him. Hence, the life of *Jesus* has become for many a mere Bible story, understood like other stories as Bible mythology. Yet the writings of the canonical Gospels have been questioned and challenged by comparative religion scholars, based upon recent archeological findings.

Ancient mythology is not to be taken literally, and as such we cannot be sure, outside of hard evidence, that we are not mistaking antiquated metaphors and mythologies pertaining to Christ for historical facts. There must therefore be some way for each generation to confirm their faith with evidence that whatever is recorded in ancient history is remembered correctly as history and is not just myth. The doctrine of the physical and spiritual incarnation of *Christ* is affirmed both by Orthodox/Catholic and or Oriental Eastern/Esoteric Christianity. Since we reject the complete reliability and authenticity of the available scriptural writings, the Bible lacks an interpretation that lends itself to the skeptical rationalistic minds of today. Therefore, to both schools of Christianity, it is a matter of very real importance that the lineage and history of *Jesus* be firmly established, in terms of a Divine incarnation in an organic structure.

Numerous groups and communities have, in an effort to live out the example of the ancient gnosis, internalized aspects of the Essene daily communions of the Tree of Life (as explained below). There are also a variety of Christian-oriented mystery schools and philosophical societies that have found a need to employ Essenian theological teachings and rites in their dogmas and lifestyles. They would claim to be actively involved in what is called The *Great Preparation* for the return, the second coming of the Christ. Throughout history, the ages have been strewn with both blatant and sublime influences from the Essenes. The group most aligned with the cosmic vibration of these early Christians is the Rastafarians.

> Yea, the Essene Nasarean messianic prophecies will all come to pass, albeit in three stages. Behold: The first stage is the coming of the Priestly Mashiakh with the Holy Spirit at His side; they shall lay the foundation for all that follows. Then, toward the end of the age inaugurated by the Priestly Mashiakh, the second stage begins: a Kingly Mashiakh, the seed of David through Solomon and the Ethiopian woman, comes forth... And He shall be a Conquering Lion...
>
> *The Holy Megillah: Nasarean Bible of the Essene Way*

In terms of beliefs, the Rastafarians have long accepted two messiahs, Yahowshua, as the Priestly Messiah, and Haile Sellassie I, as the Kingly Messiah.

The Ordinances of the True Church

The gathering of the one hundred and forty-four thousand (144,000) reincarnated souls is a major spiritual development that must take place in this age. In this organized effort, ancient wisdom will be reintroduced to the general public, wisdom that has been lost in obscurity for centuries. This organ will exist to promote the universal kinship of humanity under the Fatherhood and Motherhood of the Almighty God. Compared to the many other groups that are presently preparing for the re-emergence of a Kingly *Christ*, Rastafarians are set apart as unique in that they have accepted the Biblically prophesied Christ returned in the Glory of Ethiopia. Rastafarians are evidently the Way-Keepers of today.

> And one of the elders answered, saying unto me, What are these which are arrayed, in white robes? And whence

The Gathering

came they? And I said unto him, Sir, thou knowest. And he said to me, These are they which came out of great tribulation, and have washed their robes, and made them white in the blood of the Lamb. Therefore are they before the throne of God, and serve him day and night in his temple: and he that sitteth on the throne shall dwell among them.

Rev. ch. 7, vv. 13-15

Metaphysically, this body of people, who know the name of the One revealed as the Kingly Mashiakh, who will usher in the age of the Divine Mother Omega, represent the Church. The *True Church of Christ* in our time will be sounding this message, engaging in a worldwide mission of delivering to all nations and to peoples everywhere the truth, the whole truth of the gospel, and the particular truth about the Lord's return. This Church was founded on the principle of *Christ* in the *new name*, through the Two Witnesses who are at the right and left hand of the Throne of God. *Many are called, few are chosen.* (Matthew ch. 22, v. 14). Rastafari is the body of those called, and it is from them that this chosen group has come to prepare the Way of the Glory of the Mother.

The power of recognition is one of the greatest powers given to us as humans. Recognition gives us a basis on which to come to conclusions and make decisions affecting the quality of our lives. To recognize the *New Gospel Church* is the duty of those peculiar people who have chosen to share in the shaping and development of human salvation. This is the loftiest privilege granted to the children of the earth in any age.

The Church was revealed as a woman clothed with the glory of the sun (Rev. ch. 12, v. 1). In the Ethiopian-Italian conflict, we saw the attempts of earthly rulers to destroy the tabernacle of the King of Kings. The Church fled from them into the wilderness to escape the persecution of Rome, later to be gathered together as the remnant of Israel.

This gathering of the dispersed will indeed be *The Church*, the Daughter of Zion, and Mother through the birth of the Son, the King of Kings. Zion as the Mother will be the giver of the traditions of the New Way. All the tests prescribed by the Bible for the fulfillment of prophecy have been met in the years between 1935 and 1941 in Ethiopia. As a consequence, this manifestation has been demonstrated to be the restoration of the genuine life of the Biblical *Christ* in our day. Through supreme tests, fidelity to the Bible, and loyalty to the Lord, Yahowshua has been felt in all that Ethiopia has done. She has been loyal to all that He taught, to all that He is and to all that He is to become. As Zion, the whole tendency of Her life is to exalt Her savior, to glorify Him, to lead the multitudes to Him. She has been unfalteringly true to the historic *Christ* and Christianity, not departing from the at-one-ment, His Divine pre-existence, His Divine incarnation, or His Divinity through the Divine Mother. In the Monophysite theology of Ethiopia, His Divine and human nature are eternally one.

It would appear that the Rastafarians represent a preservation and purification of the anciency of Christian Ethiopia, our Mother. Jamaica, the *Daughter of Zion* by giving birth unto the Rastafarians, is actually paving the way for the resurrection of the Mother, through the consciousness of the Father Haile Sellassie I as the First Principle.

The Rastafarians, Ethiopians in exile, represent the restoration of true Christian dignity to the world, through the ancient precepts made practical in the Kingly Mashiakh. We read in Genesis ch. 49, vv. 10-11 of the blessing Father Israel gave his sons:

> The scepter shall not depart from Judah, nor a lawgiver from between his feet, until Shiloh come; and unto him

shall the gathering of the people be. Binding his foal unto the vine, and his ass's colt unto the choice vine...

In Israel's blessing, we see that the scepter shall eventually depart from Judah, but not until Shiloh comes. (*Shiloh* in Hebrew means: *to whom it belongs*.) When He comes, He will take the scepter and seal it immediately, closing one door while opening another. Shiloh, in His fulfillment as the Kingly Mashiakh, being from the line of Judah, has taken the rod of David and given it to the people of Zion in the form of a written constitution, thereby putting an end to the line of the literal King of Judah in Ethiopia. So the scepter has departed, but only after having been sealed in the name of the Elect.

The above verse says: *unto Him, shall the gathering of the people be, binding His foal unto the vine and His ass's colt unto the choice vine*. It is because of the falling away from the true teachings of Yahowshua ha Mashiakh, *the vine*, that his followers have been cut off from the source, and mankind has been denied the salvation which comes through the experience of the *Christ* life. Therefore, a need arises for the redemption unto salvation that Yahowshua represented.

Metaphysically, Shiloh is the Good Shepherd King, who symbolizes redemption unto salvation in *Christ*. In binding His *foal*, which is the nation he leads into greener pastures of *Christ*-consciousness, the Good Shepherd becomes the *choice vine*, the *elect*. The *ass's colt* is symbolic of the ass ridden into Jerusalem by the about-to-be crucified *Christ*; only this time the *ass's colt* is the body, the Church, that carries the head, which is Shiloh Himself, the *choice vine*. This *choice vine* also represents the *New Way* to which the *Witness* and the *ass's colt* are eternally bound. This elect body of people, the body of the Rastafarians, has gathered in the spirit of the *new wine*, from the *choice vine*, fulfilling ancient Essenian prophecies.

It is in the name of Haile Sellassie I that Ethiopia and the continent of Africa were united; also it was from Him that the Rastafarians did rise, bearing witness that His Imperial Majesty exemplifies in word and deed the life of Yahowshua ha Mashiakh. Biblically, this example fulfills the witness that the Father shall bear unto the Son:

> However when he, the spirit of truth, is come, he will guide you into all truth: for he shall not speak of himself; but whatsoever he shall hear, that shall he speak: and he will show you things to come. He shall glorify me: for he shall receive of mine, and shall show it unto you. All things that the father hath are mine: therefore said I, that he shall take of mine, and shall show it unto you. A little while, and ye shall not see me: and again, a little while, and ye shall see me, because I go to the father.
>
> Yahowshua speaking to His disciples
> in the Gospel of John ch. 16, vv. 13-16

This is the promise upon which all Christian messianic movements are based. In the wake of this New Gospel of the Second Coming, the Rastafarians arise as the true covenant-keepers in a mystery that perplexes some of the most brilliant minds of the theosophical societies. From the ancient prophecies we can determine that Ethiopia played a very important and sacred role for the Essenes, as it has for the Rastafarians, the only people who see Ethiopia as the Biblically prescribed Zion, the garden paradise of Eden, the Promised Land. This perspective, far beyond rational understanding and intellectual articulation, has been something of a mystery to spectators in terms of Rastafarian convictions about Ethiopia as Zion and Haile Sellassie I as the Almighty.

Vegetarianism

Vegetarianism is one radical practice found among the Howellites and Rastafarians from the beginning. I say radical because flesh-eating has long been habitual for the general public in Jamaica, even for some Seventh-Day Adventists (although consumption of pigs was strictly forbidden for them). Some Rasta brothers would not use leather in any form, even to put goatskin on their drums. All animal by-products were outlawed as *deadas*,[85] and were forbidden in every form, especially for use as something sacred, as in drum making.

Ital, pronounced (i-tol), is taken from the English word *vital* and means *pure, natural* and *unrefined*. Ital can be used to indicate clean rather than unclean, or healthy rather than unhealthy. Terminology like this originated in Jamaica among the Rastafarians in the early nineteen-thirties.

The word *ital* was formed by the common practice of Rastas of dropping the first syllable of a word and replacing it with *I*. This practice brought into being a new vocabulary; it created a language within a language: e.g., create — ireate, universe — iniverse, spirit — irit, meditate — ititate, vital — ital etc. *Ital* is to the Rastafarians what Kosher is to the Jews and Halal is to the Muslims. It is the natural way of Rasta. *Ital* is a consciousness that dictates the discipline that Rastas call *livity*.

In the theology of Rastafari, human carnivorous appetite arises from a fallen nature, steeped in unconsciousness of self or of the environment. In contrast, the *Italist* knowledge of self empowers them to educate themselves about herbs and botanicals and the benefits thereof. When we are better developed, our awareness of the connection between self and environment forbids us the killing of fellow animals for food. The intelligent choice, the one that creates minimal impact on the environment, is eating consciously of non-Genetically Modified Organism (GMO) herbs, nuts, fruits, grains, legumes, roots and vegetables; this has been an age-old tradition of the Rastafarians. The foundation of these

---

85 *Deadas* is the Rastafarian term that refers to any animal flesh that is eaten or used in any way.

botanical principles is, according to Rastas, the *Ital* consciousness of the prefallen nature.

Like the early Essenes, the Rastafarians are non-conformists who rebelled against the clergy, the government and the corrupt. As a reclusive movement, Rastafarian campsites spread out through the countryside as well as the shantytowns of Kingston, and to those youths newly convicted of the Rastafari faith, would retreat after being condemned by their parents and the society at large. Such youths were seen as non-ambitious, black-hearted madmen with no place in the newly developing middle-class colonial society. The salutation of *Peace and love*, as well as *One heart*, were the greetings of this distinctive sect, with the symbolic two-finger hand gesture for peace. *Hail I* is also a popular greeting and can still be heard in almost all circles. Peace and Love are the essence of this fear inducing, dreadlocked and *black-hearted* group.

In *The Holy Megillah*, Yahowshua prophesied:

> ...And His bread will be the Essene Nasarean scriptures, His drink, the Essene Nazarite disciplines. Yea, the Priestly Mashiakh will then make the Lion who conquered Himself into a living immortal: for He must live long to fulfill His mission. Behold, His mission: when 144,000 Essene Nazarites are made ready through the Essene Nasarean scriptures, the Kingly Mashiakh will reveal Himself in Egypt and call the 144,000 unto Him. The Immortal Lion will lead them in a Great Walk back to His homeland, Ethiopia, where He will sit upon His throne. And He will restore the paradise of Eden to Ethiopia and all the world, with help from the 144,000. And He will prepare the world to receive the Divine Mother, the Holy Spirit; for the Lion will prepare the world to greet Her with great joy, even the same world that rejected Her upon Her first coming in flesh...This will be the third stage of the messianic manifestation.

Behold: by the end of Her thousand-year reign, ushered in by Him, the earth will have become an angelic realm; human beings will have become baby angels! I tell you truly, the first stage of the messianic manifestation is now upon you; yea, it is right before your eyes!

We can search all of Christendom, asking: Where are the Nazarite mystics today? Where are the consecrated dreadlocked ascetics in the assembly of the Christian Church? We have looked for them in Western Christianity and they could not be found; but we have found them in Ethiopia, in the mountains of Gondar and Lalibela. They can be seen amongst the rocks and caves, living out their lifetime devotion unto Yahowshua ha Mashiakh. With matted tufts of hair, draping down their shoulders and backs, the Bahtawis (hermits) are the living example of the Christian mystics of the ages gone by. As Nazarite Nazarenes, they have given us the truest pattern of Essenian lifestyle to date.

The main difference between Rastafarians and Bahtawis is that, for the Rastafarians, Haile Sellassie I is the second coming of the Mashiakh. Despite this major difference, the similarities between the two make them often indistinguishable when seen together. Thus, like the Bahtawis, the Rastafarians succeed the Nazarite Nazarenes, by walking in the light of the Son and in the name of the Father, Haile Sellassie I, who has led them to the bosom of Mother Divine, His Bride, His Empress and the Mother of His children.

The Tree of Life

Gifted with the power of choice, humanity now embodies the Tree of the Knowledge of Good and Evil. As such, humanity is caught in the world of duality, and thus in a perpetual struggle with the so-called good and evil forces within. Among the fruits of the Tree of Knowledge is the awareness of evil, which in the end brings forth the experience of death and hellish realms. But another fruit of the Tree of Knowledge is the comprehension of

THE FRUITFUL ESSENE TREE OF LIFE
With the Morning and Evening Communions

good, which is the basis of hope for oneness through redemption, and for the possibility that all humankind will ultimately return by choice to the Tree of Life. The Essenes practiced devotions of communion with the Tree of Life which realigned them with the consciousness of their Divine birth. This is what is meant by *at-one-ment*, which comes through continuous consciousness of the good forces of the universe. In the science of *Rastheology*, the mystical vibrations of the medicinal *Cannabis sativa* plant, an herb commonly called *ganja*, which Rastas smoke as a sacrament, represent the Tree of Life.

The Tree of Life is believed to have seven branches, which represent the seven locks of the Nazarite, of which Samson's seven locks are an example; the seven seals of Revelation; and the seven branches of the menorah or branches of light. It is worth noting that in Kabbalistic systems the Tree of Life is at the core of Messianic consciousness.

The Fruitful Essene Tree of Life represents fourteen positive forces, seven of them heavenly or cosmic forces, and seven earthly or terrestrial forces. Along with its seven branches, the Tree is pictured as having seven roots descending into the earth, representing the water, the life force within the Earth Mother. Its seven branches likewise ascend toward the heavens, representing flames of fire, the life force of the Heavenly Father. Thus the tree symbolizes humanity's relationship to male and female as well as to earth and heaven.

Each root and branch of the Tree represents a different force or power. The roots represent the earthly forces and powers of (1) the Earthly Mother and Her Angels: (2) Earth, (3) Life, (4) Joy, (5) Sun, (6) Water, and (7) Air. The seven branches represent the cosmic powers of the (1) Heavenly Father and His Angels of: (2) Eternal Life, (3) Creative Work, (4) Peace, (5) Power, (6) Love, and (7) Wisdom. These were the angels of the visible and invisible worlds.

It is evident from *The Promise Key* that the Tree of Life was of great significance to Founding Father of Rastafari Leonard P. Howell. In their rites of fasting, the Howellites vowed to bear witness to the Tree of Life. For them the Tree of Life represented the seven-fold Peace Path of the ancient Essenes, as refined and depicted above, which is a seven-day cycle of conscious meditation on the elements that govern the created order, and which embodied their communions with the Heavenly Father and the Earthly Mother. Every Essene devotee lived out his/her discipline day by day through this Peace Path. In the consciousness of the Rastafarian, every individual Rastafarian is the *Tree of Life planted by the rivers of water, which bringeth forth fruits in due season, whose* locks, symbolic of *leaves, shall not wither.*[86] The Tree of Life, in fact, is the Pre-Adamic consciousness that stands in the midst of the garden, in the earthly paradise, beyond duality. Rastafari, the Way, the tradition, and the culture, is the path by which we have come into this light. Thus the ancient Essenes and the Essenes incarnated today both practiced similar devotions of communion with the Tree of Life.

The fruitful Tree of Life represents the Divine Feminine consciousness, and ultimately, self-sufficiency. The nursing mother in a very practical way manifests the Tree of Life, which *brings forth her fruits in due season*. This is a universal icon, one present throughout the centuries in cultures and civilizations from East to West, as timeless as life itself. And human existence is dependent on the earth's vegetation, so trees and groves are some of the earliest deities.

Holy Baptism

> This pole is black supremacy, owned by King Alpha, the King of Kings. Now Ethiopia knew the perfect value of holy baptism under water, for King Alpha taught us how to appreciate the power of holy baptism. Now we the black people have no pardon to beg white supremacy, no favor to ask her, for she is an acknowledged deceiver. From B.C. 4004 to A.D. second score, she faked all Christianity. Black Supremacy, the Church Triumphant, has denounced her openly, for baptism is a very important subject to black supremacy.
>
> Taken from *The Promise Key,* "*Royal Notice*"

---

86 Psalm 1, v. 3. And he shall be like a tree planted by the rivers of water, that bringeth forth his fruit in his season; his leaf also shall not wither; and whatsoever he doeth shall prosper.

Another tenet of Father Howell was baptism by total immersion in water, after the examples of the Essene masters John the Baptist and Yahowshua ha Mashiakh. John the Baptist was of that company, linking the Old Testament and the New. He baptized Yahowshua in the Jordan River, near the Dead Sea, in the vicinity of one of the Essene monasteries. The rite of baptism practiced by John was a sacramental ceremony which became a central part of the Christian Church. It was not so much a ceremonial Jewish rite as an individual initiatory act that sprang naturally from the Essenes' own ritual bathing practices.[87]

In fact, various forms of water immersion were basic practices of the ancient Essenes. They kept up a rigorous daily routine of bathing in cold water early in the morning, thus keeping their minds sharp and alert. It also exposed the body to a kind of shock therapy that empowered the spirit to overcome the carnal aspects of the body. Baptism was just one of these Essene water rites, the specific rite by which one was symbolically cleansed, initiated, and made ready to embark upon the system of self-development which was the *Seven-fold Peace Path*.

Humans have long harnessed the power of water in its many aspects. For example, since water was used to cleanse, it represented purification for the *Therapeutae* worshippers. In Egyptian hieroglyphs, the figure of a man behind the symbol for water signifies a priest, as *one who purifies*. In the Genesis story of the creation of the heavens and the earth, water was the only element that was recognizable before God created light:

> In the beginning God created the heavens and the earth. The earth was without form and void: and darkness was

---

[87] The same was true of the Essene custom of partaking of bread and wine, which indeed was a practice of the ancient Melkizadek Order before Yahowshua solemnized it at the Last Supper. This is the equivalent of the *holy feast* of the Howellites. But for the Howellites, this *holy feast* took place in the conviction that the name of the Kingly Mashiakh was Haile Sellassie I, King Alpha, who rules along with his Queen Omega.

on the face of the deep. And the spirit of God moved upon the face of the water.

Genesis ch. 1, vv. 1-2

Esoterically, these verses describe the chamber of the womb, which is the true primordial soup from which all life arose. *The earth was without form and void* means that the basic elements of creation existed in that watery darkness, pregnant with all manifestations, but they had no form, as the word of the Most High had not yet been spoken.

The Spirit of God moved upon the face of the water... For the water represents the feminine. The spirit of God moved upon the face of the water; thus, it is out of water that the earth was born. This is symbolic of the baptism of *Christ,* who was immersed into the water and rose up as the Anointed Son, in whom God the Father was well pleased. This can be understood as the rising of the sun from behind the horizon of an oceanic or watery womb.

After the spirit of God moved upon the face of the water, God said: *Let there be light, and there was light;* and thus the earth and its forms came into being through the power of the word of God.

Baptism by immersion in water was for the ancient Essenes a form of sacred rebirthing and anointing of the initiate. After His baptism and subsequent fast, Yahowshua straightly went into the act of preaching the wisdom of God's Kingdom, recognizing baptism as a holy rite of purification in the fashion of the Essenes. Thereby He became the purifier of the covenant, and the light of the earth, which proceeded from the womb of the Divine Mother.

Water baptism was not the only baptism mentioned by Yahowshua. He mentioned an even higher baptism, which would purify pollution that remained after water baptism. The *baptism of fire* was this promised higher baptism, a baptism in the

Divine spirit of truth, the Holy Spirit. The Holy Spirit represents the fire key, the scepter of righteousness, and the opener of the seven seals of adversity. The fire key purifies and enlightens, functioning simultaneously as a spiritual disinfectant and as luminescence. It empowers by burning up illusions and bringing to light all things hidden in the lurking darkness. Outside of fire baptism, one remains in the filth of ignorance and is still not totally cleansed, because the water of baptism itself can be polluted. Many are baptized in such pollution, feeling all the while that this baptism is sufficient.

Careful study shows the Bible to be basically about the evolution of the god of the Hebrews through His unique relationship with the children of Abraham and of Israel. Close scrutiny reveals that Yahweh changes from a crude, judgmental god, whose fierce anger caused a flood to bury the earth and everything on it,[88] to a more tolerant and forgiving god.

The god of the Old Testament vowed that no longer would He destroy the earth with water, but the god of the New Testament, though more refined than the Old Testament god, would prescribe another form of judgment. The god of the Old Testament was the pure and incorporeal fire god worshiped earlier by the Melkizadek order, the god who baptizes each initiate with the fire of the Holy Spirit. It was He who would turn water into wine, representing the spirit of fire and truth.

For in actuality, fire baptism is the true baptism, through the circumcision of the heart chakra[89] it effects. This baptism or rebirth is essentially the Immaculate Conception. Through the purification process of fire baptism, one is exempted from the so-

---

[88] Except Noah, the only one found worthy of life, and his family

[89] *Chakra* — A Sanskrit word meaning *wheel* or *turning*. The concept of *chakra* has its origins amongst the Hindus. It is believed that the *chakras* are centers, what we might call nerve centers, found at various points on the surface of the human body, which act as portals for the reception and transmission of energies.

called final judgment of fire meted out by the god of Revelation, and one becomes the supreme initiate whose power of endurance brings him/her into the totality of the power of the All. Such an initiate is the beginning and the ending, the purifier and the unapproachable fire, the Elect of God.

Water baptism is of the flesh, in that it can cleanse the body only, not the spirit. It was prescribed by the Divine will in like manner as the circumcision of Abraham, and, like circumcision, it will become obsolete, since, like circumcision, it does not ensure righteousness.

A number of polarities, or what I call parallel oppositions, are evident in the Bible. These correspond to the flesh and the spirit. I will briefly list some of these parallel oppositions:

Flesh/Carnal	*Spirit/Divine*
1. Adam and Eve	1. Alpha and Omega
2. Cain	2. Abel
3. Esau/Edom	3. Jacob/Israel
4. Phallic circumcision	4. Heartical circumcision
5. Levitical priesthood	5. Melkizadek priesthood
6. Blood of animal sacrifice	6. Blood of the sacrifice of Christ/self
7. King Saul	7. King David
8. Baptism in water	8. Baptism in fire/spirit
9. Old Jerusalem (in Palestine)	9. New Jerusalem (in Africa)
10. Old Covenant (10 Commandments)	10. New Covenant (One 2fold Commandment of love)

These parallels illustrate how, all throughout the Bible, every order or form of law that was introduced only set the stage for something more Divine and refined to replace it. *Behold I make all things new* (Rev. ch. 21, v. 5): not to cast away the old, but to purify it through the application of the science that explains how to activate the transformation process within a particular entity.

Levitical Priesthood

With this in mind, let us take a critical look at the Levitical priesthood. We saw how, shortly after its formation, it manifested the seeds of its own demise.

> Now when the people saw that Moses delayed coming down from the mountain, the people gathered together to Aaron, and said to him, "Come, make us gods that shall go before us; for as for this Moses, the man who brought us up out of the land of Egypt, we do not know what has become of him." And Aaron said to them, "Break off the golden earrings which are in the ears of your wives, your sons, and your daughters, and bring them to me." So all the people broke off the golden earrings which were in their ears and brought them to Aaron. And he received the gold from their hand, and he fashioned it with an engraving tool, and made a molten calf. Then they said, "This is your god, O Israel, that brought you out of the land of Egypt." So when Aaron saw it, he built an altar before it. And Aaron made a proclamation and said, "Tomorrow is a feast to the Lord." Then they rose early on the next day, offered burnt offerings, and brought peace offerings; and the people sat down to eat and drink, and rose up to play.

> And the Lord said to Moses, "Go, get down! For your people whom you brought out of the land of Egypt have corrupted themselves ... So it was, as soon as he came near the camp, that he saw a calf and the dancing. So Moses' anger became hot, and he cast the tablets out of his hands and broke them at the foot of the mountain. Then he took the calf, which they had made, burned it in the fire, and ground it to powder; and he scattered it on the water and made the children of Israel drink it. And Moses said to Aaron, "What did this people do to

you that you have brought so great a sin upon them?" So Aaron said, "Do not let the anger of my lord become hot. You know the people, that they are set on evil.

>   Exodus ch. 32, vv. 1-7, 19-22

The Levitical Priesthood was destined to fall short of the true glory that was reserved for the Most High. A critical look and a thorough examination of this particular order during the Old Testament period exposes its weaknesses, as the above verse illustrates.

The carnal nature of the Levitical priesthood under Aaron the Levite, brother of Moses, was a crude stage, a body of raw materials necessary to establish the premise for that which was to come. How else would we be able to distinguish the Divine and sacred from the unholy and profane? But the carnality and corruption of this priesthood was only matched by the level of self-awareness and spiritual development of the whole people called Israel: a people rebellious and corrupt, a nation bent on evil and fornication, always backsliding from the precepts showing them how to live as the children of Yahweh. They were a nomadic tribal people governed in their early days by Priest-Judges like Samuel, but who found themselves at war with each other and with the *uncircumcised* neighboring tribes they found themselves living amongst.

As stated in an earlier chapter, Samuel, the last Priest-Judge to oversee the nation of Israel, felt the pressure of the people's desire to have an absolute leader and commander in chief, a King, to lead them in battle and fight on their behalf. Samuel relented and, against his advice, the people elected the first king to lead them. They chose Saul, a Benjaminite, as king, but like the Levitical priesthood he was not destined to have his throne established over Israel.

Consider: messianic movements like those we find in Israel respond primarily to the voice of prophecy, considered the voice of the deity, Yahweh. The Hebrew prophecies allotted the office of anointed King exclusively to the tribe of Judah, which was to give birth to the *Messiah*, whose priesthood however belongs to none of the tribes of Israel but is of the Order of Melkizadek — an order, not a tribe, which was established before the arrival of Abraham in Canaan. Consider: the patriarch Abraham paid tithes and homage to this obscure mystic order, acknowledged its priesthood, and received the blessings of the Priest/King in Salem, before he ever had offspring: a king who supposedly had nothing to do with the subsequent formation of the nation of Israel out of a family of nomadic tribes.

Why was the mysterious submission of Abraham to Melkizadek so essential to the author that he included it in the Torah, the first five books of the Bible? I believe it points to a standard and sets a platform for the Most High to establish an older and more mystical priesthood to raise the *Messiah* from, a priesthood untainted by the corruption that befell these people called the Israelites under the leadership of the Levitical priesthood. Subsequently, when the time was right, the *Messiah* appeared, whose priesthood was of an order of priests that their forefather Abraham had already acknowledged and honored on his return from the battle of the slaughter of kings.[90] This Melkizadek order was destined to become the pure fire and refiner's soap that would, at last, cleanse the filthiness of the tribe of Levi and restore the people to the royal tribe of Judah and the true priesthood of Yah. For upon the coming of the *Messiah*, the priesthood of Levi becomes null and void. The priesthood from henceforth came under the authority of the King of Israel, whose tribe is Judah.

---

90 Genesis ch. 14, vv. 14-20 gives an account of the meeting of Abram (Abraham) with Melkizadek on his return from rescuing his brother from captivity after slaying the kings from Dan to Damascus.

The Sabbath and the Number Seven

The universal operation of the Seven-fold Peace Path, with its seven cycles of growth, was fundamental for the Essenes, as it was seen as possessing a particular mystical importance to spiritual development. The wisdom they strove for was connected with the mystery of numbers. Certain numbers, such as seven (7), were especially significant to them.

The Essenes followed a mystical path with forty-two (7x6) clearly defined degrees or steps. Once these were passed, the devotee was freed from the world of sins (flesh) and reached the point where their spirit was united with the Divine center. After six cycles of seven comes the seventh, where everything learned in the sixth cycle comes to full fruition in the seventh level of consciousness. These forty-two steps correspond to the forty-two generations from Abraham to Yahowshua chronicled in the *Gospel of Matthew* and the *Essene Book of Peace*.

In Rastheology, seven represents the seven seals to be broken, through the seven spirits that revolve around the Throne of Haile Sellassie I. These seven seals are: the two (2) eyes, two (2) nostrils, two (2) ears, and one (1) mouth, apart from which one cannot truly be aware of self. For Rastafarians the opening of the third eye is the ability to see and overstand[91] in the spirit what you actually see on the physical level. When all seven seals are broken, one ascends into the Divine illumination of the I AM, the seventh power.

Seven also represents the number of completion, the last day of the week and the Day of Atonement (at-one-ment). *Sabbath* is the

---

91 *Overstand* means to have a full comprehension of any particular concept or thing. It is Rastafarian idiom for "understand" which is considered to imply the Babylonian perspective or version of truth and reality. In Rastas' minds one cannot "under-stand" to fully know truth. To understand is to be brainwashed with no headroom to stand up in knowledge. One would have to "over-stand" and get a bird's-eye view of the subject matter. As long as you are "under," in Rastas' perspective, you will never be free or truly educated. One must rise above to overcome in order to overstand.

Hebrew word meaning *seventh, atonement, completion, perfection, wholeness, repose* and *rest*. The Sabbath represents the stage of one's perfect spiritual unfoldment. In the Mosaic Law, the seventh day of the week was set aside as a day of rest, on which no one was allowed to work. This was based on it being the day that Yah rested after creating the heaven and earth and all that is therein. Thus, the true Sabbath is the state of man when he has fulfilled the Divine law in thoughts and deeds through the Seven-fold Peace Path.

When man lays hold of the in-dwelling *Christ*, he is raised out of the Adamic consciousness and into *Christ* consciousness. It is in this, the seventh, level of consciousness that he finds peace and rest.

For the Jews, and some Christian Ethiopians, the Sabbath is traditionally from sunset on Friday until the following sunset on Saturday. The true Essenian Sabbath is a Sabbath to be observed every day, after one transcends the prescribed discipline of a sabbatical one day a week. The understanding of the Sabbath as from sunset Friday to sunset Saturday is found in some groups of Rastafarians, such as the Bobo Shanti, the manifest priestly order within the people of Rastafari. The Bobo Shantis' Sabbath emerged from the observance of the precepts of *The Promise Key* and the ideals of Leonard Howell through their founder Emmanuel (Charles Edwards).

In the context of the Rastafarian people, the Bobo Shantis could be viewed as the true Sabbatical order, as their precepts on the Sabbath are more Levitical, as well as more Ethiopic, than just about any other group of Rastafarians.

As was said, for the Bobo Shantis, like the Jews, the Sabbath begins at sunset on Friday and ends at sunset on Saturday. It is strictly and consciously observed, with men, women and children all wearing a white robe and turban. Work is terminated at mid-day Friday, with the rest of the day devoted to preparation for the sabbatical observance. At sunset on Friday, the sounding of drums and the chanting of successive Psalms usher the Sabbath in. Priests and priestesses stand outside of the tabernacle in a circle around it, facing the sea towards the east. Priestly voices rise, chanting in a call and response pattern unto holy Emmanuel/Haile Sellassie I. This liturgy continues until twilight, with a closing ceremony marked by the sounding of the thunder drum three times in each direction.

The Bobo Shantis, Sabbath is one of total abstinence from all work or labors except those pertaining to the observance of the Sabbath. No water is carried, no food is prepared, no fire is kindled — not even an electric light is switched on in the community. Priests and priestesses, barefoot and clad in ceremonial robes, honor and hail each other with *Blessed my Lord* in all reverence and humility. This communal Sabbatical order is presided over by the head priest, King Emmanuel, affectionately called Melkizadek. For them, he is Haile Sellassie I, reincarnated now as High Priest to establish the Melkizadek Order in Rastafari. Hence, he functions as part of the body of the Holy Trinity, according to Bobo Shanti theology: Haile Sellassie I, *the King*; Holy Emmanuel (Melkizadek), *the Priest*; and the Honorable *John* (as in John the Baptist) Marcus Garvey, *the Prophet*.

Black Market Triangle

CHAPTER 13

REASONINGS IN BLACK AND WHITE

> ... Entire systems of colonialism are being wiped out from the continent. We now have our destiny in our own hands, but we must never slacken in our determination never to allow new forms of colonialism, whatever their guise may be, to take hold of any of us, in threat to the hard-won independence and, indeed to the stability and peace of the world. African leaders must, in self-abnegation, press forward the economic, political and spiritual welfare of their peoples in the interest, not merely of national gain, but of that transcendent continental unity which alone can bring to a close the era of colonialism and Balkanization.
>
> — Haile Sellassie I
> Second Africa Conference, June 15, 1960

Europe vs. Africa

It is clear that there is an active conspiracy to exploit and undermine Africa and especially the country of Ethiopia. With regard to Ethiopia, the Christian world apparently does not have a clear understanding of the situation nor is it adequately concerned. Little is being done by international structures to alleviate the great strains that affect the lives of the African peoples. The HIV epidemic that runs rampant all over Africa, as well as the sub-standard living conditions of the average native, in a land whose resources helped build Europe and the Americas into powerful empires, are seen by the citizen of those empires as mundane facts. The present African condition is largely based on European colonization of the continent, which took many decades of strategic planning by some of the most respected nations, who sacrificed the lives of their citizens and squandered their resources to expand their illegitimate claims to Africa. Mussolini conspired to justify his illegal invasion of Ethiopia through a propaganda machine his fascist goverment in Rome put in motion during the war years of 1935-41, implementing a plan to violently take power on the continent and eliminate Africa's history from human consciousness — or at least warp it, so that Her children would be ignorant of who they truly are.

African history is still not adequately represented in the learning institutions of the world. Most people learn a lot about Hitler and Lenin before they have even heard of Marcus Garvey or Haile Sellassie I. Why is that? The reason is that providing information about great Africans is not a part of Babylon's[92] program for anyone. This is undeniably the case. Yet how can world history be taught with African history deleted?

Concern about this lack of information must be cultivated and developed; if it is, Africa will experience the positive impact. Only a few were concerned when Italy invaded Ethiopia in 1935. It is not ludicrous to believe that, if the intelligent nations of the world had been sufficiently concerned, the terrible history of those years might have taken an entirely different course. It is urgent that the situation in Africa be studied and understood, particularly by the Christian Church at large.

As a movement, Rastafari has served as a tool of empowerment for disenfranchised Africans, who were conditioned by slavery to worship a *blond-haired, blue-eyed,* bearded image of the only begotten son of a white supremacist god. A god that, from the history that Europe shares with Africa, has no love for the *less-than-human* blacks. It is difficult to believe that such a *white* god would

---

91 *Babylon*, in Rastafarian vernacular, is the system of oppression which rules the planet, from antiquity until today, through the construct of the Church and State.

sacrifice his lily white son to save *savages*, such as they claimed that the Africans were. This is an outright lie. Yet, the Bible and the sword conquered, and more than many Africans continued their bondage by religious means through Christianity — waiting to die and go to a heaven up in the fluffy white clouds of the sky, where ruddy white angels dressed in white robes, with golden hair and trumpets, herald and minister to a bearded old white man dressed also in white. You can still hear the black church congregation singing their hearts out, *Whiter than snow, whiter than snow... wash me and I shall be... whiter than snow*. The illusion that the oppressors and their god, who forced a tortured existence upon the Africans here on earth, would share an equal place in his heaven with all the slaves he despises, is another cruel joke upon people of color everywhere. Another farce in the illusive mind games of the oppressor.

Mental slavery is part two of the William Lynch[93] strategy. The result — an oppressed continent and a world of mis-educated and victimized subjects spiraling on its own self-destructive axis for over five hundred years. The voice of Rastafari echoes the teachings of Marcus Garvey calling on Africans to break the shackles of the mind and free oneself from the illusions of colonial conditioning. Yet, Marcus wasn't trying to start a religion as much as he was trying to resuscitate a consciousness in a slumbering people — an awakening and a quickening that would give rise to an indepedent African movement. In the immediacy, Marcus envisioned a nation within a nation — not unlike the Chinese or any other nationals within the parameters of (albeit not limited to) the Americas. Over the centuries of dehumanizing

---

93 *William Lynch* — popularly known as *Willie Lynch* — was a British slave owner in the West Indies and the author of the definitive tome on the *Making of a Slave*. Lynch was invited to the United States and made an address on the banks of the James River in Virginia in 1712 on how the U.S. slave owners could save money and create a perpetual source of income from their Negro investment by simply applying his methods. Lynch was to become the grand architect of a set of principles that was used as a system for gaining full control, by breaking the *Negro* slaves, a system designed to last for hundreds of years. Willie Lynch became very important to the slave owners in the South of the United States, and his series of letters/speeches became the blueprint for the syndrome of mental slavery that still affects the majority of Diaspora Africans today. See Appendix D.

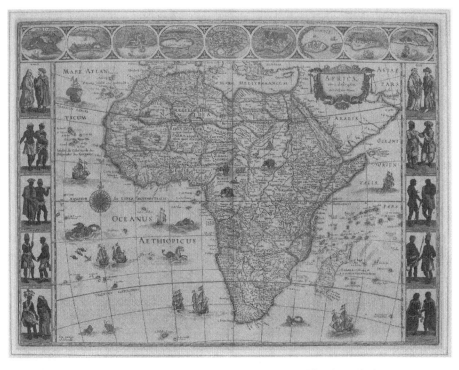

1632 Map of Africa. Photo used by permission courtesy of Sanderus Antiquariaat.

and strategically demonizing Africans, many invaluable aspects of identity were systematically destroyed and replaced with misinformation and lies, upheld by a system and enforced by laws.

The scramble for Africa and the outcome of that scramble after 1870 disrupted the balance of power amongst the European nations, leading to many tensions. The forces that led to the outbreak of war in 1914 can only be understood in light of this history of European exploitation of Africa. We see its bitter fruit today, with the people of Africa the last to remain dependent on the will of the international imperial organ.

Maps of Africa before 1870 showed names for places and tribes that are unknown to us today. Some tribes were more developed and advanced than others. In some places, rulers could trace their lineage back through many generations of queens and kings. In the years between 1870 and 1900, England secured a broad new base for her empire in Africa. France found an unlimited source of man-power there; her holdings were larger than those of England, though not always as lush. Belgium exploited the heart of the continent; and Portugal expanded into Africa as well, gaining more and more territory when she was still a power of international importance. Even Germany carved out an empire in Africa, while Italy griped with resentment at her failure to control more than mostly barren regions. Daily the nations of colonial Europe energetically exploited Africa for Her rare metals and raw materials. Everyone had plans for how to tap into Her resources. Greed increased and tension mounted over border disputes between the colonial powers, who had divided almost the whole of the great continent between them. A conference held in Berlin in 1884 made some rules and set the terms for some agreements amongst the colonizers, while by 1900 these European powers had reached agreement on boundaries which remained in place until World War I.

African resources became essential to Europe's economic life, and the whole world sought access to Her raw materials and conspired to use Her people to supply European markets for manufactured goods. It is no secret that the Axis powers of Germany and Italy had concrete plans to impose slave labor on Africans to harvest much needed materials to feed their industries. Nor is it a secret that every European-run nation today relies still on the labor of Africans, paying wages altogether too low.

The Fascist Spirit

The colonial systems the Europeans operated in Africa provided a culture for the nourishment of fascism in Europe. No matter how one looks at it, the conditions of their operation and of their

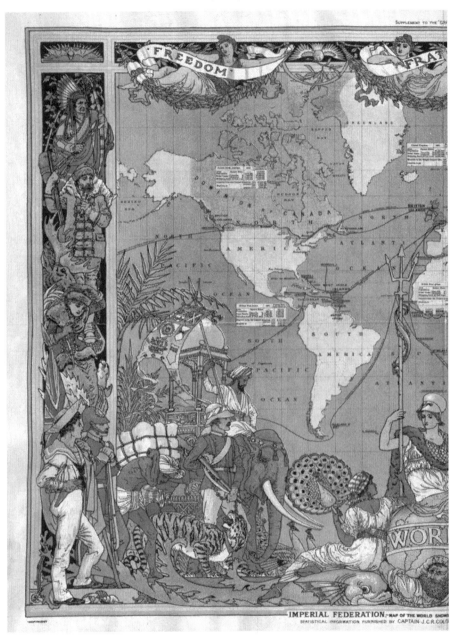

Public domain map of the world showing the extent of the British Empire in 1886. British territories colored in red. Published as a supplement for *The Graphic*, July 1886, as the "Imperial Federation". Statistical information furnished by Captain J.C.R. Colomb, M.P. formerly R.M.A.

A Journey to the Roots of Rastafari

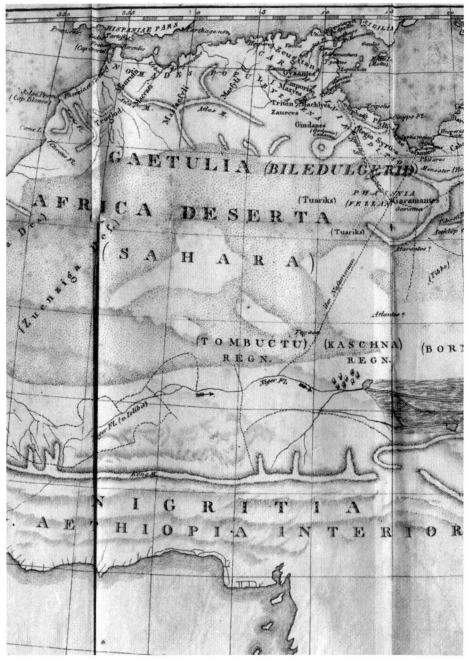

Ancient Map of Africa

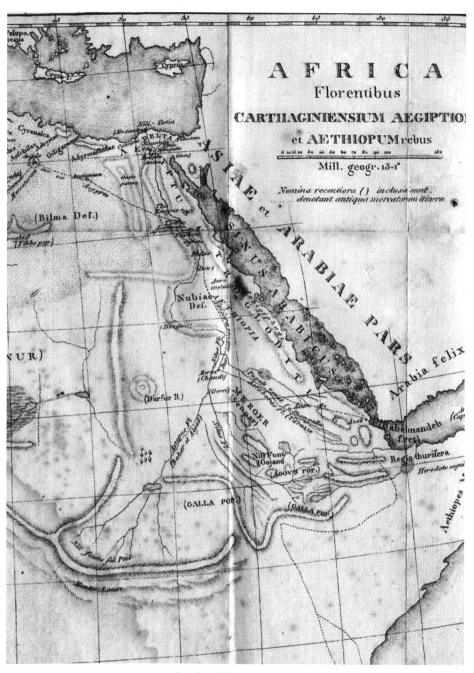

Ancient Map of Africa

exercise of control opened the way for the development of the fascist spirit in those who administered the government. There are four elements of fascism that were widely noticeable in the African colonial system. They are:

1. The manipulation of the masses for the benefit of the state.
2. Blatant disregard of the rights of the individual to security on their land, to freedom of movement in the cities and towns, to participate in the government; as well as denial of the individual's opportunity for unfettered expression.
3. Arrogance and sense of superiority that is developed in the ruling class, which is a minority of the population.
4. Control by force, often ruthless in its application.

Some of these elements of fascism still exist in varying forms in countries still under the colonial influence, such as was recently witnessed in South Africa under apartheid. The present situation in Palestine breeds and reflects the same fascist sentiments, and it will continue to grow unless some radical system of cure and prevention is enacted. Colonialism laid the groundwork for fascism to spread, the world has since been unable to control or change its spread; but efforts must be made to take action now. Like many diseases, it cannot be merely isolated. Fascism must be exterminated before we will be able to process the problems and challenges that face Africans and the world at large.

When fascist elements consciously or unconsciously dominate colonies in a particular section of the world, there can be no guarantee that the same spirit will not break out at home. Even if some colonizing persons may begin their careers with a spirit of concern to do the best thing for the natives of the country (or what they determine to be the best thing whether the natives like it or not), it almost always ends as simply the manipulation of people for the benefit of a political-economic overlord. This is not a simple matter of the individuals involved. It is a complex system of collective conspiracy implicating the colonial government.

Officials who may exert themselves in a more positive direction are often overwhelmed by that system.

It may surprise many to learn it, but demonic forces were active in the turn of events that triggered both World Wars. The spiritual powers of darkness gathered the nations to war in Europe under the illusive guise of Christianity. Only so could the nations sit back and watch the rape of Christian Ethiopia by another so-called Christian country, the one which housed the seat of the Pope. With bombs, tanks and a mass of heavy artillery blessed by the Pope and his cardinals, fascist Italy trespassed on the independent African sovereign, the seat of David, King of Kings and Lord of Lords.

Colonial Christianity

In the wake of colonialism, colonial, imperialistic Christian missions processed whole continents of indigenous cultures out of existence. These missions left a trail of devastation. To assess the full damage done by colonial Christianity would take a lifetime of intense study by the most devoted and educated scholars. It is not sufficient to say that the continent of Africa, with Her diversity of unique tribes and cultures, has experienced many destructive blows at the hand of colonial Christianity. She was devastated, and is overwhelmingly the land most affected by colonialism in the world.

The great irony of our time is that the contemporary Jews and metropolitan Christians of the globe, in their search for a superior religious cultural tradition and a Divinely legitimate political structure, never recognize the kingdom of Judah in Ethiopia. And extensive observation even of Africans, at home or abroad, shows them too to be more receptive to European Christianity than to the indigenous Christian faith of their own continent.

Let us take a moment to look at the psychological effects Colonial Christianity has had on people throughout the world.

Christianity under Rome can be seen as, in effect, a contraceptive, preventing its progeny from being born again into the consciousness of Yahowshua and thus becoming a part of the true body of the Mashiakh. Behind the intricate complexities of Christian dogma, Jesus consistently surfaces as the only begotten Son of God the Father, thus making it blasphemous for anyone to equal Him. Christianity, as we know, functions from a Patriarchal Trinity which excludes the Mother. Thus, the psychology of Christians is imbalanced and incomplete. The feminine face of God is viewed as heretical and cloaked under a veil of ambiguity and taboos.

Under Christian psychology, salvation is supposed to be the living out of the principle of Christ in one's personal life; the individual experiences salvation only when they have a radical transformation from one state of mind to another, and have changed for the better. This is alchemy in every sense of the word. This experience is also the individual's Immaculate Conception. Yet this essence and core of Christian theology is not actually realized in the lives of the faithful today.

The Popes, Priests and Pastors have throughout the ages created and established a sort of bondage over the psyche of humanity that calculatedly prevents the true birth or rebirth sought by the faithful. This is contradiction and deception, gelled into one as a contraceptive. One cannot be born again on any level unless one is reborn through the power of the Mother; whether internally or externally, the maternal energy is needed. Recognizing that the denial of the maternal is a block to rebirth, we conclude that this contraceptive is a vice, which will ultimately disillusion the followers of the Christian belief system.

This contraceptive psychology is not unique to Christianity; in fact a similar spirit is evident in many religions. It was similarly repressive minds that falsely accused Yahowshua and crucified Him in the olden days of Jewry. What was the charge? Nothing less than blasphemy for affirming Himself in the Power of the Mashiakh, making Himself One with God. By executing Him on such a charge, they that slew Him bore witness to the Immaculate Conception (properly understood) of Yahowshua ha Mashiakh.

We read in Mark ch. 14, v. 61-64:

> ...Again the high priest asked him, and said unto him, Art thou the Christ, the Son of the Blessed? And Jesus said, I am: and ye shall see the son of man sitting on the right hand of power, and coming in the clouds of heaven. Then the high priest rent his clothes, and said, What need we any further witnesses? Ye have heard the blasphemy: what think ye? And they all condemned him to be guilty of death.

It was in faithfulness to this understanding and practice of the Immaculate Conception that apostles of Yahowshua built the Essene monasteries, to faithfully await His rebirth as the Kingly Mashiakh at His Second Coming in Glory. However, Christianity across the centuries has had no consensus on any alleged returns of Yahowshua; in fact, every claim or proclamation of a return is viewed as sacrilege. In this respect, the Christians of today are like the Jews of the Old Testament animal sacrifice cult. Both await a Mashiakh that, up to the present, has not arrived nor thereby affirmed that their god is real.

Because of this psychological contraceptive, should the Savior or Mashiakh be present among those most devoted to this form of colonial Christianity, He could not be acknowledged as such. Any such proclamation would in fact lead to the murder of the

Individual making it. They would have to remove the Witness that would testify to their falsehood, to keep their well-guarded secret safe.

The inquisitive mind naturally wants to know: What is the secret that all the machinery of Catholicism was designed to suppress? According to the Rastafarians, the concept of God cannot be truly realized outside of humanity. But the elite, educated minority, which holds the monopoly on Christian theology, sees the need to secure themselves in power over the poor ignorant majority by means of a false hope of salvation. The secret that Catholicism aims to keep from people is that woman-and-man, in the consciousness of love, is the manifest God.

Armageddon

> And He gathered them together into a place called in the Hebrew tongue ar-ma-ged'don. Rev. ch. 16, v. 16.

The battle of the great day of God Almighty is called Armageddon after the Megiddo Valley in northern Palestine. For over three thousand years it has been a battlefield; Israel and the Philistines fought each other there for centuries. *Megiddo* is Hebrew for *place of many troops, rendezvous* or *crowded place*. The prophet Zechariah spoke of it as a valley of great mourning. The scriptures use the name to signify the final battle of the world, which will center on Zion, the Holy Land.

According to Bible prophecy, the powers of evil on earth will gather together to fight against the Lord and His anointed saints in His second coming. These evil forces have in fact organized a league to oppose the Christ and they will lead their armies in a great fight against Him, for they are the spirit of devils, working miracles which go forth unto the kings of the earth and the whole world, to gather them to the battle for that great day of God Almighty.

The Battle of Armageddon, the apocalyptic clash between the forces of good and evil, is, according to Biblical prophecy, the sign of the coming of the Lord: ...*And there was a war in heaven; Michael and his angels fought against the dragon, and the dragon fought, and his angels, and prevailed not, but was cast out of heaven...* (Rev. ch. 12, vv. 7-8).

This prophetic battle has been interpreted and viewed from many perspectives by the spiritualists, theologians, religious fanatics and learned minds of the ages. They all put much emphasis on Rome and the Roman Empire as a key element in the unfolding of the catastrophic events of past, present and future. Many have singled out Christianity under colonial Rome as the mask for an agenda of destruction, yet few of these observers have pointed to significant other perpetrators of organized criminality, such as Nazism. The real cause of both world wars has not really been explored on the spiritual level, and the obvious evidence of these spiritual causes, such as demonic forces behind Nazism and other Fascist movements, merely browsed over by writers and world leaders alike.

Many books and articles by respected, educated minds have singled out the system of the Papacy as the prophetical fulfillment of the beast and dragon of the Books of Daniel and Revelation, a sign of the end. Billboards express anti-Papal sentiments around the world on a continuous basis as well. Round-the-clock effort is put into telecommunications and social media that point out the apocalyptic fulfillment of ancient prophecies. In recent centuries, foundations and institutions such as the Jehovah's Witnesses, Seventh-Day Adventists, Mormons, Rosicrucians and a world of others have published in various media a universe of information on the subject. Many of these are quite informative and factual — dogmatic as well, but for the most part true. Every individual and organization that is aware of the full meaning of the impending Armageddon is looking to it as a way out, a means to an end —

the end being the return of the Christ to confirm His Kingdom and re-establish the paradise of Eden, according to an ongoing tradition inherited by Christianity, Christ-consciousness groups and various other cults.

At the root of the Battle of Armageddon and of the Apocalypse in general are friction, tension and conflict that will lead to the disaster of the ultimate clash, defined and declared as war. Thus Armageddon will not be just one battle, but a series of battles, leading to an international explosion. The same pattern is evident in the two great World Wars of the twentieth century, both taking place within one generation, exactly eighteen years apart, from 1918 to 1936. World War II is really a continuation of the first, and both were fought on the basis of the expansion of European colonial interests in Africa.

Esau and Jacob

The Battle of Armageddon will not be fought over commercial supremacy, nor over territory, but over something deeply esoteric and spiritual. Esoterically, this battle was fought to dethrone God, and we speak in the past tense even as the scriptures do, *There was a war in heaven.* We see in this war spoken of by John in the Book of Revelation congruence with another story of the Bible. This takes us back to the Book of Genesis, to the time of the birth of Esau (Edom) and Jacob (Israel), who were twin sons to Rebekah and Isaac son of Abraham.

> ...And Isaac intreated the Lord for his wife because she was barren: and the Lord was intreated of him, and Rebekah his wife conceived. And the children struggled within her; and she said, If it be so, why am I thus? And she went to inquire of the Lord. And the Lord said unto her, Two nations are in thy womb, and two manner of people shall be separated from thy bowels; and the one people shall be stronger than the

other people, and the elder shall serve the younger... And the first came out red, all over like an hairy garment; and they called his name Esau. And after that came his brother out, and his hand took hold on Esau's heel; and his name was called Jacob...

Genesis ch. 25, vv. 21-23, 25-26

The struggle of the children within the womb of Rebekah represents the war prophesied in Revelation. Their struggle then was a struggle for power, as is our struggle now, which will lead to Armageddon. Esau symbolizes the forces of the dragon or beast, which is metaphysically the immature carnal consciousness in man, driven by desire: the undeveloped man arrogantly satisfies this appetite, regardless of higher law. The threat Esau posed to Jacob represents the internal rebellion we humans experience when we try to change our mode of thought to a more spiritual one. This resistance takes form in the birth, and then in the casting out, of Esau. From him comes the nation of the Edomites who would become the archenemy of the Israelites. Hence Esau represents, in a sense, the substance of ultimate evil. Thus it is said in Revelation ch. 12, v. 12:

Woe be unto the people of the earth; because the devil has come down to you, having great wrath...

The birth of Jacob with his hand holding his brother's heel metaphysically represents the salvation promised in the coming of Christ.

Jacob means *bringing to an end, recompenser, reward,* or *supplanter.* As such, he is the hope by which the beastly nature, as Edom, will be subdued. Esau in his hairiness typifies the animal self, which comes to expression first as force or friction. Most of humankind allows this force to rule their consciousness, but in order to follow the path of human development, a higher force, called Jacob or rather Israel, must subdue the carnal personality and its instincts. Jacob represents the I AM identity, from which the Divine king of Israel will come. This is the promise, but also the cause of the war. Ultimate power is to be given to the King of Kings, as the *Christ* will be known, to establish a never-ending kingdom and govern the earth as the sovereign Elect of God. He will be the standard-bearer and the ultimate authority.

The struggle of the twins, beginning in the womb, is over the birthright, the precedence which according to tradition goes to the first-born. Now almost every war has been about land, a priceless commodity coveted, and then owned, by the one who can use force and violence to take it. Land is what every ambitious power-seeker wants at any cost. But morality should be the standard by which any ruler administers authority over others, and harmony with the natural order must be the outcome of human endeavors. When it is not, all of life's creatures suffer along with the earth as a whole.

Esau sold his birthright to his brother in a moment of weakness, as he swore, gave his word, to his brother in agreement for food and drink. Deep down Esau had no intention of fulfilling his agreement, and so Jacob had to use cunning to obtain his share of the bargain. Because he did, Jacob is often viewed as a trickster, one who stole his brother's birthright. It is not justified, however, thus to attack Jacob's character. In those days, oral oaths and covenants were understood as binding commitments. A man's word was his life, as is shown by Yahweh's displeasure with the Israelites for failing to keep their vows, for which they experienced the hardships prescribed as punishments for disobedience, what, following Hindu/Buddhist tradition, we may call *karma*. Thus the birthright belonged to Jacob once Esau traded and promised it to him.

Enmity with Jacob developed in Esau when he realized the gravity of the covenant he had made; he kept this matter secret from his father. The agreement did not however deliver to Jacob what he had bargained for; he had to acquire it by any means necessary, which included the deception through which he received Isaac's blessing. Esau had no intention of informing his father that he had sold Jacob the blessing of the firstborn, the actual birthright, which would have been the moral action to take. As events unfolded, twelve sons were born to Jacob, who formed the tribes of Israel, and sons were also born to Esau; we clearly see two nations and two manner of people developing from the patriarchal twins.

The blessing Jacob received from Isaac was in fact his anointment as heir to the father's wealth and power. With this inheritance, the son could launch whatever projects his heart desired. This was his legal right, with all his father's property and servants put in subjection under him. This is the meaning of the birthright, which ultimately, in the higher realms of reasoning, represents the very Throne of God.

In time, Edom (Esau) fathered many powerful nations, ruled by dukes and kings long before the people of Israel had a mortal king and throne. Some of the nations that were to war against the Israelites later, such as the Amalekites (whose name means *warlike*), were in fact descendants of Esau. The nation of Edom itself, dwelling about their chief city of Bozrah, gained much wealth and power. The Edomites became very powerful in the earth, gaining dominion by force and tyranny.

According to the blessing Isaac gave Esau, he would dwell in the fatness of the earth, living by the sword, and eventually gain dominion. Jacob, however, received the blessing of the firstborn, with the promise of the pearl[94] (the golden seed) that would embody all Divine attributes. This means that the Glory of the Godhead would belong to his seat. On another level, the conflict between the brothers would play out once again between King Saul and David, as they struggled to establish their throne in Israel.

In Judah is God known; his praise is great in Israel...

Psalm 76, v. 1

Judah, the seed of Jacob, became, in the form of David, the seat and body of the pearl. Wars are often fought for a royal crown and throne, and it is precisely for this that Europe (esoterically Edom) found herself in later centuries positioned for battle, for an attempt to take the birthright of the Ethiopians (Israel) by force. This birthright belongs to Africa, and it is only through total surrender to Her, the birthplace and Mother of all creation, that nations receive their proper blessing. Through mutual recognition and acceptance, everyone can have their branch in Her family tree.

If Africans seek salvation, and they do, it must include salvation from the hands of their oppressors, who for hundreds of years have been colonial imperialists, governing by force and deadly violence in the name of Christianity. But Africa's salvation could not come in the form of the colonial Christ God, because it is in the name of Jesus Christ that the colonialists executed every cruel and heartless atrocity against Her indigenous peoples. Africa's

---

94 "There is extant in Ethiopian literature a legend to the effect that when God made Adam, He placed in his body a 'Pearl,' which He intended to pass from Adam into the bodies of a series of holy men, one after the other, until the appointed time, when it should enter the body of Hanna, and into the substance of her daughter the Virgin Mary. Now the 'Pearl' passed through the body of Solomon, an ancestor of Christ; Christ and Menyelek, the son of Solomon by the Queen of Sheba, were sons of Solomon, and according to Ethiopian ideas kin to each other. But Christ was the Son of God, and, therefore, being the kinsman of Christ, Menyelek was divine...and the kings of Ethiopia who were descended from Menyelek were of divine origin, and their words and deeds were those of Gods." Taken from the Preface of *The Kebra Nagast*, translated by Sir E. A. Wallis Budge.

spiritual civilization was targeted and branded by the colonial minds as Pagan. The Catholic Church, whose head is in Rome, has done more than her fair share to delete African consciousness from the world, in part through the colonization of the minds of Africans, imposing both physical and mental slavery upon them.

Africa and the world now need redemption from the yoke of colonial salvation, which can only come through a new faculty of interpretation. This entails the Christian Church, as it is presently known, being arrested and charged with murder, pillaging and a score of other inhuman crimes against Mother Nature and Her children. But we are sure that the atmosphere of the Christian world is not conducive to such unconventional viewpoints, nor prepared to face this reality. One must remember that the peacekeeping League of Nations could be viewed as a Christian governmental body, the international political church, designed as it was to uphold world peace by means of the highest Christian ideals. Nevertheless, in June 1936, they were paralyzed, unable to live out the principles of the Covenant, which would have prevented the Italian Church and State from raping Ethiopia. World War II was the result of their hypocrisy, and Haile Sellassie I remains a voice to be reckoned with until this day.

White Privilege

This article appeared in the *Baltimore Sun* newspaper, written by Robert Jensen, a white professor at the University of Texas:

> I'm sitting in my University of Texas office, talking to a very bright and very conservative white student about affirmative action in college admissions, which he opposes and I support. The student says he wants a level playing field with no unearned advantages for anyone. I ask him whether he thinks that being white has advantages in the United States.

Jensen continued:

> Have either of us, I ask, ever benefited from being white in a world run mostly by white people? Yes, he conceded. There is something real and tangible we could call white privilege. So, if we live in a world of white privilege — unearned white privilege — how does that affect your notion of a level playing field? I asked. He paused for a moment and said, "That really doesn't matter." That statement, I suggested to him, reveals the ultimate white privilege: the privilege to acknowledge that you have unearned privilege but to ignore what it means.
>
> That exchange led me to rethink the way I talk about race and racism with students. It drove home the importance of confronting the dirty secret that we white people carry around with us every day: in a world of white privilege, some of what we have is unearned. I think much of both the fear and anger that comes up around discussions of affirmative action has its roots in that secret. So these days, my goal is to talk openly and honestly about white supremacy and white privilege.
>
> White privilege, like any social phenomenon, is complex. In a white supremacist culture, all white people have privilege, whether or not they are overtly racist themselves. There are general patterns, but such privilege plays out differently depending on context and other aspects of one's identity (in my case, being male gives me other kinds of privilege).
>
> Rather than try to tell others how white privilege has played out in their lives, I talk about how it has affected me. I am as white as white gets in this country. I am of northern European heritage and I was raised in North

Dakota, one of the whitest states in the country. I grew up in a virtually all-white world surrounded by racism, both personal and institutional. Because I didn't live near a reservation, I didn't even have exposure to the state's only numerically significant nonwhite population, American Indians. I have struggled to resist that racist training and the racism in my culture. I like to think I have changed, even though I routinely trip over the lingering effects of that internalized racism and the institutional racism around me. But no matter how much I "fix" myself, one thing never changes — I walk through the world with white privilege.

What does that mean? Perhaps most importantly, when I seek admission to a university or apply for a job, or hunt for an apartment, I don't look threatening. Almost all of the people evaluating me look like me — they are white. They see in me a reflection of themselves — and in a racist world, that is an advantage. I smile. I am white. I am one of them. I am not dangerous. Even when I voice critical opinions, I am cut some slack. After all, I'm white…

But, all that said, I know I did not get where I am by merit alone. I benefited from, among other things, white privilege. That doesn't mean that I don't deserve my job, or that if I weren't white I would never have gotten the job. It means simply that all through my life, I have soaked up benefits from being white.

All my life I have been hired for jobs by white people. I was accepted for graduate school by white people. And I was hired for a teaching position by the predominantly white University of Texas, headed by a white president, in a college headed by a white dean and in a department with a white chairman that at the time had one nonwhite tenured professor. I have worked hard to get where I am, and I work hard to stay there. But to feel good about myself and my work, I do not have to believe that "merit," as defined by white people in a white country, alone got me here. I can acknowledge that in addition to all that hard work, I got a significant boost from white privilege. At one time in my life, I would not have been able to say that, because I needed to believe that my success in life was due solely to my individual talent and effort. I saw myself as the heroic American, the rugged individualist. I was so deeply seduced by the culture's mythology that I couldn't see the fear that was binding me to those myths…

There is not space here to list all the ways in which white privilege plays out in our daily lives, but it is clear that I will carry this privilege with me until the day white supremacy is erased from this society.

We live in a time when the barriers and boundaries drawn in the past, coming from a time of precisely defined control through the racist strategies and oppressive means of Jim Crowism, are now seemingly blurred by affirmative action and contemporary political correctness. In our time there is an appearance of civil justice and equal rights for all human beings regardless of race, ethnicity, sex or class, of a balanced playing field. That everyone can make it and we all have equal access to opportunities. Some of us believe that things have never been better, that we have overcome the oppressive evils of a colonial past and are collectively forging ahead towards a bright future, free of racism, sexism or social phobias. I too would like to believe that this analysis is accurate.

White privilege, as the ultimate by-product of white supremacy, is the best example and evidence of a time-honored tradition and legacy that continue to secure the progenies of the past oppressors. Many inheritors of this culture today appear oblivious to their contribution as shareholders in the worldwide conspiracy to secure an empire at the expense of a Continent and its People. Today's societies are controlled by the same influencing forces as were the minds of the founders that sowed the first seeds of this racist regime: a legacy of prejudice unsurpassed in human history, a savage machine of greed and hate contrived and assembled from the coldest cruelest parts of the beastly nature of the human animal.

Black Supremacy vs. White Supremacy

As small a volume as it is, *The Promise Key*, outlining the philosophies, opinions and concepts of Leonard Percival Howell, is one of the strongest original sources of Rastafari. The early Rastafarian concept of black supremacy could be viewed as a racist counterpart to the notorious dictatorship of white supremacy, just as negative, and with equal potential for destruction. From a distance, this appears to be a valid point; however, close and objective scrutiny of white supremacy has given us grounds to believe otherwise.

White supremacy surfaces in the racist colonial Christian thought patterns that made blackness the color of the devil and gave us a blond-haired, blue-eyed image of the only begotten Son of God. This image is the core of white supremacy, the doctrine of the superiority of the white race, and establishes that race as Divine, with the right to dominate and enslave the so-called inferior races or peoples of color. Proponents of white supremacy use elements of the *Holy Bible* to strengthen their racist position. Two examples are in the book of Genesis and the Epistle to the Colossians:

> Now the sons of Noah who went out of the ark were Shem, Ham, and Japheth. And Ham was the father of

Canaan. These three were the sons of Noah, and from these the whole earth were populated... And Ham, the father of Canaan, saw the nakedness of his father, and told his two brothers outside... So Noah awoke from his wine, and knew what his younger son had done to him. Then he said: Cursed be Canaan; a servant of servants he shall be to his brethren.

Genesis ch. 9, vv. 18-25

Servants, obey in all things your masters according to the flesh; not with eye service, as men pleasers; but in singleness of heart, fearing God: and whatsoever ye do, do it heartily, as to the Lord, and not unto men; knowing that of the Lord ye shall receive the reward of the inheritance: for ye serve the Lord Christ.

Colossians ch. 3, vv. 22-24

Based on these and other scriptures, millions of people have been slaughtered and many more made to serve the white man's ideas and concepts in the name of *Jesus Christ our Lord*. The institution of white supremacy, with its history of crimes against nature and humanity, still propagates the doctrine of white superiority in every possible way. White supremacy, in the form of a Eurocentric value system, is so ingrained in our societies that every culture around the globe today has internalized aspects of it through the direct influence of colonialism. If we look realistically at the world at large in this light, we see colonialism as a ruling force embedded deep in the unconscious psyche of the world.

Colonialism may in fact have been snuffed out on some levels or in some forms, believe it or not, but it persists in the institutions and the minds of those who govern the world. Nothing but war, death and destruction has come of the white man's rule over the peace-loving peoples of the earth. The only good that can come from it is its death, from which new life may spring forth in acknowledgment of the reality of the Living God.

The manifestation of this true consciousness of God is, according to the Divine will, indigenous to Africa, and specifically the Kingdom of Ethiopia. It is out of Her that the standard of supreme authority, dignity and morality did come under the name of Haile Sellassie I. The doctrine of Black Supremacy was consequently born as more than just a reactionary response to white supremacy, but as the inevitable implication of a superior order, the Church Triumphant, the Assembly of Rastafari. That is, at least, how Howell understood Black Supremacy.

For people like Marcus Garvey and Leonard Howell, Black Supremacy was the truth, the reality of a natural moral order. If God's Law is the standard by which humans should live, then God's Law is the superior Law and the Ultimate Reality of life. As the early Rastafarians saw, Jah's manifestation in history was, according to prophetical fulfillment, Haile Sellassie I, and through Him Jah gave rise to a new people, a new language and a new Church which confesses the supremacy of a Christ who is African, the so-called Black Christ.

> Black Supremacy has taken charge of white supremacy by King Alpha and Queen Omega, the King of Kings. Instead of saying civilization hereafter we all shall say Black Supremacy. Just take this drench of indomitable fury and move for the Church Triumphant right from the bridge of supreme authority. Black Supremacy will promote the morals of every shade according to our power to go. The Black museum will be open day and night for life. Education will be free and

compulsory to all mortal beings, if you are not an enemy of Black Supremacy.

> Taken from Howell, *The Promise Key*, *"Government"*

One can see clearly from the words of The Gong that he was not a racist, but that his idea of Black Supremacy was of the supremacy of the highest moral standard.

The zenith of African civilization took place when Europe was still naked and groped in the darkness of her civilization's incubatory stages. The blueprint Africa gave to the world was not based simply upon the supremacy of the Black Race, but upon moral, indeed macrocosmic, law. At the peak of Her international power, Africa saw no need to conquer and subjugate the people of neighboring lands.

It has been said that the pyramids of Egypt were built by slaves of the powerful Pharaohs, but archeological evidence indicates otherwise. Recent archeologists have found that those who engineered and labored on the pyramids lived in choice dwellings surrounding these great monuments. The laborers were equivalent to the working class, the nine-to-fivers, of today, with only minor differences. Slaves under the Pharaonic dynasties were afforded basic civil privileges, allowing them to ascend to positions of power, as Joseph, son of Israel, did after having been sold into bondage in Egypt. There is no parallel to these opportunities in the white man's colonial rule. The Europeans took slavery to a much lower level. Under white supremacy, even basic human rights are denied to people of color, contravening the Divine nature of all human beings. White supremacy is thus an invention of the destructive nature of man, not a fruit of the nurturing, creative element of the Divine. Africans could not foresee or fathom such a low level of consciousness, which is why the white man could take them by surprise and export them to distant lands as a kind of sub-human cargo.

African civilization, throughout history, has proven itself to be based upon totally different principles than the European dictatorship with its Christian façade. Searching out the matter thoroughly reveals absolutely no justification for white racism on any level. One cannot argue that it is a reaction to any form of black supremacy or African nationalistic conspiracy. In fact, white supremacy, as a form of government or as a moral standard, is the most pronounced symptom of an acute inferiority complex ever seen, one which is without parallel in recorded history.

The underpinnings of Black Supremacy are directly opposite to those of white supremacy, so that the two should not be compared or viewed as one and the same or even similar. The idea of race superiority is usually alien to the cultures of people of color, as is evident from the pages of their history; in fact it appears to be a trait unique to Europeans, their trademark, even though they are, genealogically speaking, the new kids on the block. If race superiority had been a concept held by Africans, the history of that continent, and indeed of the world, would have followed a completely different plot — a plot in which Europeans would not have had the leading roles.

Because of the many evil fruits which white supremacy bore, however we, The Royal Apostles of Haile Sellassie I in Mother Divine, do not want to be associated with any form of supremacy, apart from the supremacy of the Divinity itself. Through Haile Sellassie I, and the pure fire of His transforming love and forgiveness, the gate of Zion is open wide for all to enter in. Therefore, we choose to not use language that could easily be misconstrued as proclaiming a black counterpart to an evil white device.

The Classic Image of Jesus

Jesus: The Myth vs. Yahowshua: The Life

The name *Jesus* is synonymous with Western Christianity, and inseparable from the Eurocentric image of the Savior. That is the image that has imprinted itself upon the psyche of humanity, in such a way that, if you hear the name with your eyes closed, you automatically bring this Eurocentric image into focus. Few Africans in the Diaspora deny that the sound of the name *Jesus Christ* conjures a European image. More than a few scholars of the Bible and of history are aware that this image does not represent the true identity of the Christ. Nevertheless Jesus Christ, understood as God, continues to condition the minds of millions through the painted image.

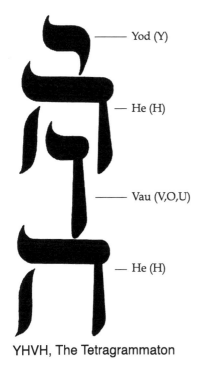

YHVH, The Tetragrammaton

I have declared that the Jesus Christ of the King James Version (K.J.V.) differs greatly from the Essenian teacher of righteousness named Yahowshua, and that they are not one and the same. The name *Jesus Christ* is English, though we are sure that we are not talking about an Englishman. Therefore we must ask ourselves, what was the true name of this historical figure? And, from what country did he come? It is said that he was born a Jew, of Hebrew heritage. Thus it is evident that he must have had a Hebrew name, and looked more or less like the people that came from the eastern part of the world. His name could not have been Jesus.

Some might argue that it is not significant whether one says Jesus, Iesus, or Yahowshua, but it is important to note that English was not the language of the authors of the Bible and, as such, English does not carry the intended meaning or feeling in many cases. While it is sometimes possible for one language to be translated into another and still maintain its original meaning and purpose, Hebrew, considering its Kabalistic nature, cannot be completely translated into a new tongue such as English, which has its roots in German, Dutch, and the Scandinavian languages, though it has an uncanny ability to assimilate words from other languages such as French and Latin. English, in comparison to Aramaic and

Hebrew, is quite a young language, and some Hebrew words and phrases have no exact counterpart in English.

In the Bible, the Hebrew god is called by many names, usually of Hebrew or Aramaic origin, and oftentimes surrounded by strong taboos. Great emphasis is placed, however, on his proper Name, and one was forbidden to utter the Name unless one was prepared to absorb the immense power the sound conjured. Yahweh is this proper Name of God given in the Bible, said to be Hebrew for *He who is eternal, the Self-existent one,* the *I AM.* In the American Standard Version and some other translations, Jehovah is used where Yahweh appears in the Hebrew text. According to Hebrew scholars, however, the original name in Hebrew is יהוה (YHVH), for Biblical Hebrew was written without vowels, not Yahweh, Jehovah, or any other form that is used in English Bibles. This name is called the Tetragrammaton, from the Greek *tetra* meaning four and *gramma* meaning letter.

In the Authorized Version of 1611 and many modern translations, the name Yahweh is improperly translated *Lord*. Many other names — Yah (Jah), Adonay, and Elohim, to name a few — are used in the Hebrew Bible in addition to, or to substitute for, the most sacred name. Yah (Jah) is Hebrew meaning *everlasting, eternal,* and *unchangeable*. It is one of the most ancient names given to any deity. (See Psalm 68, v. 4.)

Baal is another word, translated as *Lord* in English Bibles, but it was used by Hebrews as the name for a god of those who attributed form to divinity, and whose worship was therefore considered pagan.

Jesus is a Greek rendering of the Hebrew Yahowshua. Yet Jesus is Greek for *son of Zeus*, who is best known as a Greek god. Therefore whenever we utter the words *Jesus Christ* we are actually invoking the spirit of a pagan Greek god.

Originally, however, Zeus was an Ethiopian king, whom the Greeks came to worship as the god of the sun. *Webster's Dictionary* says that Zeus is the sky god of the Greeks and known in Latin as *Deus*, in Italian as *Dio*, and in Spanish as *Dios*.

Thus, in our Bibles, the names Yahweh and Yahowshua are replaced by the names of the pagan deities of the nations amongst whom the Hebrews dwelt. For Yahweh is replaced by Baal, the Babylonian deity, or Adonay, the Canaanitish deity of the Phoenicians, both of which have the meaning of the English word *Lord*.

Such names as Lord, God, Jesus and Christ in no way represent the true meanings of the Name of the Most High revealed to Moses and the patriarchs. Such translations mislead the worshipper, transferring the praise of the Almighty and diverting energy to pagan gods. This form of idolatry is the most mischievous there is, in that it appears to have the form of true worship, but in actuality subtly absorbs the life force of the individual, channeling it in a way that distorts the truth and binds the individual to illusions. Similar things happen in all forms of religion, but nowhere as overtly as in Christianity.

One could argue that, if the meaning of a word is forgotten, or if the meaning is absent from its sound, then the word cannot be properly or practically used, rendering it dead. In the case of Hebrew and Aramaic, words are associated with an intricate system of symbols and numbers, which many scholars have tried to translate literally. But Hebrew is an idiomatic language and cannot be literally translated into a classical or modern language. One Hebrew word may have anywhere from three to ten different meanings, depending on the context, therefore, whole thoughts and not mere words must be translated.

Much, if not all of the confusion that Bible readers of today face can be attributed to the mistranslation of the scriptural texts by Greek and other scribes and scholars. The foundation of modern Christianity is based upon commitments to some of these interpretations. Subsequently, questions pertaining to the authentic meaning of the scriptures, especially the New Testament, are viewed as sacrilegious, making it difficult to correct the errors of the past. The Church is built upon hermeneutics erroneously arrived at long ago; what will its future be if past errors are not corrected?

We have concluded that the name of the man known as the Christ definitely was not *Jesus*. There is also newfound evidence that His life and teachings were radically different from those that we have come to accept based on the New Testament. If newfound evidence, such as that found in the *Dead Sea* and *Nag Hammadi* scrolls, is what it seems, we are compelled to ask questions which will shake the foundation of the Christian belief system: questions such as, Who was this Jesus of Nazareth? And from whence did He come? What was His childhood like? When was He really born? What did the Immaculate Conception mean to the founders of the early Church? Was Jesus just an enlightened Jew?

The *Essene New Testament* presents a number of stories and concepts conflicting with the New Testament of the K.J.V. These conflicts compel us to come to grips with our accepted beliefs about the life and works of Christ.

The conflicts are that, according to the Essenes:
1. Joseph was the legitimate biological father of Yahowshua.
2. Mary and Joseph had sex in order to conceive the Divine Child.
3. He was born into the Jewish ascetic group called the Essenes.
4. He was a vegetarian like his Essene mother and father.
5. He taught the equality of women and acknowledged the feminine in the Divine.

6. Yahowshua was married at eighteen years of age to Miriam, a virgin of the tribe of Judah, who died seven years after they wed.

> And in the eighteenth year of his age, Iesus was espoused unto Miriam, a virgin of the tribe of Iudah with whom he lived seven years, and she died, for God took her, that he might go on to the higher things which he had to do, and to suffer for the sons and daughters of men.
>
> Taken from the *Essene New Testament*

If the ancient Essenes were, as believed by many historians, the forerunners of the so-called Christian Church, then these differences or inconsistencies are in fact something to look deeper into. One may assume that the Essene version gives the more accurate and authentic depiction of the life and teachings of the Messiah.

A comparative study of the Essene Gospel and the canonical New Testament shows that the Yahowshua of the *Gospel of the Holy Twelve* is definitely not the Jesus of the *Holy Bible*. Though they would seem to have the same purpose, two quite different portraits are drawn of two similar, but different, characters. In both accounts, the conception and birth of the personalities occur in Divine fashion, but the Essene Messiah came from the seed and egg of Joseph and Mary through the act of sex, while the King James Version presents a sexless, fatherless birth. This is a fundamental difference which affects the theology and nature of the Christian Church as we know it.

The Essenian understanding of His birth is more in alignment with the natural established order of animal life as humans understand it. This one difference is sufficient to establish that the doctrines and ways of the present church is substantially different from the early church established by the Essenes. Many contemporary Jews and Christians accept and support the theory that Yahowshua, like John the Baptist, was an Essene master. If so, then, like John, He was a type of Nazarite priest and practiced strict vegetarianism in accordance with the teachings of the higher school of knowledge.

There are, as I suggested earlier, many implications of the basic difference between the ancient Essenes and modern Christians about the Christ's birth. The Essene understanding of the Immaculate Conception as the fruit of a consciously aligned sexual act between Mary and Joseph makes a more realistic foundation for a church. The reason is simple. If Yahowshua was naturally born as a result of sex, His organic physical manifestation is authenticated, bringing Him into a clearer light. If He was not born through sex, but through other, obscure and unnatural means, as described by the Gospels of the K.J.V., then His humanity is totally lost, and His believers are alienated and confused. Therefore, one must look at this issue objectively, and with great care and sensitivity.

The concept of the (literally) immaculately conceived Christ, which is commonly accepted by the general Christian public, denies Christ a human sexual nature, and in so doing, ultimately denies to their humanity their true Divine Christ nature. Without sex, Christ cannot experience the first birth, which is a carnal birth of a biological nature. Only through the first birth does he learn, and become able to teach, how to transform crude material into the refined astral body that is the reborn body of Christ, which is immaculately conceived in a mystical sense. This reborn body is not biological by nature, nor does it claim descent from any lineage through father or mother. It is God, the Father and Mother within, who gives birth to this higher conscious substance known as the body of Christ.

> ...And Iesus began at this time to be thirty years of age, being after the flesh indeed the Son of Ioseph and Mary; but after the Spirit, the Christ, the Son of God,

the Father and Mother Eternal, as was declared by the Spirit of holiness.

Taken from the *Essene New Testament*

If the clergy close the door through which the initiate can enter into union with Christ on the spiritual and the personal level, then, by virtue of doing so, they deny to the spirit of Christ a body or vessel through which the work of the Divine can be expressed.

The fact that the founding Rastafarians accepted Jesus Christ as a precursor to Haile Sellassie I in no way meant that they accepted him in the same fanatical way as the Christians who were their predecessors. In fact, these Rastafarians held strongly to the idea that the King James Version was not complete and could only be read correctly by those whose third eye was open. It would appear that they had views of the Bible conflicting with those of Christians. Such views as: *The white man did not edit the Bible for the benefit of the black man*[95] did not prevent them from pointing out many passages in the Bible which supported their belief in Haile Sellassie I as the prophesied Second Coming. The Bible was (and still is) their most sacred text, above all other books besides the autobiography of Haile Sellassie I.

At some point in the nineteen-fifties, continuing until the seventies, the mythical *Maccabee Bible* was rumored in Jamaica to be the lost Bible of the black man, the book containing the true teachings of the Christ. The Maccabee Bible represented Rastafarians' knowledge that there was another version of the ancient tradition, one that, to them, was more profitable to Africans who had been severed from their roots. This sacred book was banned in Jamaica, in order, the Rastafarians asserted, to keep the oppressed black masses in the dark about their true identity and presence in the Bible.

---

95 Words of the late great Reggae superstar, Bob Marley.

Abraham was a black man, as were Jesse and David and Solomon and all the prophets. Jesus Christ himself was a black man, but the white man stole the Bible from black people, superimposed his image on it, and re-translated it in such a way as to enforce white supremacy over black people. These are fundamental Rastafarian beliefs about the Bible and its origins.

The future of Africa depends on whether Africans at home and abroad are ready to face themselves, first as Africans, and then as people controlled and manipulated by an alien force. The lobotomizing of the African mind by Christian missionaries has gone a long way towards disconnecting Africans from the African spirit, while injecting the saving grace of Jesus Christ into the psyche of African natives. Jesuit priests, in particular, systematically reshaped the perspective of Africans, while subjugating them to the Christ of the white supremacists. Thus the Christians, through their domination of African peoples, alienate them from their true birthright, which is their African cultural heritage.

For example, the popular religious icon of the Mother (or Madonna) and Child, common to just about every Christian denomination, continues to depict them as Europeans. If they are depicted as Africans, or as anything other than Europeans, the icon is automatically dubbed and dismissed as a *Black Madonna and Child*, although the European icon is never called a *White Madonna*. It is important to note that the Egyptian image of Horus nursing at the breast of his mother Isis is the most ancient and archetypal image of mother and child there is. The same is true for icons of Jesus, who because he is depicted as European, forces the African version to alone be called a *Black Christ*.[96] A paperback entitled *The African Presence in the Bible*, was written in direct reaction to the Eurocentric

---

[96] Ironically, there is a book about the life and work of Marcus Garvey called *Black Moses*. As we have seen, Moses was black, so it's ironic that a book about the life and work of Marcus Garvey was called *Black Moses*.

overtones of the modern Christian scriptures. Why is there no book on *the European presence in the Bible*?

All this is to illustrate the fact that the white man has hegemony over Christianity and controls all aspects of it, so that, whenever Africans adopt, or convert to, Christianity, they need to apply corrective measures to see and to show the African presence in the Bible. By doing so, however, by recognizing and opposing the white supremacist overtones of mainstream Christianity, they are seen as fanatics. Some critics go as far as to label such reactions by Africans as *blackening* history.

The situation with Judaism is very much the same as with Christianity. The European Jew has done much to convince the world that Jewishness is more than a religion, but a race of white people. Believe it or not, they have more or less succeeded. Whenever an African calls himself a Jew, he or she is seen as some rare phenomenon — certainly as someone who converted to that faith. Even most Africans are surprised at the claim that there are age-old communities of black Jews; this is ironic when we consider that Judaism's roots are in Egypt.

The scriptural Book of Exodus declares that some Hebrews in Egypt did not know that Moses, who was brought up in the house of the pharaoh, was a Hebrew. They thought he was an Egyptian. The point is this: If ancient Egyptian civilization was indigenously African, as may be clearly seen in the ruins and monuments at Luxor and Gaza, then Moses, the Hebrew, must have looked like an Egyptian. Specifically, he must have been one of the Semitic Nubians native to North East Africa. The African origins of Jewish civilization have been masked by European images and influences, and this can only have come about as the result of conspiracy. This is not news to most Bible students, nor to renowned scholars of Judaeo-Christian history, and it should certainly not be news to people of African descent today.

Judaism is the only major religion claiming to be a race as well as a religion. Although Judaism makes this claim, calling a group comprised solely of Europeans *Jews for Jesus* is oxymoronic. Once a Jew becomes a Christian, he or she ceases to be a Jew in the traditional sense. The acceptance of Jesus Christ as the Savior makes one a Christian, regardless of race, creed or previous religious preoccupation. A Jew who accepts Christ and then calls himself a *Jew for Jesus* claims exemption from this rule. By pretending to keep the privilege of being a Jew, they want to have their cake and eat it too.

If the European Jews are allowed their claim that Judaism is a race as well as a religion, then only a certain group of Europeans and a certain group of non-Europeans can be considered Jewish. This makes Judaism a narrow tribal religion, exclusive to the chosen few, and the Jew's god is not the living God but only the god seen from the prejudiced perspective of Jewish interpretation. Christianity, on the other hand, claims just about everything that makes a Jew a Jew, but embraces an existential philosophy that makes it a universal religion. The missionaries care not whether one is black, brown or yellow. Their only mission is to convert the poor ignorant soul to fulfill its duty to breathe life into a Eurocentric value system through Jesus Christ.

Through their investigations, the early Rastafarians found in the scriptures detailed descriptions of current events. The central figure, Haile Sellassie I, was hidden in veiled prophetical allusions. They saw their sect's origin, life, purpose and glorious destiny all to have been preordained, being laid out in the predictions of the ancients. But only the aligned, those who had eyes to see, could discern how the truth of these mysteries has been revealed at this moment in time. The secrets of the Bible could only be rediscovered by those whose seals were broken in the spirit of truth. As they saw it, if one did not acknowledge how prophecy had been fulfilled, especially where Haile Sellassie I was concerned, then one could not claim to know Jesus Christ either. They saw this to be so because, while Jesus was thousands of years ago, Haile Sellassie I's presence was revealed in the here and now. For Rastafarians, the two could not be separated. Jesus, the Son, always presupposed a Father, who, for the Rastafarians, is the true King of Kings and Lord of Lords, Haile Sellassie I.

The monopoly that Europe has claimed on Judaism and Christianity leaves Africa and Africans bound up in strings, under a white supremacist hierarchy headed by rabbis and popes. Essenism, associated with both Judaism and early Christianity, is key to understanding mystic Judaism and the pioneers of the early Church. Therefore, while some groups, who were invested in later, false teachings, put much effort into suppressing the Essene writings, others, radicals, wanted to expose them to public scrutiny. Through the efforts of the radicals, the *Dead Sea Scrolls* have been published in many languages.

In 1928, Edmond Bordeaux Szekley, who earned his Ph.D. from the University of Paris, published his translation of the Essene Gospel of Peace, based on a sacred ancient manuscript that he found in the secret underground archives of the Vatican. He released it in four volumes: Book 1, *The Essene Gospel of Peace*; Book 2, *The Unknown Book of the Essenes*; Book 3, *The Lost Scrolls and the Essene Brotherhood*; and Book 4, *The Teachings of the Elect*.

These books reveal the Essene interpretation of the life and teaching of Yahowshua, which contradicts foundational beliefs of Christianity, as discussed. But, once we admit to the major differences between the Jesus of conventional Christianity and the Yahowshua revealed in the earliest sources, we must ask: Why do the same blond-haired blue-eyed images so saturate Szekley's books? Pages upon pages of skillfully illustrated depictions of angels and prophets impress themselves upon the psyche of the reader. These represent the most puissant strategy of racial indoctrination through iconographic propaganda ever used by religious zealots or political leaders. The fact that Eurocentric racial domination perpetuates itself through the printed word and images shows that the authors and translators get to choose what goes in and what stays out of these books, which leads us to see European power over the presses. Yet, one cannot blame the Europeans for representing themselves in the ways in which they have done over the centuries. It is their prerogative to do so. If Africans were in their position today, things might or might not be different, considering how many Africans presently function from a Europeanized psyche. In any case the facts should prevail over opinions, race, gender and illusions, or anything that would pervert the truth.

Whenever we come across Essene literature or books on the subject of Yahowshua, we consistently encounter the same physical images, yet the text portrays Him as undeniably and uniquely different from what is commonly believed of Him. As ready as most scholars are to dispute and debate the issues that surround the mysteries of His life, they have not yet come to the point of unraveling the accepted fabric upon which this image is painted. Rather, we witness a total whitening of all images pertaining to Judaeo-Christian persons. European monopolization of religion and spirituality also claims Essenism, shaping its image and worldviews as pertaining to them. It is therefore important to see how the Rastafarians, through Ethiopianism, hold fast to something uniquely black African, which when explored in depth, reveals a certain victory over Eurocentric value systems and gods.

The Rastafarians already declared the divinity of the African blood within the context of the Bible through the lineage of David, the lineal ancestral father of Yahowshua, as well as of Ras Tafari, the Ethiopian prince who claims the heritage and lineage of the biblical Hebrews. This, for the Rastafarians, exposes the witty but cunning invention of a white Christ to prevent Africans from knowing God in their own image. The blackness of the

Solomonic kings of Ethiopia confirms that Jesus must have been just as black, if he ever existed at all.

Earlier I mentioned the ancient image of a dreadlocked Ethiopic Christ, but I must clearly state that, even in Ethiopia, this image of Christ does not necessarily typify the views of the general public. For that matter, most Ethiopians of today see King Solomon not as a black or dusky ancestor, but rather like the Jews that now occupy Jerusalem. This is one of the ongoing issues between Rastafarians and the Ethiopian Orthodox Church, which some Rastafarians claim is now being colonized by European Christianity and its icons. They argue that Ethiopia evaded the colonization process of old but is now succumbing to another form of colonization, colonization by a non-Ethiopian image of the Son of God. By thus succumbing to Europe, Ethiopia today is giving Europe even greater hegemony, a power that can only be counteracted by the anciency of the Ethiopian Church.

If Ethiopians, while claiming descent from David, deny the blackness of *Iyesus Cristos*, how can they claim that their rulers for more than two thousand years have been descendants of Abraham via the union of King Solomon and Queen Makeda of Sheba? *Dem no know dem selves, dats why dem suffah,* says Rastafarian icon Bob Marley, who, though his father was a white Englishman, claimed African roots through his Jamaican mother. He said this in response to Ethiopians who denounced Rastafarians for worshipping Haile Sellassie I as the returned Christ, the Black God.

Rastafari would appear to be the only world religion, for lack of a better word (unless you count certain West African spiritual traditions), that Africans have any claim to or any autonomy with. The Rastafarians claim legitimacy as a Messianic Order through Ethiopia's authentic claim to Judaism, as well as through its Orthodox Coptic Christianity. Rastafari, as a Way, gives Ethi-

Here is a sticker, commonly found hanging in kiosks, car windows, and bumpers of taxis and buses all over Ethiopia. I bought these on the back streets of Merkato, Addis Ababa in 1997, and surprisingly enough, this kind of imagery has only increased over the years. It is a prime example of what I mean in terms of Ethiopia's diversion from her roots. This sticker depicts Jesus, centered on the shape of Ethiopia against a backdrop of the country's national colors with a caption in Amharic: *Medihani alem Ethiopian ye TebiKatal* = "The savior of the world will protect Ethiopia."

opians the opportunity to now embrace what they deny in their Christian conviction, and it launches a whole new path through the now-Westernized dogmas and traditions of the once ancient faith. Rastafarians radically dismiss the idea of a white Christ. They will reinterpret any and all scriptures through the spectacles of Africans and make it fit into their pro-Ethiopian conviction. To Rastafarians, Ethiopians are the people chosen to preserve the glory of the Living God, a glory Rastafarians now inherit through their acceptance of Haile Sellassie I — making Rastafarians, who, after all, consider themselves Ethiopians, the New Israel and the few, the chosen, the elect of Jah.

Like the early Christians under the empire of Caesar, the vanguards of Rastafari, dubbed *Nyahmen*,[97] refused to participate in the armed forces of Jamaica on the ground that such service

---

[97] *Nyahman* is short for the term *Nyahbingi* man *Nyahbingi* is the name of a West African warrior princess who gave her life as a sacrifice in battle against colonialism. The name is used in Rastafari to mean death to black and white oppression, and is also the term used to identify a particular sect of Rastafarians, as well as any Rastafarian gathering expressing the *churchical* drumming and chanting of the culture. *Nyahbingi* was also a secret order made up of black African leaders and headed by Haile Sellassie in order to fight European colonization on the African continent.

contradicted the teachings of Christ. Rastafarians declared that Africa was their home. It would have been useless for them to build up treasures in Babylon because repatriation was at hand. They became societal dropouts, burning the fire of apocalypse in the heart of Babylon-Jamaica.

Here we see another in the classic iconographic European style, in the same Ethiopian motif as the previous sticker, but this time the caption says; *Ime berhan ye Ethiopia.TebaKi nat.* which means "Mother light will protect Ethiopia" These images are not unusual in the Ethiopia of today. It has become commonplace, and can be seen, in various motifs, on commercial minibuses and taxis all over Ethiopia.

The religious leaders of their day condemned them as being of Satan, the victims of hallucinogenic visions induced by marijuana, an herb that the Rastafarians call a religious sacrament. Fear grew when locks-men increased in numbers and could be seen regularly in public places. The Rastafarians pointed to what they saw as the spiritual and moral bankruptcy of the colonial government, and the wickedness and corruption of Babylon, which led to wars and rumors of wars as prophesied by Christ in the Gospel of St. Matthew ch. 24, v. 6: *And ye shall hear of wars and rumors of wars: see that ye be not troubled: for all things must come to pass, but the end is not yet.*

If the Ethiopian Orthodox Church should claim her true and complete African glory in Christ, she would automatically propel herself into the center of the Judaeo-Christian world. Unless Ethiopia fully asserts her mystical claim on Christ, white supremacy in the name of Jesus will continue to hold complete authority in Christendom and Christianity. Only Ethiopia can stand up to the papacy in Rome, and only She has the authority and antiquity to claim for real what is called the Black Christ. Many historians and biblical scholars are aware of this. If Ethiopia fails to return to Her original value system, her African Christian ideal, then she undermines her lineal claim to King David's Divine legacy.

The fervent revival of Ethiopianism that flourished in the 1930s among diasporic Africans in the West Indies led to the popular belief that Ethiopia is the Black People's Zion. Although this concept was popular among early twentieth-century black nationalists and pan-Africanists, it soon dwindled into a sectarian and political idea among certain devotees descended from the Garvey era, the ones we now know as the Rastafarians. Ethiopia shoots herself in the foot when, though she claims so much along the lines of her descent from ancient Jewry as well as early Christianity, she yet continues to look outside herself, to the ruins of Palestine, certainly, but also to the seat of Rome for her spiritual and religious heritage and inspiration.

In many modern paintings which depict the legendary encounter of King Solomon and Queen Makeda, although the Ethiopian artist paints the Queen a chocolate brown, Solomon is rendered as a pink-skinned European King. We also observe that Menelik, the son from the union, is shown in some paintings today as the same pink skin color as his father. This wasn't always so. As it happens, Ethiopia has preserved some of the most ancient and beautiful religious icons of the exalted Mother and Child that have ever been painted anywhere, as well as some of the most solemn portraits of Christ. Many images of saints of Ethiopia's Christian Orthodoxy are skillfully painted onto the interior walls of the monolithic churches. Some surviving images date as far back as the thirteenth and fourteenth centuries,[98] and they portray a variety of sacred images and symbols, but all depict the facial features of the Ethiopian in the style of the Solomonic Amhara. This can be seen in the big melancholy eyes of the angels, which gaze out of big round black faces. This iconographic style is unique to Ethiopia in the world of religious art. It is said that a German painter once painted an icon of Jesus modeled on Haile Sellassie I. It would be good for Ethiopia to follow his lead.

These modern Ethiopian artists perpetuate a drastic change in tradition by embracing and crystallizing the relatively new idea of the Europeans that to be Hebrew or Jew means to be pink-skinned. Ethiopia, for thousands of years the only Jewish monarchy, has always in Her history proudly claimed a rulership on the Davidic throne; she never imagined King David and Solomon as European Jews. For hundreds, even thousands of years, Judaism thrived as the state religion of the land of Judah-Ethiopia. As almost everyone now knows, the heirs to the Ethiopian Throne have always claimed lineage from King Solomon and Queen Makeda of Sheba. If the Greek name *Ethiopia* means burnt or black faces, then there is a legitimate so-called black Jewish Empire established in Ethiopia, and it has been established since before the concept of Jesus was ever contrived.

Why was this kingdom established in Ethiopia? What is the spiritual value and meaning of it? If the scriptures are right in characterizing the Ark of the Covenant as Yahweh's Shekinah[99] amongst the Israelites, then Ethiopia's claim of royal and

---

98 Many of Ethiopia's ancient artifacts were either stolen or destroyed by warring foreign invaders, such as Imam Ahmad Ghrand in 1531, who penetrated Ethiopia's borders and destroyed the oldest church (4th century), St. Mary of Zion, and precious relics along with it. Many other such sackings as a result of various wars fought on the basis of European colonial intentions cost Ethiopia dearly in the department of records and ancient artifacts. The Derg, a Communist government that overthrow Haile Sellassie I's government in 1975, did its fair share in destroying much of Ethiopia's ancient Christian heritage.

99 Shekinah is Hebrew for YHVH's habitation or presence, something like God's spirit. Like the related concepts, Zion and (God's) wisdom, it is of feminine gender. Proverbs chap. 8 speaks at length of wisdom as a female power.

Messianic ancestry points the finger to Herself as the habitation of the living God. *Ethiopia shall soon stretch forth her hand unto God*[100] is far more than a "clue" to the mystery of God's abode on earth. Obedience to the direction in which She points leads every curious and inquisitive mind to the heart of Her bosom.

The icon of the Queen of Sheba and her only son Menelik gave birth to an identical portrait of the Christian Mother and Child. How significant is this? In no other part of Judaism was there such an image. This age-old Ethiopian image shows the Judaic Christianity of the land through the prism of Mother and Child in a manner unmatched and unclaimed anywhere else in the world.

Christian Ethiopians, and certain astute historians and biblical scholars as well, regard Lalibela as a New Jerusalem, a Zion. However, for many Ethiopian Christians and Jews alike, Palestine continues to be the birthplace of their forefathers and the cradle of their faith. Consequently they esteem Israel as the Holy Land and Jerusalem, the Sacred City. The Falashas, or Beta Israel as they prefer to be called, are a unique Jewish community indigenous to Ethiopia. Their Jewish faith was established there in Ethiopia before Christ was even born, yet they proved that they had no attachment to Ethiopia when they declared that they were exiles there and that Israel was their rightful home and Zion on earth.

This is ironic, for even though Europeans have known for centuries about the Ethiopian Jews, the latter appear to have been largely unaware of the European Jews, with their belated and reformed writs and rites. The centuries of isolation of the Ethiopian realm long helped to shroud these forgotten descendants of Ham with thick clouds of mystery. When to this was added the loss of their political stronghold in a Hebraic empire that rapidly became a Christian empire, desperate

---

100 Psalm 68, v. 31

conditions developed in their dwindling communities. But once Europeans filtered into the interior of modern Ethiopia, the outside world made a new connection to the Beta Israel. Ashkenazi Jews became their allies, culminating in *Operation Moses*, the repatriation of Ethiopian Jews to the Holy Land of Palestine, which commenced on November 21, 1984 and continued until January 5, 1985.

The Ethiopian Jews that migrated to Israel encountered contempt and prejudice as they came face to face with their pink-skinned brothers and sisters in the faith. For the Beta Israel, life in Palestine has not been what they expected. Their day-to-day social experience in their newfound reality contradicted their spiritual ideals, these Black Jews in a white-run-Zion. Operation Moses is a perfect example of Ethiopians looking to the outside world for fulfillment, only to get caught in a web of religious disillusionment.

Rastafarians view the exodus of these Jews from Ethiopia with disdain, exclaiming, *Many are called, but few are chosen*. It leads one to ask major questions, such as: What Zion or heaven can be prepared for Africans by a white-dominated religion and culture? Can Africans possibly continue to worship a god who requires them to subjugate their psyches to a white supremacist belief system, rendering the possibility of developing an African spirituality moot? These questions and many others are the reason this book was written, in an attempt to explore the answers and to examine, using a new faculty of interpretation, the possibilities for Rastafari as the solution and ultimate alternative.

African people worshiping the white man's god have yet to create a truly independent and autonomous nation, rather, Christianity and other religions have used the misinformed masses of Africans as an instrument by which to develop white men into a powerful world order. If the enemies of indigenous spirituality were able to create a concept, give life to it, and use it to mastermind a conspiracy to enslave the globe, binding its peoples to the illusion of salvation in Jesus, then Ethiopia surely can and must cultivate a deeper consciousness around Her true reality in Christ. By doing so, Ethiopia alone can give Africans, and in particular diasporic Africans, an ultimate alternative to the contraceptive mentality of Western Christianity, and by doing so claim Her rightful place in the developing spectrum of Judaeo-Christian thought.

Should Ethiopia make such a paradigm shift, the many that are called by the new name Rastafari, the Essene Nazarites, through these ancient Gnostic Essene teachings, will return home to Zion, as more than prodigal sons and daughters, indeed as the royal fruits of the ancient mysteries, and the future womb for the seeds of the chosen few.

The Journey continues...

APPENDIX A:
THE AUTHENTICITY OF THE BIBLE

"Masoretic" is the name given to a text of the Bible that is distinguished particularly by the system of vowel signs which was developed by the Jewish Ben Asher family and applied to the Hebrew Bible between the 7th and 10th centuries A.D. The word "Masoretic" comes from the Hebrew *masorah*, meaning transmission of a tradition — in this case, the copying, editing and distribution of the Hebrew scriptures.

One of the best examples of the Masoretic text is the Leningrad Codex, which is considered to be the oldest complete Hebrew Bible that exists. It contains all the books now included in Jewish bibles, and dates from circa 1009 A.D., most likely in Egypt. There are older codices,[101] such as the Aleppo, which can be used as references for correcting the Leningrad Codex, but they are incomplete. The importance of the Leningrad Codex is that it is used as the basis for most modern translations of the Hebrew Bible. It has been reproduced in the Biblia Hebraica (1937) and Biblia Hebraica Stuttgartensia (1977).

The King James Version (KJV), the most famous English Bible, is considered by many to be the greatest piece of English literature of all time, as well as its number-one best seller. It began in October of 1603 when, at the behest of King James, 54 scholars from the Church of England were appointed to edit the previous English Bibles. The job was completed in seven years, in 1611, with 47 of the original appointees working on it to completion. The KJV therefore was 400 years old in 2011. King James instructed the scholars as follows:

> 1. The ordinary Bible read in the Church, commonly called the Bishops' Bible, to be followed, and as little altered as the original will permit.

---

101 "Codices" is the plural form of "codex" which means "book."

2. The names of the prophets and the holy writers, with the other names in the text, to be retained, as near as may be, accordingly as they are vulgarly used.

3. The old ecclesiastical words to be kept, as the word *church,* not to be translated *congregation.*

4. When any word hath divers significations, that to be kept which hath been most commonly used by the most eminent fathers, being agreeable to the propriety of the place and the analogies of faith.

5. The division of chapters to be altered either not at all, or as little as may be, if necessity so require.

6. No marginal notes at all to be affixed, but only for the explanation of the Hebrew or Greek words, which cannot, without some circumlocution, so briefly and fitly be expressed, in the text.

7. Such quotations of places to be marginally set down as shall serve for the fit reference of one Scripture to another.

8. Every particular man of each company to take the same chapter or chapters; and, having translated or amended them severally by himself where he thinks good, all to meet together to confirm what they have done, and agree for their part what shall stand.

9. As any one company hath dispatched any one book in this manner, they shall send it to the rest, to be considered of seriously and judiciously; for his Majesty is very careful on this point.

10. If any company, upon the review of the book so sent, shall doubt or differ upon any places, to send them word thereof, to note the places, and therewithal to send their reasons; to which if they consent not, the difference to be compounded at the general meeting, which is to be of the chief persons of each company, at the end of the work.

11. When any place of special obscurity is doubted of, letters to be directed by authority to send to any learned man in the land for his judgment of such a place.

12. Letters to be sent from every bishop to the rest of his clergy, admonishing them of this translation in hand, and to move and

charge as many as, being skillful in the tongues, have taken pains in that kind, to send their particular observations to the company, either at Westminster, Cambridge, or Oxford, according as it was directed before in the king's letter to the archbishop.

13. The directors in each company to be the Deans of Westminster and Chester, for Westminster, and the king's professors in Hebrew and Greek in the two universities.

14. These translations to be used, when they agree better with the text than the Bishops' Bible: Tyndale's, Coverdale's, Matthew's [Rogers'], Whitchurch's [Cranmer's], Geneva.

15. By a later rule, "three or four of the most ancient and grave divines, in either of the universities, not employed in translating, to be assigned to be overseers of the translation, for the better observation of the fourth rule."

These physicians of theology, doctors and scholars were some of the most brilliant and accomplished men of their time. Among these learned men and translators were:

- Dr. Launcelot Andrewes, Dean of Westminster, presided over the Westminster company. Fuller says of him: "The world wanted learning to know how learned this man was, so skilled in all (especially Oriental) languages, that some conceive he might, if then living, almost have served as an interpreter-general at the confusion of tongues." He became successively Bishop of Chichester, Ely and Winchester. Born 1555, died 1626.

- Dr. Edward Lively, Regius Professor of Hebrew at Cambridge, and thus at the head of the Cambridge company, was eminent for his knowledge of Oriental languages, especially of Hebrew. He died in 1605, having been Professor of Hebrew for twenty-five years. His death was a great loss to the work, which he had helped to begin, but not to complete.

- Dr. John Overall was made Professor of Divinity at Cambridge in 1596, and in 1604 was Dean of St. Paul's, London. He was considered by some the most scholarly divine in England. In 1614 he was made Bishop of Litchfield and Coventry. He was transferred to the see of Norwich in 1618. Born 1559, died 1619.

- Dr. Adrian de Saravia is said to have been the only foreigner employed on the work. He was born in Artois, France; his Father was a Spaniard, and his mother a Belgian. In 1582 he was Professor of Divinity at Leyden; in 1587 he came to England. He became Prebend of Canterbury, and afterward Canon of Westminster. He was noted for his knowledge of Hebrew. Born 1531, died 1612.

- William Bedwell, or Beadwell, was one of the greatest Arabic scholars of his day. At his death he left unfinished MSS. of an Arabic Lexicon, and also of a Persian Dictionary.

- Dr. Laurence Chadderton was for thirty-eight years Master of Emanuel College, Cambridge, and well versed in Rabbinical learning. He was one of the few Puritan divines among the translators. Born 1537, died 1640 at the advanced age of one hundred and three.

- Dr. John Reynolds, who first suggested the work, was a man of great attainments in Hebrew and Greek. He died before the revision was completed, but worked at it during his last sickness as long as his strength permitted. Born 1549, died 1607.

- Dr. Richard Kilbye, Oxford Professor of Hebrew, was reckoned among the greatest Hebraists of his day. Died 1620.

- Dr. Miles Smith was a student of classic authors from his youth, was well acquainted with the Rabbinical learning, and well versed in Hebrew, Chaldee, Syriac and Arabic. He was often called a "walking library." Born about 1568, died 1624.

- John Boyse, or Bois, at six years of age could write Hebrew elegantly. He was for twelve years chief lecturer in Greek at St. John's College, Cambridge. Bishop Andrewes, of Ely, made him a prebend in his church in 1615. He was one of the most laborious of all the revisers. Born 1560, died 1643.

- Sir Henry Saville was warden of Merton College, Oxford, for thirty-six years. He devoted his fortune to the encouragement of learning, and was himself a fine Greek scholar. Born 1549, died 1622.

- Dr. Thomas Holland was Regius Professor of Divinity in Exeter College, Oxford, and also Master of his college. He was considered a prodigy in all branches of literature. Born 1539, died 1612.

> Taken from Isaac H. Hall, ed., *The Revised New Testament and History of Revisions*. Philadelphia: Hubbard Brothers, 1881.

The KJV of the Bible issued in 1611 by these learned men was primarily based upon the Textus Receptus, a codex compiled by a Dutch theologian named Desiderius Erasmus (circa 1466-1536). Some scholars take a critical view of this manuscript and dismiss it as being hurriedly put together with "thousands of typographical errors." These errors made their way into the 1611 King James Version of the Bible.

Despite the recent findings of earlier, more authentic documents, ardent fundamentalist Christians and millions of other believers assert that the KJV contains the infallible words of God. Nothing could be further from the truth. The original writers of the manuscripts that comprise the Bible may have been divinely inspired, but the same cannot be said for the many copies from various translations in Greek, Latin and other languages that make the scriptures of the *Holy Bible*. The reliability of the bible has been under suspicion and has been questioned for centuries by more than just renowned scholars but also by the general public. Of course these objections are more popular today than they were in the dark ages of medieval Europe.

Today, the Bible is under serious scrutiny by objective and critical minds from all walks of life. Many outrightly denounce much of it as a compilation of ancient writings flawed and defective by time and translations. Men of vision, who are deemed inspired by God, originally scribed the majority of the writings that comprise the books of the Bible, in Aramaic or Hebrew and in Greek. They were, however, individuals with their own insights, opinions and interpretations of Jewish history and traditions and had not meant for their writing to be compiled with the writings of other authors, much less called the word of God.

Some of the authors accredited with writing many of the books in the Bible, from Genesis, supposedly written by Moses, to the four Gospels of Matthew, Mark, Luke and John, are known to be wrong.

It is thought by some historians that many of these writings may be the works of ghostwriters, who customarily penned manuscripts and credited names like Solomon or Enoch as the authors because they felt that the writings were vicariously inspired by these greats. This was a common practice in those days.

The idea that the Bible is the infallible irrefutable word of God has been the conservative Christian doctrinal position for ages. To dispute the inerrancy of the Bible, however, has more or less become the order of today's tech-savvy minds, stirring heated and passionate discussions between conservative Christians and objective forward-thinking radicals. Bible inconsistencies are a popular subject, and are pointed out by many bible students and scholars as showing the very fallible nature of its authors. This is not a new subject for Bible skeptics.

One of the primary agitators for objectivity about the Bible is Thomas Paine, with his 17th century publication of *The Age of Reason* written in three parts. Following in the footsteps of eighteen-century British deists, Paine's book's main point is that the bible is the fantastic imagination of man and is without doubt flawed by his nature. Paine declared that the government and the church were in cahoots to manipulate and monopolize the minds of the public without considering the people's interest. Men who, like Thomas Paine, I consider forward-thinking, emerged out of Europe's Age of Enlightenment, believed that the Bible was not exempt from public scrutiny, but should be held to the same tests of logic and reason applied to any other piece of literature.

At the beginning of Part I of the *Age of Reason*, Paine lays out his personal creed:

> I believe in one God, and no more; and I hope for happiness beyond this life.

I believe in the equality of man; and I believe that religious duties consist in doing justice, loving mercy, and endeavoring to make our fellow-creatures happy.

But, lest it should be supposed that I believe many other things in addition to these, I shall, in the progress of this work, declare the things I do not believe, and my reasons for not believing them.

I do not believe in the creed professed by the Jewish Church, by the Roman Church, by the Greek Church, by the Turkish Church, by the Protestant Church, nor by any church that I know of. My own mind is my own church.

All national institutions of churches, whether Jewish, Christian or Turkish, appear to me no other than human inventions, set up to terrify and enslave mankind, and monopolize power and profit.

I do not mean by this declaration to condemn those who believe otherwise; they have the same right to their belief as I have to mine. But it is necessary to the happiness of man that he be mentally faithful to himself. Infidelity does not consist in believing, or in disbelieving; it consists in professing to believe what he does not believe.

In 1792 when the first part of the Age of Reason was composed, Paine was on the run from England, after the British dubbed his latest book, *Rights of Man, Part II* seditious. While in France, he published *The Age of Reason* in 1793, copies of which sold for three pence a piece. It was to become somewhat of a bible for deists and bible skeptics of subsequent centuries. Pointing out the inconsistencies and contradictions of the Bible, Paine hoped to effect change in how the religious system works and how the masses view it. This religious change, he thought, would eventually effect positive change in the political system as well.

Inconsistencies in the Bible prompt some to wonder, should they be viewed as errors of men or as the imperfection of God? Either way one chooses poses threats to the established understanding and acceptance of the Bible as it is.

The following quotations from the Bible are taken from the King James Version of 1611:

Genesis 1:3-5

[3] And God said, Let there be light: and there was light.
[4] And God saw the light, that it was good: and God divided the light from the darkness.
[5] And God called the light Day, and the darkness he called Night. And the evening and the morning were the first day.

Genesis 1:14-19

[14] And God said, Let there be lights in the firmament of the heaven to divide the day from the night; and let them be for signs, and for seasons, and for days, and years:
[15] And let them be for lights in the firmament of the heaven to give light upon the earth: and it was so.
[16] And God made two great lights; the greater light to rule the day, and the lesser light to rule the night: he made the stars also.
[17] And God set them in the firmament of the heaven to give light upon the earth,
[18] And to rule over the day and over the night, and to divide the light from the darkness: and God saw that it was good.
[19] And the evening and the morning were the fourth day.

Which of the above should we believe to be the correct understanding? On the first day light and darkness was separated and day and night created, but the sun, which separates night from day, wasn't created until the fourth day.

Here is another example:

Genesis 16:15

¹⁵ And Hagar bare Abram a son: and Abram called his son's name, which Hagar bare, Ishmael.

Genesis 21:1-3

21 And the Lord visited Sarah as he had said, and the Lord did unto Sarah as he had spoken.
² For Sarah conceived, and bare Abraham a son in his old age, at the set time of which God had spoken to him.
³ And Abraham called the name of his son that was born unto him, whom Sarah bare to him, Isaac.

Galatians 4:22

²² For it is written, that Abraham had two sons, the one by a bondmaid, the other by a freewoman.

Hebrews 11:17

¹⁷ By faith Abraham, when he was tried, offered up Isaac: and he that had received the promises offered up his only begotten son,

Hebrews ch. 11, v. 17 states that Abraham gave up his only begotten son, meaning that he had only one son, Isaac. Yet Genesis ch. 16, v. 15 states that Abraham had a son with Hagar. Is there some esoteric explanation for this?

Or are these merely superfluous assertions and concerns? There are many more inconsistencies or contradictions in the Bible, contained in over a hundred passages. Yet these issues by no means nullify the value of the Bible or its importance in the minds of the faithful, as they call upon their God today.

Ancient manuscripts recently discovered, such as the *Nag Hammadi Library*, the *Dead Sea Scrolls* and the *Essene New Testament* are all documents that are considerably older than those used to translate the Bible as we know it. These ancient documents may confirm aspects of the KJV, but for the most part, contradict it. As stated before, the Gospel of the Holy Twelve, for example, controversial for many decades amongst scholars, gives us a vegetarian version of Yahowshua as well as a sexual conception of his immaculate birth and record him as being the spouse of Miriam Magdalene. The Bible doesn't specifically say that he was a Nazarite, but Essene Gospels clearly declare his Nazariteship.

> *Then said Miriam unto the angel, How shall this be, seeing I know not a man? And the angel answered and said unto her, The Holy Spirit shall come upon Ioseph thy spouse, and the power of the Highest shall overshadow thee...Therefore ye shall eat no flesh, nor drink strong drink, for the child shall be consecrated unto god from his mother's womb, and neither flesh nor strong drink shall he take, nor shall razor touch his head.*

What if you had read this verse before you read the version in the Bible, what would you think when you finally come in contact with a much later version of the annunciation, such as the one written in the KJV, and compare them? Would you choose to believe the fantastic latter version, or the one that seems to flow with and is governed by nature? Divine laws govern nature, and the same laws govern humanity. As we continue to read in the Essene Gospels:

> *And the same day the angel Gabriel appeared unto Ioseph in a dream and said unto him, Hail, Ioseph, thou that are highly favoured, for the Fatherhood of god is with thee...Then Ioseph being raised from sleep did as the angel had bidden him, and went in unto Miriam, his espoused bride, and she conceived in her womb the Holy One.*

However, the Bible will not agree with any of these assertions of these much older documents, as they are in direct contradiction with what is written in the Bible, and also with what most Christian believers believe. As shown above, the Essene gospels paint a totally different portrait of Yahowshua than the KJV. And if one is to take the Bible, that conditioned most Christian minds, as the literal words of God, written in stone, then one will have a difficult time accepting something as simple as natural childbirth that brought forth the Christ, but will accept the sci fi-like, supernatural phenomenon of sexless birth. This same mind will justify their incredible beliefs with FAITH, and a popular cliché: Nothing is impossible with my God. The Bible or any book, held in the same reverence by any variety of personality types, can become a vice if one is not able or willing to go above and beyond the teachings and conditionings of their religious persuasion. If nothing is impossible with God, then why not a sexual birth? Can't God do that?

The Essene gospel of the Holy Twelve goes further to say:

> And Iesus began at this time to be thirty years of age, being after the flesh indeed the son of Ioseph and Miriam; but after the Spirit, the Christ, the son of God, the father and mother Eternal, as was declared by the Spirit of holiness with power. And Ioseph was the son of Jacob Elisheba, and Miriam was the daughter of Eli (called Joachim) and Anna, who were the children of David and Bathsheba, of Judah and Shela, of Jacob and Leah, of Issac and Rebecca, of Abraham and Sarah, of Seth and Maat, of Adam and Eve, who were the children of God.

APPENDIX B:
LITTLE-KNOWN FACTS
ABOUT THE APOSTLES OF YAHOWSHUA

The Apostles knew Mary Magdalene as the Apostle of the Apostles because She, said to be Yahowshua's beloved, was the one who announced to them His resurrection. This makes her the first Apostle — a Greek word meaning messenger.

Peter was early Christianity's first champion. In the Acts of the Apostles, we hear of him performing some of the same miracles as Christ, such as healing the lame and raising the dead, as well as executing a supernatural death sentence upon one he considered to have cheated God.

The first martyr, according to the Bible, was Stephen, a vigilant young evangelist who chastened a Jewish community with words of Christ's return to destroy the temple in Jerusalem. For this he was condemned to death for blasphemy around the year 35 as he died praying for his accusers.

Before Saul of Tarsus became the apostle we know as Paul, he was a leading persecutor of Christians and observed Stephen's stoning.

Paul is said to have claimed the title apostle for himself, as he believed he had seen the Lord and received spiritual commission from him. His letters to the various pockets of converts around the Mediterranean became the substance of most of the books that make up the New Testament.

Only two of the four canonical Evangelists (writers of Gospels), Matthew and John, were among the original apostles. The other two, Mark and Luke, gained the equivalent of apostleship through their important contribution in writing Gospels of the New Testament.

St. Mark, whose symbol is a winged lion with his paw upon the open Gospel, is the founder of the Copts in Egypt. St. Mark became the nucleus and essence of the Venetian church as well as of the Alexandrian church. Tradition tells us that he died a martyr in Alexandria, from whence his remains were stolen in 828 by two Venetian merchants Bono da Malamocco and Rustico da Torcello and brought to Italy. In 1968, the Vatican returned a bone fragment said to be St. Mark's to Egypt in a gesture of apology for the ninth-century theft of the saint's remains.

King Herod Agrippa I beheaded James the Greater in the year 44.

Tradition states that Thomas founded the first Christian church in India in A.D. 52.

In the year 64, the Roman Emperor Nero accused the emerging Christian movement of arson and executed scores of early believers in his private arena with savage deaths. The condemned was torn limb from limb by ferocious wild beasts, burned in a pit of fire, or nailed to a cross.

According to tradition, 11 of the Twelve Apostles were martyred. Phillip, Andrew and Peter were crucified.

In the year 110 under the emperor Trajan, Ignatius, the bishop of Antioch, was arrested and brought to Rome to be condemned to death by beasts at the public games. This kind of bloody violence would be perpetuated for the next two hundred years.

Even Hindus pray to St. George, the dragon-slayer, believing he may offer their children protection from cobras.

APPENDIX C:
NOTES ON ORIGINAL ART

The First Supper
Oil on canvas © 1999
43.5" x 57"
page 124

Leonardo Da Vinci's rendering of the Last Supper, the symbolic final Passover meal of Yahowshua and his disciples, is probably the most famous representation of the Mashiakh's ceremonial feast before his crucifixion.

> *And he took bread and brake it, and gave unto them, saying, This is my body which is given for you: This do in remembrance of me. Likewise also the cup after supper, saying, this cup is the New Testament in my blood, which is shed for you*
>
> Luke chapter 22, verse 19

Yahowshua ha Mashiakh's Last Supper has come to be seen as embodying his love and compassion, as well as the prelude to his final and ultimate act of selflessness. However, our preoccupation with the Last Supper has all but overshadowed the sacrifices made by the Mother in giving the First Supper, his Mother, but also all Mothers Illuminating Love and Kindness (M.I.L.K.).

The First Supper is the most fitting title for this piece as it portrays the nursing mother as youthful and voluptuous, reminiscent of the image of the Goddess Auset (Isis) breast-feeding her messiah-son Heru (Horus). The image of Mother and Child, often representing Miriam and Yahowshua the Son of God, is in fact a universal image and is in no way unique to Christianity.

The sun, the element sustaining our globe, consistently has a harmonious relationship with Mother Earth. We humans quickly came to recognize the significance of both to our existence, so the earth and the sun became our first Gods, Mother Earth and Father Sun.

The First Supper represents the mother as the Tree of Life, sacrificing her essence and body as food for her offspring, made from her blood. The Blood of Christ is the blood of his mother and the flesh he gave was also Hers. It was She that was crucified in Him, feeling the pain that only a mother can know.

As the Queen Mother, Her lap symbolizes the throne, and as She nurses Her man-child destined to be king, Her milk represents wisdom. She looks lovingly down upon His face as She cradles Him with enlarged protective hands, a symbol of Her strength and guidance.

She is a Nazarite, like Her son, as may be seen in Her locks, and she is therefore a vegetarian according to the stipulations of the Nazarite vow.

The First Supper represents the fundamental food prescribed by nature for humans. It is only through Her nurturing milk that the first-born Son from the Divine Mother's womb was able to fulfill the Last Supper.

The Divine Mother's so-called Blackness represents the fertile primordial womb pregnant with life; and as the first mother in the genesis of the human race, she embodies the totality of the human species, first in the line of motherhood and divinity. All things emerge from the dark void or the black womb.

Behold an Ethiopian
Oil on canvas ©2002
24" X 30"
page 64

Who do men say that I am?

Luke chapter 9, verses 18-21

This portrait was done to provoke the question, Who is depicted in the work? The halo, purple robe, and upraised palms suggest a holy mystic. Some say it is the true Christ, others speculate that it is a reactionary interpretation of Jesus Christ.

At a lecture I gave at U.C. Berkeley, a student, who called it "the Black Jesus," argued that the color of his skin did not matter after all. Without the scarification of the crucifixion it is difficult for the viewer to be certain, but every other detail points to a conclusion that it is indeed a painting of the prophesied son, the Mashiakh.

For certain, it is not an image of *Jesus*. In-depth investigation into the history and image of Jesus begins and ends with the European translation of a non-European language giving the spiritual and religious history of a people, namely the Israelites.

Many of the images that we've grown accustomed to identifying with the Bible are actually from a world alien to it, the frigid climate of Europe. The dominance of these images has, in fact, been contrived to enforce European domination of the planet's psyche.

Moses the Israelite was born and bred in Egypt, was an African. His fellow Hebrews mistook him for an Egyptian, which implies that the Egyptians and the Hebrews were of one and the same stock of people.

The Ethiopian royal house is founded upon Hebrew and Semitic blood, which flowed in the bodies of the last emperor and empress, Haile Sellassie I, and Tegene Menen. Both were Africans who lived out every aspect of what Europeans claim to know as *Jesus Christ*. Yet, the name *Jesus* and the image of *Jesus* are completely invalid in the context of the ancient manuscripts. *Jesus* only arose after those manuscripts were translated into Greek, and from Greek into Latin, and from Latin into English, from which texts our modern *Holy Bible* was compiled.

The biblical images we grew up with in the West are out of alignment with the portraits the scriptures paint. For example, it is understood that the savior was a Nazarite, yet until now we had not seen any, not even one, portrait of Jesus with dreadlocks, the outward sign and seal of the Nazarites' vow.

Samson, Samuel, Ezekiel and John the Baptist were of the same order, which was, at the time, the highest and most mystical part of Judaism. But we have yet to see any European, and have seen only a few Afrocentric, images of these judges and prophets with dreadlocks.

Numbers chapter 6 contains the ordinances of the Nazarite vow stating, *All the days of his/her separation thou shall be holy unto the Lord and no razor shall come upon thine head . . . And thou shall let the locks of thine hair grow long.* The mothers of all the above judges and prophets over Israel dedicated their sons with this vow.

The scriptures tells us that Samson had seven locks; in Rastafarian idiom we call that *Congo natty*, representing thereby that these were thick locks outstanding from the much smaller, finer dreadlocks, that are more common.

Thus the skin color and locks in this portrait *Behold an Ethiopian*, brings us closer to a historical rather than the common mythological likeness of the man Yahowshua. It is important to be aware of his pigmentation as this will help to determine what part of the world he was from and who his mother actually was.

The Gathering
Oil on canvas ©1999
49" X 71"
page 249

The Gathering of the one hundred forty-four thousand (144,000) of the Book of Revelation has been a subject of discussion for centuries. This painting depicts the enthroned primordial Divine aspects of humanity as mother and father, with the human family as children. The Emperor and Empress sit in union on one throne, representing the power of the Holy Trinity, as male and female, through the power of the same unseen energy of spirit.

Their union is represented in the eclipsing sun and moon, with the consequent rebirth of the earth through an African consciousness, namely Ethiopia.

It is the conscious awareness of our spiritual umbilical ties to our first parents, from our African roots, that will foster us humans in our return to the very source of our spiritual and physiological existence. Archeological findings confirm the African origins of the human species, as is now common knowledge.

The writings in the Book of Genesis chapter 2, verses 7-13 also place Adam and Eve in the garden paradise geographically located in Ethiopia, making Africa the mother of our biblical First Parents. This fact speaks distinctly of the Divine birthright of the African womb, and the right of every individual to be reborn through the recognition of Her, in order to come full circle to Divinity.

It is out of the denial, suppression and oppression of the African woman's Divine motherhood that the term *Black Madonna* is derived, and something similar may be said of the term the *Black Christ*.

Over five hundred years of internalized African oppression has catalyzed a number of self-destructive reactions to the forced assimilation of colonial Christianity. For example, when we as Africans exalt God as European, depicting the holiest symbols, such as the Madonna and Child and the Holy Trinity, in European flesh, we already deny our own mothers, but we also deny ourselves of our own birthright as first fruits of the earth's womb.

The *Holy Bible*, with all its conventional icons, has become the ideal for many of us, who are still under the disillusioning force of colonialism and Christianity. However, if we continue to be distracted by false ideologies, we ignore the reality that images which do not empower us as individuals, divide and conquer us as a people.

The *White Madonna*, along with the *White Christ*, for lack of a better term, is the accepted norm in the dominant Christian world, even though the historical evidence proves the image is false. There is no question about skin color when it comes to images of the Christ and his mother until they are painted black or brown; then all of a sudden they become the *Black Madonna* or the *Black Christ*. This is ironic because the icons should convey the first, as well as the highest human ideals. This being so, all humanity should be able to see their spiritual and biological roots in these icons as prototypes. How is this possible, unless they represent accurately, in image and likeness, the primordial parents? How can the African woman, descended directly from Eve, identify with a redemption that comes from a womb that does not resemble her own?

As the Mother of humanity, the African mother and her womb become our common denominator and point of reference. The word "prototype," which is Greek, was coined by St. Basil in the fourth century to mean the sacred personage whom an icon represents. Applying this concept to humanity itself casts an extraordinary light on the *sacred personage* of the African woman (or W.O.M.B.M.A.N.[102]) as literally the earliest figure we can draw. Our enlightenment will come when we as humans surrender to our true nature, the African nature within all of us, which is our natural birthright. As long as the term *Black Madonna*, exists among us, and therefore the idea that such an image is peculiar, we are in denial of the reality that God is the mother of humanity, who happens to be African by nature.

Revelation 12
Oil on canvas © 2002
57" X 43 1/2"
page 133

And there appeared a great wonder in heaven, a woman clothed with the sun, and the moon under her feet, and upon her head a crown of twelve stars; and she being with child cried, travailing in birth, and pained to be delivered . . . and when the dragon saw that he was cast unto the earth he persecuted the woman, which brought forth the man child.

The woman in this painting of Revelation 12 symbolizes the geographical mother of the anointed child, literally Zion, the embodiment of the Shekinah and home of the Ark of the Covenant. According to esoteric Judeo-Christian theology, the Ark of the Covenant represents Miriam, Mother of the Lord, Mother of Zion and in truth the Holy Grail. She is the source and container of His bloodline, and only through Her could He be reborn in order to literally ascend the promised Throne.

---

102 Woman Of My Birth, Mothering All Nations.

The expectant Mother, pregnant with unlimited potential, poses a threat, as Her child within Her womb embodies the epitome of the law contained in the pure golden vessel called the Ark of God in the Bible. After enduring tribulation and countless self-sacrifice She conceived, nurtured, and protected Her progeny, giving birth to the revolutionary change of a new age. The rose that She holds so delicately symbolizes the promise of Her chief city, Addis Ababa, which means *new flower*. The scars in Her palms are stigmata turned into pearls; across her bosom is painted the word Ethiopia in Amharic, the Ethiopian national language

Six angels plus one guards Her, signifying the seven spirits of the Most High. Clothed in the glory of Her ascended son, with the moon under Her feet, She is crowned with twelve golden six-pointed stars, a sign that She has triumphed over the perils of the dragon and the beast, which Her son, as the Lion King, is destined to slay.

Though it may be relatively unknown amongst the masses, many renowned historians and scholars have been aware of the Ethiopian claim to the biblical Ark of the Covenant, which was brought to Her by Menelik I, the son from the union of King Solomon and the famed Queen of Sheba. It is out of this union that Ethiopia's Davidic sovereignty was established hundreds of years before Christ was born. This created a legitimate Jewish state in Ethiopia, where Kings and Queens sat upon the throne of David, ruling as King of Kings, Lion of the Tribe of Judah, Elect of God, Light of the World and King of Zion. The Hebraic traditions inherited from the ancient kingdom of Solomon laid the foundation for a unique Hebrew Christian heritage to develop in virtual isolation in Ethiopia, which boasts no less than eleven monolithic churches hewn from solid volcanic rock in the thirteenth century during the reign of King Lalibela. This remote mountain village, which was once Ethiopia's capital, became known as Lalibela or the *New Jerusalem*.

Escaping European colonialization, Ethiopia, with her ancient sovereignty rooted in biblical history, stood as the only independent African state that could pose a threat to the conquering colonial imperialism that plagued the globe leading up to the Second World War. Ethiopia and Her fiercely independent people became the hope of a continent and those scattered throughout the African Diaspora, seeking strength, dignity and identity in something African that was unconquerable by Europeans.

Ethiopia was recognized by many as the exception to European rule in Africa, and as our Zion by Marcus Garvey, who fathered the Pan-Africanism and Ethiopianism that helped shaped the consciousness of Jamaicans and many others towards an Ethiopian perspective on Divinity. Thus were born the first Rastafarians, the generation that would see through clouds of illusion to embrace the Divine prophecies fulfilled in Ethiopia through the birth of Lij Tafari Makonnen in 1892 — the child that would survive the onslaught of the Italian invasion, and glory in the triumph of the famous battle of Adowa four years later in 1896. In 1930 — thirty-four years later — the Negus Tafari Makonnen ascended the Ethiopian throne and was crowned Haile Sellassie I (that is, *Might and Power of the Trinity*), King of Kings, Lord of Lords, the Conquering Lion of the Tribe of Judah, and King of Zion.

In light of the rise of this King, I painted this painting as a metaphor pointing to the higher, more esoteric meaning of the prophecies in the book of the Revelation, when we read:

> She bore a male Child who was to rule all nations with a rod of iron. And her Child was caught up to God and his throne.
>
> Revelation chapter 12, verse 5

APPENDIX D:
THE WILLIAM LYNCH LETTERS

This speech was said to have been delivered by Willie Lynch on the bank of the James River in the colony of Virginia in 1712. Lynch was a British slave owner in the West Indies. He was invited to the colony of Virginia in 1712 to teach his methods to slave owners there:

Greetings,

Gentlemen. I greet you here on the bank of the James River in the year of our Lord one thousand seven hundred and twelve. First, I shall thank you, the gentlemen of the Colony of Virginia, for bringing me here. I am here to help you solve some of your problems with slaves. Your invitation reached me on my modest plantation in the West Indies, where I have experimented with some of the newest, and still the oldest, methods for control of slaves. Ancient Rome would envy us if my program were implemented. As our boat sailed south on the James River, named for our illustrious King, whose version of the Bible we cherish, I saw enough to know that your problem is not unique. While Rome used cords of wood as crosses for standing human bodies along its highways in great numbers, you are here using the tree and the rope on occasions. I caught the whiff of a dead slave hanging from a tree, a couple miles back. You are not only losing valuable stock by hangings, you are having uprisings, slaves are running away, your crops are sometimes left in the fields too long for maximum profit, you suffer occasional fires, your animals are killed. Gentlemen, you know what your problems are; I do not need to elaborate. I am not here to enumerate your problems, I am here to introduce you to a method of solving them. In my bag here, **I HAVE A FOOLPROOF METHOD FOR CONTROLLING YOUR BLACK SLAVES.** I guarantee every one of you that, if installed correctly, **IT WILL CONTROL THE SLAVES FOR AT LEAST 300 YEARS.** My method is simple.

Any member of your family or your overseer can use it. **I HAVE OUTLINED A NUMBER OF DIFFERENCES AMONG THE SLAVES; AND I TAKE THESE DIFFERENCES AND MAKE THEM BIGGER. I USE FEAR, DISTRUST AND ENVY FOR CONTROL PURPOSES.** These methods have worked on my modest plantation in the West Indies and it will work throughout the South. Take this simple little list of differences and think about them. On top of my list is "**AGE**," but it's there only because it starts with an "a." The second is "**COLOR**" or shade. There is **INTELLIGENCE, SIZE, SEX, SIZES OF PLANTATIONS, STATUS** on plantations, **ATTITUDE** of owners, whether the slaves live in the valley, on a hill, East, West, North, South, has fine hair, coarse hair, or is tall or short. Now that you have a list of differences, I shall give you an outline of action, but before that, I shall assure you that **DISTRUST IS STRONGER THAN TRUST AND ENVY STRONGER THAN ADULATION, RESPECT OR ADMIRATION**. The Black slaves after receiving this indoctrination shall carry on and will become self-refueling and self-generating for **HUNDREDS** of years, maybe **THOUSANDS**. Don't forget, you must pitch the **OLD** black male vs. the **YOUNG** black male, and the **YOUNG** black male against the **OLD** black male. You must use the **DARK** skin slaves vs. the **LIGHT** skin slaves, and the **LIGHT** skin slaves vs. the **DARK** skin slaves. You must use the **FEMALE** vs. the **MALE**, and the **MALE** vs. the **FEMALE**. You must also have white servants and overseers [who] distrust all Blacks. But it is **NECESSARY THAT YOUR SLAVES TRUST AND DEPEND ON US. THEY MUST LOVE, RESPECT AND TRUST ONLY US**. Gentlemen, these kits are your keys to control. Use them. Have your wives and children use them, never miss an opportunity. **IF USED INTENSELY FOR ONE YEAR, THE SLAVES THEMSELVES WILL REMAIN PERPETUALLY DISTRUSTFUL**. Thank you, gentlemen.

LET'S MAKE A SLAVE

It was the interest and business of slave holders to study human nature, and the slave nature in particular, with a view to practical results. I and many of them attained astonishing proficiency in this direction. They had to deal not with earth, wood and stone, but with men and, by every regard they had for their own safety and prosperity, they needed to know the material on which they were to work, conscious of the injustice and wrong they were every hour perpetrating and knowing what they themselves would do. Were they the victims of such wrongs? They were constantly looking for the first signs of the dreaded retribution. They watched therefore with skilled and practiced eyes, and learned to read with great accuracy, the state of mind and heart of the slave, through his sable face. Unusual sobriety, apparent abstractions, sullenness and indifference, indeed, any mood out of the common, was afforded ground for suspicion and inquiry. **LET'S MAKE A SLAVE** is a study of the scientific process of man-breaking and slave-making. It describes the rationale and results of the Anglo Saxons' ideas and methods of insuring the master/slave relationship.

The Original and Development of a Social Being Called "The Negro." Let us make a slave. What do we need? First of all, we need a black nigger man, a pregnant nigger woman and her baby nigger boy. Second, we will use the same basic principle that we use in breaking a horse, combined with some more sustaining factors. What we do with horses is that we break them from one form of life to another; that is, we reduce them from their natural state in nature. Whereas nature provides them with the natural capacity to take care of their offspring, we break that natural string of independence from them and thereby create a dependency status, so that we may be able to get from them useful production for our business and pleasure.

CARDINAL PRINCIPLES FOR MAKING A NEGRO

For fear that our future generations may not understand the principles of breaking both of the beast together, the nigger and the horse: We understand that economics based on short-range planning results in periodic economic chaos; so that to avoid turmoil in the economy, it requires us to have breadth and depth in long-range comprehensive planning, articulating both skill and sharp perceptions. We lay down the following principles for long range comprehensive economic planning. Both horse and niggers [are] no good to the economy in the wild or natural state. Both must be **BROKEN** and **TIED** together for orderly production.

For an orderly future, special and particular attention must be paid to the **FEMALE** and the **YOUNGEST** offspring. Both must be **CROSSBRED** to produce a variety and division of labor. Both must be taught to respond to a peculiar new **LANGUAGE**. Psychological and physical instruction of **CONTAINMENT** must be created for both.

We hold the six cardinal principles as truth to be self-evident, based upon following the discourse concerning the economics of breaking and tying the horse and the nigger together, all inclusive of the six principles laid down above. NOTE: Neither principle alone will suffice for good economics. All principles must be employed for orderly good of the nation. Accordingly, both a wild horse and a wild or natur[al] nigger is dangerous even if captured, for they will have the tendency to seek their customary freedom and, in doing so, might kill you in your sleep. You cannot rest. They sleep while you are awake, and are awake while you are asleep. They are **DANGEROUS** near the family house and it requires too much labor to watch them away from the house. Above all, you cannot get them to work in this natural state. Hence, both the horse and the nigger must be broken; that is breaking them from one form of mental life to another. **KEEP THE BODY, TAKE THE MIND!** In other words, break the will to resist.

Now the breaking process is the same for both the horse and the nigger, only slightly varying in degrees. But, as we said before, there is an art in long range economic planning. **YOU MUST KEEP YOUR EYE AND THOUGHTS ON THE FEMALE** and the **OFFSPRING** of the horse and the nigger. A brief discourse in offspring development will shed light on the key to sound economic principles. Pay little attention to the generation of original breaking, but **CONCENTRATE ON FUTURE GENERATIONS**. Therefore, if you break the **FEMALE** mother, she will BREAK the offspring in its early years of development; and when the offspring is old enough to work, she will deliver it up to you, for her normal female protective tendencies will have been lost in the original breaking process. For example, take the case of the wild stud horse, a female horse and an already infant horse and compare the breaking process with two captured nigger males in their natural state, a pregnant nigger woman with her infant offspring. Take the stud horse, break him for limited containment. Completely break the female horse until she becomes very gentle, whereas you or anybody can ride her in her comfort. Breed the mare and the stud until you have the desired offspring. Then, you can turn the stud to freedom until you need him again. Train the female horse whereby she will eat out of your hand, and she will in turn train the infant horse to eat out of your hand, also.

When it comes to breaking the uncivilized nigger, use the same process, but vary the degree and step up the pressure, so as to do a complete reversal of the mind. Take the meanest and most restless nigger, strip him of his clothes in front of the remaining male niggers, the females, and the nigger infants; tar and feather him, tie each leg to a different horse faced in opposite directions, set him afire and beat both horses to pull him apart in front of the remaining niggers. The next step is to take a bullwhip and beat the remaining nigger males to the point of death, in front of the females and the infants. Don't kill him, but **PUT THE FEAR OF GOD IN HIM**, for he can be useful for future breeding.

THE BREAKING PROCESS OF THE AFRICAN WOMAN

Take the female and run a series of tests on her to see if she will submit to your desires willingly. Test her in every way, because she is the most important factor for good economics. If she shows any sign of resistance in submitting completely to your will, do not hesitate to use the bullwhip on her to extract that last bit of [b----] out of her. Take care not to kill her, for in [killing her], you spoil good economics. When in complete submission, she will train her offsprings in the early years to submit to labor when they become of age. Understanding is the best thing. Therefore, we shall go deeper into this area of the subject matter concerning what we have produced here in this breaking process of the female nigger.

We have reversed the relationship; in her natural uncivilized state, she would have a strong dependency on the uncivilized nigger male, and she would have a limited protective tendency toward her independent male offspring and would raise male offsprings to be dependent like her. Nature had provided for this type of balance. We reversed nature by burning and pulling a civilized nigger apart and bullwhipping the other to the point of death, all in her presence. By her being left alone, unprotected, with the **MALE IMAGE DESTROYED**, the ordeal caused her to move from her psychologically dependent state to a frozen, independent state. In this frozen, psychological state of independence, she will raise her **MALE** and female offspring in reversed roles. For **FEAR** of the young male's life, she will psychologically train him to be **MENTALLY WEAK** and

DEPENDENT, but **PHYSICALLY STRONG**. Because she has become psychologically independent, she will train her **FEMALE** offsprings to be psychologically independent. What have you got? You've got the nigger **WOMAN OUT FRONT AND THE** nigger **MAN BEHIND AND SCARED**.

This is a perfect situation of sound sleep and economics. Before the breaking process, we had to be alertly on guard at all times. Now, we can sleep soundly, for out of frozen fear his woman stands guard for us. He cannot get past her early slave-molding process. He is a good tool, now ready to be tied to the horse at a tender age. By the time a nigger boy reaches the age of sixteen, he is soundly broken in and ready for a long life of sound and efficient work and the reproduction of a unit of good labor force. Continually through the breaking of uncivilized savage niggers, by throwing the nigger female savage into a frozen psychological state of independence, by killing the protective male image, and by creating a submissive dependent mind of the nigger male slave, we have created an orbiting cycle that turns on its own axis forever, unless a phenomenon occurs and re-shifts the position of the male and female slaves. We show what we mean by example. Take the case of the two economic slave units and examine them close.

THE NEGRO MARRIAGE

We breed two nigger males with two nigger females. Then we take the nigger males away from them and keep them moving and working. Say one nigger female bears a nigger female and the other bears a nigger male; both nigger females — being without influence of the nigger male image, frozen with an independent psychology — will raise their offspring into reverse positions. The one with the female offspring will teach her to be like herself, independent and negotiable (we negotiate with her, through her, by her, negotiate her at will). The one with the nigger male offspring, she being frozen in subconscious fear for his life, will raise him to be mentally dependent and weak, but physically strong; in other words, body over mind. Now, in a few years when these two offsprings become fertile for early reproduction, we will mate and breed them and continue the cycle. That is good, sound and long-range comprehensive planning.

WARNING: POSSIBLE INTERLOPING NEGATIVES

Earlier, we talked about the non-economic good of the horse and the nigger in their wild or natural state; we talked out the principle of breaking and tying them together for orderly production. Furthermore, we talked about paying particular attention to the female savage and her offspring for orderly future planning; then more recently we stated that, by reversing the positions of the male and female savages, we created an orbiting cycle that turns on its own axis forever unless a phenomenon occurred and reshifts the positions of the male and female savages. Our experts warned us about the possibility of this phenomenon occurring, for they say that the mind has a strong drive to correct and re-correct itself over a period of time if it can touch some substantial original historical base; and they advised us that the best way to deal with the phenomenon is to shave off the brute's mental history and create a multiplicity of phenomena of illusions, so that each illusion will twirl in its own orbit, something similar to floating balls in a vacuum. This creation of multiplicity of phenomena of illusions entails the principle of crossbreeding the nigger and the horse as we stated above, the purpose of which is to create a diversified division of labor; thereby creating different levels of labor and different values of illusion at each connecting level of labor. The result of which is the severance of the points of original beginnings for each sphere's illusion.

Since we feel that the subject matter may get more complicated as we proceed in laying down our economic plan concerning the purpose, reason and effect of crossbreeding horses and niggers, we shall lay down the following definition terms for future generations. Orbiting cycle means a thing turning in a given path. Axis means that upon which or around which a body turns. Phenomenon means something beyond ordinary conception and inspires awe and wonder. Multiplicity means a great number. Means a globe. Crossbreeding a horse means taking a horse and breeding it with an ass and you get a dumb, ass backward, long-headed mule that is not reproductive nor productive by itself. Crossbreeding niggers mean taking so many drops of good white blood and putting them into as many nigger women as possible, varying the drops by the various tones that you want, and then letting them breed with each other until another circle of color appears as you desire.

What this means is this: Put the niggers and the horse in a breeding pot, mix some asses and some good white blood and what do you get? You got a multiplicity of colors of ass backward, unusual niggers, running, tied to ass backward long-headed mules, the one productive of itself, the other sterile. (The one constant, the other dying, we keep the nigger constant for we may replace the mules for another tool.) Both mule and nigger tied to each other, neither knowing where the other came from and neither productive for itself, nor without each other.

CONTROLLED LANGUAGE

Crossbreeding completed, for further severance from their original beginning, **WE MUST COMPLETELY ANNIHILATE THE MOTHER TONGUE** of both the new nigger and the new mule, and institute a new language [learning which will be] the new life's work of both. You know language is a peculiar institution. It leads to the heart of a people. The more a foreigner knows about the language of another country the more he is able to move through all levels of that society. Therefore, if the foreigner is an enemy of the country, to the extent that he knows the body of the language, to that extent is the country vulnerable to attack or invasion of a foreign culture. For example, if you take a slave, if you teach him all about your language, he will know all your secrets, and he is then no more a slave, for you can't fool him any longer, and **BEING A FOOL IS ONE OF THE BASIC INGREDIENTS OF ANY INCIDENTS TO THE MAINTENANCE OF THE SLAVERY SYSTEM**.

For example, if you told a slave that he must perform in getting out "our crops" and he knows the language well, he would know that "our crops" didn't mean "our crops" and the slavery system would break down, for he would relate on the basis of what "our crops" really meant. So you have to be careful in setting up the new language; for the slaves would soon be in your house, talking to you as "man to man," and that is death to our economic system.

In addition, the definitions of words or terms are only a minute part of the process. Values are created and transported by communication through the body of the language. A total society has many interconnected value systems. All the values in the society have bridges of language to connect them for orderly working in the society. But for these language bridges, these many value systems would sharply clash and cause internal strife or civil war, the degree of the conflict being determined by the magnitude of the issues or relative opposing strengths in whatever form. For example, if you put a slave in a hog pen and train him to live there and incorporate in him to value it as a way of life completely, the biggest problem you would have out of him is that he would worry you about provisions to keep the hog pen clean. [If you] make a slip and incorporate something in his language whereby he comes to value a house more than he does his hog pen, you got a problem. He will soon be in your house.

BIBLIOGRAPHY

Ancient Scripture

The Apocrypha
Authorized (King James) Version
Translated out of the original tongues and with the former translations
      diligently compared and revised by His Majesty's special command
Appointed to be read in churches
Cambridge, England: University Press
Pitt Brevier edition
Being the version set forth 1611
International Standard Book Number (ISBN) 0-521-50674-3 hardback

The Oxford Annotated Apocrypha of the Old Testament
Revised Standard Version
Translated from the Greek and Latin tongues
Edited by Bruce M. Metzger
New York: Oxford University Press, Inc., 1965
Being the version set forth 1611, revised 1894, compared with the most
      ancient authorities and revised 1957
Library of Congress Catalog Number (LCCN) 65-12463

The Bandlet of Righteousness: An Ethiopian Book of the Dead
(Luzac's Semitic Text and Translation Series, vol. 19)
Translated from the Ethiopic and edited by Sir E[rnest] A[lfred] Wallis
      Budge, Kt, from two manuscripts in the British Museum
London: Luzac & Company, 1929
ISBN 0-404-11349-4

The Holy Bible
(Gideons Bible)
Authorized (King James) Version
Containing the Old and New Testaments
Translated out of the original tongues and with the former translations
      diligently compared and revised [by His Majesty's special command]
[Appointed to be read in churches]
Nashville: National Publishing Co., 1978
For the Gideons International
Being the version set forth 1611

The Dead Sea Scrolls in English
G[eza] Vermes, translator and editor
Third edition
London: Pelican Books, 1987
Reprinted in Penguin Books, 1990
ISBN 0-14-013544-8 paperback

The Book of Enoch the Prophet: An Apocryphal Production
Translated for the first time from an Ethiopic manuscript in the Bodleian
 Library by Richard Laurence
Third edition, revised and enlarged
Oxford, England: John Henry Parker, 1838
Hard-bound

The Book of the Secrets of Enoch
Translated from the Slavonic by W[illiam] R[ichard] Morfill
Edited by R[obert] H[enry] Charles
Oxford: The Clarendon Press, 1896
(Also included in *Lost Books of the Bible*)

Essene Holy Bible
The Holy Megillah: The Nasarean Bible of the Essene Way, English
 translation available through www.essene.org/essnmstr.html
 Dec.21, 2013. Includes: *Essene New Testament: The Gospel of the Holy Twelve*
Translated from the original Aramaic by Gideon Jasper Ouseley
 in the late 1800s
Pamphlet produced c/o Rev. Brother David Owen, Creswell, Oregon, 1980

Essene Gospel of Peace: Book 1
The Aramaic and Old Slavonic texts compared, edited and translated by
 Edmond Bordeaux Szekely
San Diego, California: Academy Books, Publishers, 1975

Essene Gospel of Peace: Book 2: The Unknown Books of the Essenes
Translated by Edmond Bordeaux Szekely
Nelson, British Columbia: International Biogenic Society, 1981
ISBN-13 978-0895640017 paperback

The Essene Gospel of Peace: Book 3: Lost Scrolls of the Essene Brotherhood
The original Hebrew and Aramaic texts translated and edited by Edmond
 Bordeaux Szekely
San Diego, California: Academy Books, Publishers, 1977

Essene Gospel of Peace: Book 4: The Teachings of the Elect
Translated from the Aramaic by Edmond Bordeaux Szekely
 and brought forth by Norma Nilsson Bordeaux
Nelson, British Columbia: International Biogenic Society, 1981

The Fetha Negast
The Law of the Kings
Translated from the Ge'ez by Abba Paulos Tzadua
Edited by Peter L. Strauss
Addis Ababa, Ethiopia: Haile Sellassie I University, Faculty of Law, 1968

The Book of Jubilees, or, The Little Genesis
Translated from the editor's Ethiopic text and edited by
R[obert] H[enry] Charles
London: Adam & Charles Black, 1902
xci 275p 23cm hardbound with bibliography

The Kabbalah Reader: A Sourcebook of Visionary Judaism.
Edited by Edward Hoffman
Boston: Trumper Books (Shambala Publications), 2010
ISBN 978-1-59030-656-7 paperback

Kebra Negast (The Glory of Kings): The True Ark of the Covenant
Compiled, edited and translated by Miguel F. Brooks
Asmara, Eritrea and Lawrenceville, New Jersey: Red Sea Press, 1995
Second printing, 1996
ISBN 1-56902-033-7 paperback

Kebra Negast (The Glory of Kings): The Queen of Sheba and Her Only Son Menyelek
First published in English by Oxford University Press 1932
E. A. Wallis Budge, translator
Chicago: Research Associates School Times Publications / Frontline Distribution International, Inc., 2000
Kingston, Jamaica: Miguel Lorne Publishers, 2000
ISBN 0-94839-042-5
LCCCN 98-66860 paperback

The Lost Books of the Bible and The Forgotten Books of Eden
[Edited by Rutherford Hayes Platt, Jr.]
[Translated by W. Wake, E. Trumpp, S. C. Malan, R. H. Charles and others]
Introduction by Frank Crane
Includes The Book of the Secrets of Enoch
USA: Word Bible Publishers [1963]
Originally published by Alpha House, Inc., 1926
ISBN 0-529-03385-2
LCCN 63-19519

Legends of Our Lady Mary the Perpetual Virgin and Her Mother Hannâ
Translated from the Ethiopic Manuscripts collected by King Theodore at Makdalâ and now in the British Museum
London: Oxford University Press (Humphrey Milford), 1933

The Nag Hammadi Library in English
Third, completely revised, edition
Translated and introduced by Members of the Coptic Gnostic Library Project of The Institute for Antiquity and Christianity,
    Claremont, California
James M. Robinson, General Editor
Richard Smith, Managing Editor
Includes the Gospel according to Thomas
New York: HarperSanFrancisco, a division of Harper Collins
    Publishers, 1990
Leiden, The Netherlands: E. J. Brill, 1978, 1988
ISBN 0-06-066935-7 paperback

Writings and Speeches of H.I.M. Haile Sellassie I

"My Life and Ethiopia's Progress" 1892-1937
The Autobiography of Emperor Haile Sellassie I
Translated from the Amharic and annotated by Edward Ullendorff
(University of London, School of Oriental and African Studies)
London: Oxford University Press, 1976
Originally published in 1972, written in 1937

"My Life and Ethiopia's Progress" volume 2, Addis Ababa, 1966
The Autobiography of Emperor Haile Sellassie I
King of Kings of All Ethiopia and Lord of All Lords
Translated by Ezekiel Gebissa and others
Edited and annotated by Harold Marcus with Ezekiel Gebissa and
    Tibebe Eshete
Chicago: Research Associates School Times Publications/
    Frontline Distribution International, Inc., 1999
First published in English at Lansing, Michigan: Michigan State
    University Press, 1994
LCCN 97-65862
ISBN 0-94839-032-8 paperback

Speeches Delivered by His Imperial Majesty Haile Selassie [the] 1st[,] Emperor of Ethiopia, on Various Occasions
May 1957 to December 1959
Addis Ababa, Ethiopia: The Ministry of Information, 1960
Printed by the Commercial Printing Press

The National Geographic Magazine

Washington: The National Geographic Society
Paper journal with illustrations

Volume 51. no. 6 (June 1925)
Harry V. Harlan, "A Caravan Journey Through Abyssinia"

Volume 54, no. 2 (August 1928)
Wilfred H. Osgood, "Nature and Man in Ethiopia"

Volume 59, no. 6 (June 1931)
Addison E Southard, "Modern Ethiopia"
W. Robert Moore, "Coronation Days in Addis Ababa"
"Present Day Scenes in The World's Oldest Empire" (27 photographs)

Modern Apocrypha

Abba Yahudah Berhane Sellassie and Abbazero
An Introduction to the Royal Apostles of Haile Sellassie I in Mother Divine: The Essene Nazarite Monastic Order of Melkizadek
Cave Junction, Oregon: The Royal Apostles of Haile Sellassie I in
    Mother Divine: The Essene Nazarite Monastic Order of
    Melkizadek, circa 1990
Bound by the authors, with illustrations

David "Brother Day" Owen / Abba Nazariah
The Holy Megillah: Nasarean Bible of the Essene Way, published by
its chief translator, Day of Greenleaf. To order a copy, write to Day at:
Essene Church of Christ, Box 516, Elmira, Oregon, 97437

Hodamyah and Hawwah-Nofeeyah
The Book of Edom (Torchlight)
Staten Island, New York: Ruach Inc. (The Aliyah Project), c. 1990
Illustrated pamphlet

The Rastafari United Theocratic House (TRUTH)
"Coronation Days in Addis Ababa"
Illustrated pamphlet, c. 1980

Other Sources

Michael Baigent and Richard Leigh
The Dead Sea Scrolls Deception
New York: Simon & Schuster, 1991
A Touchstone Book
ISBN 0-671-73454-7 paperback

A. J. Barker
The Rape of Ethiopia 1936
(Ballantine's Illustrated History of the Violent Century)
(Politics in Action No. 4)
New York: Ballantine Books Inc., 1971

Conrad Bergendoff
The Church of the Lutheran Reformation: A Historical Survey of Lutheranism
St. Louis, Missouri: Concordia Publishing House, 1967
xv 339p 24cm hardbound with bibliography
LCCCN 67-16893

Benson Bobrick
The Making of the English Bible
Published by arrangement with Simon & Schuster, New York
London: Weidenfeld & Nicolson, 2001
ISBN 0-297-60772-3

Robert H[erman] Bogue
The Dawn of Christianity: The Essene Heritage
New York: Vantage Press, 1986
ISBN 0-533-06545-3 hardbound
LCCCN 85-90005

Melvin Bolton
Ethiopian Wildlands
London: Collins and Harvill Press, 1976
221p illustrations and index 23cm
ISBN 0-00-262205 X hardbound

A. A. Brooks
History of Bedwardism
Jarett Kobek, editor
Second edition, revised and enlarged
Kingston, Jamaica: The Gleaner Press, 1917
Downloaded on August 23, 2013 from www.kobek.com

E[rnest] A[lfred Thompson] Wallis Budge
The Gods of the Egyptians: or Studies in Egyptian Mythology, volume 2
New York: Dover Publications, Inc., 1969
Originally published London: Methuen & Company, 1904
ISBN 0-486-22056-7 paperback
LCCCN 72-91925

Joseph Campbell
The Masks of God
First edition, hardbound
New York: Viking Press
Vol. 1: Primitive Mythology (1959)
Vol. 2: Oriental Mythology (1962)
Vol. 3: Occidental Mythology (1964)
Vol. 4: Creative Mythology (1968)
LCCN 59-8354

F.L. Cross, editor
The Oxford Dictionary of the Christian Church
Third edition
E. A. Livingstone, editor of third edition
Oxford, England: Oxford University Press, 1997
First published 1957

Charles Darwin
On the Origin of Species: By Means of Natural Selection; or the Preservation of Favored Races in the Struggle for Life
(The World's Classics, volume 11)
London: Oxford University Press, 1951
xxx 692p 16cm clothbound with index

The Descent of Man, and Selection in Relation to Sex
Reprinted from the second English edition, revised and augmented
(Burt's Library of the World's Best Books)
New York: A. L. Burt, 1874
vii 797p 20cm clothbound with frontispiece portrait and other illustrations

John D. Davis
A Dictionary of the Bible
Fourth revised edition
Grand Rapids, Michigan: Baker Book House, 1956
v 840p 24cm hardbound with portraits, maps and other illustrations
Originally published in 1924

Edith Deen
All of the Women of the Bible
New York: Harper & Brothers Publishers, 1955
LCCCN 55-8521 hardbound

James Dugan and Laurence Davis Lafore
Days of Emperor and Clown: The Italo-Ethiopian War, 1935-1936
Crossroads of World History
New York: Doubleday, 1973
ISBN 0385046081

Prince Emmanuel(Charles Edwards) the 7th [1898-1981]
Black Supremacy [in Righteousness of Salvation]
Saint Andrew, Jamaica: Ethiopia Africa Black International Congress
72p paperback

Robert T. Elson
(World War II)
Prelude to War
Charles Osborne, editor
Alexandria, Virginia: Time-Life Books, 1976
Hardbound, with illustrations

Final Call
"Willie Lynch Letter: The Making of a Slave" (1712)
downloaded at www.finalcall.com/artman/publish/Perspectives_1/
    Willie_Lynch_letter_The_Making_of_a_Slave.shtml on Dec.22,2013

Malcolm Forsberg
Land Beyond the Nile
New York: Harper & Brothers, 1958
232p illustrated 22cm

Marcus Garvey
Marcus Garvey: Life and Lessons
A Centennial Companion to The Marcus Garvey and Universal Negro
    Improvement Association Papers
Robert A. Hill, editor
Barbara Bair, associate editor
Berkeley: University of California Press, 1987
ISBN 0-520-06265-5 paperback

"Philosophy and Opinions of Marcus Garvey [or Africa for the Africans]"
Edited by Amy Jacques-Garvey, 1923
The Journal of Pan African Studies 2009 eBook
Downloaded on February 22, 2014 from http://worldafropedia.com/
    ~worldafr/wiki/images/6/69/Philosophy_and_Opinions_of_
Marcus_Garvey.pdf

John Gunther
Inside Africa
New York: Harper & Brothers, 1953
London: Hamish Hamilton Ltd. 1959

Isaac H. Hall, editor
The Revised New Testament and History of Revisions
Philadelphia: Hubbard Brothers; Atlanta: C.R. Blackwell & Co.; New York: A.L. Bancroft & Co.; 1881

Graham Hancock
The Sign and the Seal: The Quest for the Lost Ark of the Covenant
New York: Simon & Schuster, Inc., 1992
A Touchstone Book
ISBN 0-671-86541-2 paperback

Corinne Heline
Occult Anatomy and the Bible
Santa Monica, California:
New Age Press, 1937

Theodore Heline
The Dead Sea Scrolls*: The Essenian Forerunners of Christ*
Marina del Rey, California: DeVorss and Company, Publishers
First published in 1957
Eighth edition, 1980
ISBN 0-87613-066-X

Arnold Hermann Ludwig Heeren
Historical Researches Into the Politics, Intercourse and Trade of the Principal Nations of Antiquity
Translated at Oxford, England: 1833
Originally published at Göttingen, Sweden: 1793-1796 in German as
   Ideen über Politik, den Verkehr, und den Handel der vornehmsten Völker der alten Welt

Leonard Percival Howell (as G[angun] G[uru] Maregh)
The Promise Key
Jamaica: c. 1935
Pamphlet available as The Promised Key at www.thecarafcentre.org.uk/pdf/promised-key.pdf
Drawing from:
Fitz Balintine Pettersburg
The Royal Parchment Scroll of Black Supremacy
Jamaica: 1926

Laënnec Hurbon
Voodoo: Search for the Spirit
New York: Harry N. Abrams, Inc., 1995
ISBN 0-8109-2857-4
Illustrated paperback

Elizabeth Isichei
The History of Christianity in Africa: From Antiquity to the Present
Grand Rapids, Michigan: W.B. Eerdmans Publishing Company
    and Lawrenceville, New Jersey: Africa World Press, 1995
xi 420p clothbound illustrated 22cm
ISBN 0-86543-442-5

Jill Kamil
Coptic Egypt: History and Guide
Plans and maps by Hassan Ibrahim
Cairo, Egypt: The American University in Cairo Press, 1987
ISBN 977-424-104-5 paperback

Joseph Klausner
From Jesus to Paul
Translated from the Hebrew by William F. Stinespring
New York: The Macmillian Company, 1943
Published in Hebrew c. 1939
Hard-bound

Hans Küng
Christianity: Essence, History and Future
New York: The Continuum Publishing Co., 1998
Translated from the German by John Bowden
Published Munich, Germany: Piper Verlag, 1994
ISBN 0-8264-0884-2 paperback

Martin A. Larson
The Essene-Christian Faith: A Study in the Sources of Western Religion
New York: Philosophical Library, Inc., 1980
[I]SBN 8022-2241-2
LCCCN 79-83606

Richard Leakey
The Origin of Humankind
(Science Masters Series)
New York: BasicBooks, a division of HarperCollinsPublishers, 1994
ISBN 0-465-03135-8 paperback

Wolf Leslau
Concise Amharic Dictionary: Amharic-English English-Amharic
Berkeley: University of California Press, 1976
ISBN 0-520-02660-8 paperback
LCCCN 73-90668

Emil Ludwig
The Nile: The Life Story of a River
Garden City, New York: Garden City Publishing Co., Inc., 1943
Originally published at Amsterdam, The Netherlands: Querido Verlag N. V. 1935, 1936

Helen M. Luke
Woman Earth and Spirit: The Feminine Symbol and Myth
New York: Crossroad Publishing Co., 1984

Giuseppe Mammarella.
Italy After Fascism: A Political History 1943-1963
Montreal, Quebec: Mario Casalini Ltd., 1964
LCCN 64-23409 paperback

A. Jan Marcussen
National Sunday Law
Thompsonville, Illinois: Amazing Truth Publications, 1983
54th printing 1994

James Luther Mays, general editor, with the Society of Biblical Literature
Harper's Bible Commentary
San Francisco: Harper & Row, Publishers, 1988
ISBN 0-06-065541-0 hardbound

Sterling M. Means
Ethiopia and the Missing Link in African History
Philadelphia: Debbas Printing Co., 1980
Originally published at Harrisburg, Pennsylvania: The Atlantis Publishing Company, 1945
Paperback

Richard Pankhurst
The Ethiopians: A History
The Peoples of Africa
Oxford, England: Blackwell Publishers, 1998
Published in paperback 2001
ISBN 0-631-22493-9 paperback

Angela Partington, editor
Oxford Dictionary of Quotations: Revised fourth edition
Sara Tulloch, managing editor
Susan Ratcliffe, assistant editor
Oxford, England: Oxford University Press, 1996
ISBN 0-19-860058-5 clothbound
First edition published in 1941

Mortimo (Mortimer) "Kumi" Planno (Planner)
The Earth Most Strangest Man: The Rastafarian
Kingston, Jamaica: Unpublished monograph, 1969
Downloaded on August 10, 2013 from http://www.cifas.us/material/
    earth-most-strangest-man

Charles Ponce
Kabbalah: An Introduction and Illustration for the World Today
Wheaton, Illinois: Quest Books, 1978
ISBN 0-8356-0510-8
Paperback

Charles Francis Potter
The Lost Years of Jesus Revealed
Robbinsdale, Minnesota: Fawcett Publication, 1962
First published in 1958

George Rawlinson
[Rawlingston's Ancient Monarchies]
*The Five Great Monarchies of the Ancient Eastern World; or The History,
    Geography, and Antiquities of Chaldæa, Assyria, Babylon, Media, and Persia*
Collected and illustrated from ancient and modern sources
New York: Dodd, Mead, and Company. 1881
In three hardbound volumes, with maps and illustrations

H. H. Rowley, editor
The Old Testament and Modern Study. A Generation of Discovery and Research
Essays by members of the Society for Old Testament study
Oxford, England: Oxford University Press, 1951

Yuri Rubinsky and Ian Wiseman
A History of the End of the World
New York: Quill/An Invisible Book (William Morrow & Company, Inc.),
    1982
ISBN 0-688-01388-0 paperback

Christine Sandford
*The Lion of Judah Hath Prevailed: Being the Biography of His Imperial Majesty
    Haile Selassie I*
London: J. M. Dent & Sons Ltd., 1955
Illustrated with sixteen pages of photographs

Ruth Schumann Antelme and Stéphane Rossini
Sacred Sexuality in Ancient Egypt: The Erotic Secrets of the Forbidden Papyri
Rochester, Vermont: Innner Traditions, 2001
ISBN 0-892-818638

Enid S. Smith
"The Mystic Order of Essenes"
Originally ublished in December 1956 in *Rays from the Rose
Cross: The Rosicrucian Fellowship Magazine*
Downloaded on Feb. 23, 2014 from://rosicrucianzine.tripod.
    com/essenes.htm

William Smith
Smith's Bible Dictionary
Compiled from Dr. William Smith's Dictionary of the Bible
Philadelphia: A J Holman & Co., 1960

Evelyn and Frank Stagg
Woman in the World of Jesus
Louisville, Kentucky: Westminster John Knox press, 1978
ISBN 0-664-24195-6 paperback

Edmond Bordeaux Szekely
Essene Communions with the Infinite
Cartago, Costa Rica: International Biogenic Society, 1979

The Essene Jesus: A Reevaluation from the Dead Sea Scrolls
Cartago, Costa Rica: International Biogenic Society, 1977

From Enoch to the Dead Sea Scrolls
Cartago, Costa Rica: International Biogenic Society, 1981

David Abner Talbot
Haile Selassie I: Silver Jubilee
The Hague, The Netherlands: W.P. Van Stockum & Zoon, Publishers, 1955
Hard-bound, with illustrations

The Rastafari United Theocratic House (TRUTH)
"Coronation Days in Addis Ababa"
Illustrated compilation of materials, no date

Edward Ullendorf
From Emperor Haile Selassie to H. J. Polotsky: An Ethiopian and Semitic Miscellany
Wiesbaden, Germany: Harrassowitz, 1995
ISBN 3-447-03615-X

Robert Van de Weyer
The Monastic Community of Ethiopia
Downloaded on November 16, 2013 from tezetaethiopia.wordpress.com/2005/04/20/ the-monastic-community-of-ethiopia-by-robert-van-de-weyer
Originally published in *Ethiopia Observer* in the 1960's or 1970's

William D. Watley and Raquel Annette St. Clair
The African Presence in the Bible: Gospel Sermons Rooted in History
Valley Forge, Pennsylvania: Judson Press, 2000
x 117p 22cm paperback
ISBN 0-8170-1349-0
With bibliographic references

Robert G. Weisbord
African Zion: The Attempt to Establish a Jewish Colony in the East African Protectorate, 1903-1905
Philadelphia, Pennsylvania: The Jewish Publication Society of America, 1968
LCCCN 68-15791 hard-bound
With bibliography, index and map

H[erbert] G[eorge] Wells
The Outline of History: Being a Plain History of Life and Mankind, volume 1
Revised and updated by Raymond Postgate and G. P. Wells
Maps and plans by J. F. Horrabin
Garden City, New York: Doubleday & Company, Inc., 1971
Originally published in 1920, hard-bound

Wikipedia: The Free Encyclopedia That Anyone Can Edit (English)
https://en.wikipedia.org/wiki/Main_Page

Bahru Zewde
A History of Modern Ethiopia: 1855-1974
(Eastern African Studies)
London: James Currey
Athens, Ohio: Ohio University Press
Addis Ababa, Ethiopia: Addis Ababa University Press, 1992
First published 1991
Reprinted 1994, 1995
ISBN 0-85255-066-9 paperback

NOTES

NOTES

NOTES

NOTES

NOTES

Made in the USA
Middletown, DE
07 March 2021